THE CLIMATE EMERGENCY

and Green Spirituality Activism

A Last Chance to Change our Values?

Chris Philpott

"Ecology is about caring for the outer landscape and spirituality is about caring for the inner landscape. One is not complete without the other. Chris Philpott's outstanding book on Green Spirituality elucidates this unity of ecology and spirituality in a profound way. Green Spirituality is as informative as it is inspiring, it is a wonderful manual for the activists and a guide to address the pressing problems of our time such as climate change. I recommend the book wholeheartedly."
Satish Kumar (Director of Programmes of the Schumacher College international centre for ecological studies, and Editor Emeritus of Resurgence & ecologist.)

"Climate change and allied ecological emergencies threaten both humanity and the rest of nature. Faith communities, of diverse kinds, are often at the cutting edge of challenging this destruction and promoting adaption. Thus the relationship between spirituality and survival is a crucial area of discussion. This book will provide an important contribution to such a discussion, Chris Philpott has both eloquence as a writer and vast experience as a campaigner. This book will be both essential and interesting".
Derek Wall (former Principal Speaker for the Green Party of England and Wales.)

More from the Author
Website: www.greenspirituality.org
YouTube Channel - Climate Emergency and Spiritual Values:
https://www.youtube.com/channel/UCC-ZD5qq1Lj_MMl0mJtxaVg
For talks (for sustainable travel expenses) message Chris Philpott via his Facebook page: https://www.facebook.com/Green-Spirituality

I would like to dedicate this book to the late Hugh Fraser who helped me complete my last book *"Green Spirituality - One Answer to Global Environmental Problems and World Poverty"* (2011). I also dedicate this book to all past and present green activists who have responded to the Climate Emergency. Finally this book is dedicated to my children and grandchildren and all future generations, I pray that they may listen to the guidance in this book and live in a sustainable world.

To Kate this book is a token of gratitude for all your support in helping me continue my mission around the Climate Emergency. THANKS! May the future be GREEN!!

Chris

ACKNOWLEDGEMENTS

I first want to acknowledge this wonderful planet and its ecosystems which have given me life for 70 years. I also acknowledge all those wonderful people who have helped and inspired me to continue to be a green activist for the last 40 years. I am indebted to the help of the late Hugh Fraser, who edited my last book, and the late John-Francis Phipps who helped shape it. I would also like to give heartfelt thanks to writers who have encouraged me through the years including Mark Lynas, Vandana Shiva, Dr. Fazlun Khalid, Satish Kumar, Jonathon Porritt, Bill McKibben and Derek Wall. I acknowledge all the organisations which have helped me learn more about the Climate Emergency, particularly the Green Party, Friends of the Earth, Greenpeace, 350.0rg, World Wide Fund for Nature, Carbon Brief, The Climate News Network, Eco Watch and Extinction Rebellion.

Without the encouragement, patience and support of my wife Felicity the 5 year project to write this book would never have happened. My heartfelt thanks go to my friend Zani of zanidesign.com for the stunning cover design. I have also been blessed to have the technical support of my friend Dave Hastings in creating the YouTube channel on "Climate Emergency and Spiritual Values" which enhances the message of this book (www.dhphoto.co.uk). Lastly I would like to express deep gratitude to my Bahá'í friends, Paddy and Ann Vickers, for their advice, for editing this book so skilfully and for their continued encouragement.

Contents

INTRODUCTION

Why this book?

When you pick up this book you will probably have some questions. You wonder who is the person writing this book and what is their motive for writing it and what is "Green Spirituality" anyway? I am not an academic but a concerned citizen and green activist for almost 40 years. I also have knowledge and experience of different spiritual traditions and inter-faith. I follow a Buddhist path myself. This book is born out of the compassion I feel for the suffering in our world caused by present and future climate change.

My motive in writing this book is to add the spiritual dimension to the debate about climate change. This is done by highlighting teachings from different spiritual traditions on how we should treat the earth. In particular I wish to appeal to the many people in our world who lead a spiritual life but who may not fully know the relevant teachings within their own or other faiths. I also share easily-understood and up-to-date information about climate change and suggest some practical paths you can take to make a difference. I refer to my own experiences of green activism throughout.

What I have written in this book is correct as I far as I know to the best of my ability and fully referenced. Any profits made from this book will be used to promote the messages in this book. At the moment people need to be empowered and not overwhelmed. Access to clear information should enable people to make informed choices. Nowadays, many people get their information from social media platforms which are run by large corporations, embedded in the capitalist system, which are not usually guided by ethics or morals, but purely by profit. People using these social media can spread dangerous misinformation which cannot be validated. Corporations running the social media make their money out of distraction and focussing on the trivial. As Naomi Klein so elegantly puts it, they have you "running round in digital circles in search of the next dopamine fix." If we all became green activists then the future suffering of all people and of nature would be less. Activism to be effective needs to be on a global scale.

What is Green Spirituality?

Let me define simply what I think "Green Spirituality Activism" is. Being green means a person is concerned about the environment and social justice. However, there is no single, widely agreed-upon definition of spirituality. To me, spirituality is about recognition that there is a metaphysical reality beyond the physical reality and this can be experienced by the individual. Being spiritual means that a person adopts values based on the spiritual teachings of their particular spiritual tradition or perhaps an eclectic mix from several spiritual traditions. When you combine concern for the environment and social justice with spiritual values you live your life from a perspective of Green Spirituality. You are motivated as an activist to do something to help people and the environment because you have adopted spiritual values - you start to live the green lifestyle. Green Spirituality considers nature to be sacred, of intrinsic value, and worthy of reverent care. The climate emergency has been caused by the lesser values adopted by much of humanity. If we focus on our own "individualism" rather than the society in which we live and, for instance, value the greed and materialism of the consumerist culture, the result unfortunately is climate change.

Spiritual values have for millennia been a primary source of values in many cultures. The example can be found in indigenous peoples who realised our relationship to the Earth needs to be spiritually as well as physically sustaining. In the final analysis the climate emergency is a spiritual emergency because we have forgotten or ignored the wisdom and guidance handed down to us from different spiritual traditions over multiple generations. If we had kept our spiritual values then climate change would probably not have happened. If it had, it would be in a manageable form and not a threat to future generations. I want to add to the debate of what to do about the climate emergency by introducing spirituality and the values it brings us. In the end our behaviour is guided by the values that we hold and if they are not based on high ethics and values then climate change will be exacerbated.

The Need for Change

I am writing this introduction in isolation, with the COVID19 pandemic changing the whole world. Climate change is similar in that its effects on the economy and on people will be profound in the future. What COVID19 has taught us is that we are all dependent on each other. It also shows that great changes to societies can be made in a short time if governments have the political will to do so. What the climate emergency should teach us is that we are dependent on each other and on a stable climate.

The consequences of inaction on the climate emergency are made very clear in this book and could be terminal for most of life on earth, including humans. At least you are being given a warning of what might come and a chance to change things. Already our planet is melting, drying, acidifying, flooding and burning. Millions in the future may lose their lives through famine, war, drought and displacement, all due to climate change. This is made clear in the book when I describe the worst possible future scenario. I do not want my children and grandchildren to inherit this dire situation. For the sake of material comfort for relatively few in the present and recent past, we may well have made life very difficult for future generations. What is clear is that the standard of material plenty for future generations will be much lower. I am a pensioner, but young people and those nations which did not cause the problem in the first place could face an unfair and very uncertain future.

The drivers of this "creative self-destruction" are corporate elites who would sooner see their world destroyed rather than relinquish their power over the media and politics. The fossil fuel capitalism that they run is in the interests of capital not people. Governments will step in to protect their interests just as we are seeing with them propping up fossil fuel companies after COVID19.

Greenhouse gases are cumulative in the atmosphere. The current global warming is an effect of all greenhouse gases put in the atmosphere during the last 100 years. Even if we stopped emissions now, the accumulated levels of greenhouse gases will have an effect for perhaps thousands of years. This is certainly true of rising sea levels and rising temperatures. The longer we leave it to decarbonise our economies, the longer-lasting will be the effects of climate change on this planet.

I am in a band called the Eco Messengers and one of my songs, which I wrote a decade ago, is entitled "Last Chance Saloon for Global Warming". It says:

"This is the last chance saloon for global warming,
We have been given our final warning,
We are gonna have to change our ways,
If not everybody pays,
You don't have to be some kind of genius,
The way we are heading we will end up like Venus."

In 2018, three years ago as I write this, the International Panel on Climate Change said that we had 12 years to dramatically cut carbon emissions or face a future of climate chaos. We are in a climate emergency. What is needed now is to reclaim our power from those who are not using it in our interests. At the same time we need a dramatic change in our behaviour - in how we travel, how we grow food, how we produce energy and the things we consume.

What You will Find in this Book

This book is organised into 4 parts.

Part 1 focuses on the problems we face with the climate emergency in terms of extreme weather, food and water shortages, biodiversity loss and the effect on health. At the beginning of each chapter there is a series of quotations from different spiritual traditions which illustrate what our approach in spiritual terms should be to looking after the earth in connection with each of these topics. In the second part of the chapter there is a description of what the actual situation is with these problems, both now and into the future.

Part 2 focuses on what we can do about these problems, describing the different paths we can take – changing our own individual lifestyles, joining climate protests, supporting Non-Governmental Organisations, political activism and leading a spiritual life. We can do all of these if we wish.

Part 3 describes the possible good and bad future scenarios depending on how many changes we make as a species and as individuals.

Part 4 is a final chapter on spiritual guidance on how to avoid the worst scenarios of climate change.

At the end of the book there is a page of definitions and frequently used abbreviations which you may find a useful reference when reading through the chapters. The very last page of the book is a space where you can make your own private pledges to make a difference. Please use this, particularly as you read through the second section showing what we can do to make that difference.

I hope this book helps you navigate through the turbulent times of the climate emergency.

Chris Philpott
February 2021

POSTSCRIPT

As this book was being prepared for publication, even more extreme weather events have been reported: unprecedented heatwaves in western Canada and the NW USA; catastrophic floods in Germany, China and India; widespread wildfires in Turkey and Greece. No doubt, sadly, there will be more. The United Nations International Panel on Climate Change has produced its latest report, which concludes unequivocally that global warming is the result of our own actions. Although much of the damage has already been done – sea levels will continue to rise for hundreds of years and glaciers continue to melt – it emphasises the need to act immediately to prevent the situation getting much, much worse. I hope this book will help you to play your own, vital, part in helping us avoid complete disaster.

Part 1

Why there is a **Climate Emergency**

Chapter 1:

THE DEEPER CAUSES OF
CLIMATE CHANGE

Our planet is warning us that it cannot support our current way of life and this is expressed through climate change. The problem is that modern human activities constantly release huge amounts of greenhouse gases into the atmosphere, which are causing a swift global warming on a scale never experienced before by our planet. The risk is that it could unbalance the Earth's atmospheric and oceanic cycles on such a scale that it would have unpredictable and possibly catastrophic consequences for our climate. There are two levels of causation of climate change, the surface physical level but always the deeper level of causes arising from human behaviour.

THE ACTUAL PHYSICAL CAUSES

Earth's climate is the result of a balance between the amount of incoming energy from the sun as against the energy being radiated out into space. The sun's rays travel through the atmosphere and warm the earth's surface, generating the upward emission of infrared heat. Some of this heat is trapped on its escape to space by what are therefore called "greenhouse" gases in the atmosphere (mainly water vapour, carbon dioxide, methane, nitrous oxide and ozone) and sent back towards the surface. Greenhouse gases (GHGs) thus act like a blanket, trapping the heat. A certain level of GHGs is very necessary. In fact, without any GHGs at all the average temperature of the earth's surface would be about -18°C, rather than the present average of +15°C. However, the large quantity of greenhouse gases released by current human activities increases the thickness of this "atmospheric blanket", causing global temperatures to rise by a significant amount. This is often referred to as global warming.[1]

Problems really began in the 19th century, with progress in science and technology which resulted in the Industrial Revolution. Fossil fuels were the basis of the energy which powered the machines of industry and transport, and the greenhouse gases they emitted increased the effect of the "atmospheric blanket", so temperatures started to rise. To date, human-generated emissions since the start of the Industrial Revolution have led to global warming of 1.0°C. If these emissions continue at current rates, we are likely to reach 1.5°C of warming between 2030 and 2052 - an additional warming of 0.5°C from today's level.[1] This may not sound like a lot, but it has an enormous effect on weather patterns.

This rise in temperature is what has led to climate change. Climate change is a long-term shift in weather conditions identified by changes in temperature, precipitation (rain, snow, etc), winds, and other indicators. Climate change can involve both changes in average conditions and changes in variability, including, for example, extreme events. Over the last million years, Earth has naturally cycled in and out of an ice age every 100,000 years or so. The planet left the last ice age around 12,000 years ago and is currently in an interglacial cycle called the Holocene epoch. Earth has natural systems that help keep it cool, even during these warmer interglacial periods. But many scientists argue that due to the immense impact of humans on climate and the environment, the current geological age should be called the Anthropocene (from anthropogenic, which means originating with human activity). Although we are now only a short way through the current interglacial cycle, temperatures are now almost as hot as the maximum historical temperature recorded during such a cycle.[1]

Carbon Dioxide

Carbon dioxide is one of the major gases which traps heat. Nature emits 230 gigatons of carbon dioxide into the atmosphere each year. But it also absorbs that same amount through plants and the oceans. It remained balanced until 10,000 years ago when humans began burning wood. It slowly rose to 278 parts per million until 1850, when humans began burning coal, oil, kerosene, and gasoline.[1] Since then it has risen rapidly -

the latest figure, for October 2020 is 415 ppm.[2] This is much higher than at any time in the past 800,000 years. The countries which are the five largest emitters account for 60% of the world's carbon emissions. China and the United States are the worst, at 29.34 % and 13.77%, respectively. India contributes 6.62%, Russia adds 4.76%, and Japan 3.56%.[3] The United States has emitted more CO_2 than any other country to date: at around 400 billion tonnes since 1751, it is responsible for 25% of historical emissions.[3] On a per-person basis, the United States is the worst offender. In 2014, it emitted 16.2 metric tons of CO_2 per person.

If we look at the main sources of emissions worldwide in 2015, electricity and heat production accounted for the largest share at 30%. That was followed by transportation, which accounted for 15%, manufacturing and construction 12.4% and agriculture 9%.[4] The data shows that carbon dioxide concentrations in the atmosphere increased at a higher rate between 2015 and 2019 than in the previous five years. Currently emissions are still increasing.[5] One big reason for increases is that our addiction to fossil fuels is growing, despite the 2015 Paris Agreement, as a United Nations Report in 2019 has shown. The report stated that as of 2019 the world is on track to use about 50% more fossil fuels by 2030 than would be consistent with a 2°C global temperature increase and 120% more than would be consistent with a 1.5°C increase.[6]

Deforestation

Humans are also causing increases in carbon dioxide levels by removing trees. Trees take CO_2 out of the atmosphere, but are being removed through land use changes such as urban development, the use of trees for raw materials, and through agriculture. By removing these valuable carbon sinks, we are hastening warming even further. The global forest area fell by 3% from 1990 (4128 million hectares) to 2015 (3999 million hectares).[7] The tropics lost 11.9 million hectares of tree cover in 2019, according to Global Forest Watch. That's the equivalent of losing a patch of primary forest the size of a football pitch of every 6 seconds for the entire year. Depressingly, primary forest loss was 2.8% higher in 2019 than the year before.[8] The Intergovernmental Panel on Climate Change has a target of limiting global warming to 1.5 degrees Celsius above pre-industrial levels. They have clearly stated that planting more trees, and keeping existing trees in the ground, are both essential to meeting that goal.[9]

Boreal forests (in the sub-arctic) store 30% of all carbon stored on land. Yet we are cutting them down and killing them off with pests which prosper in rising temperatures. For instance, the mountain pine beetle alone has already wiped out forests the size of Washington State in the USA.[10]

Tropical rain forests also absorb CO_2. Deforestation in the Amazon has accelerated since President Jair Bolsonaro took office. Between January and August 2019, deforestation more than doubled compared to the same period the previous year, according to Brazil's National Institute for Space Research. The Amazon deforestation rate reached the equivalent of 3 football fields per minute according to the data.[11] This was due to the intentional setting of fires by cattle ranchers and others to clear land, something encouraged by the policies of Bolsonaro, who has weakened environmental regulations and enforcement. If current deforestation rates in the Amazon rainforest continue, the forest could be two years away from the "tipping point" after which it will no longer be able to sustain itself by making its own rain. This could trigger a rapid conversion of much of the forest to savanna or grassland ecosystems, thereby emitting large amounts of carbon to the atmosphere.[12]

According to findings in the journal *"Science"*, we can mitigate climate change by planting lots of trees. A trillion of them in fact, maybe even more. Swiss scientists indicate this unprecedented, large-scale tree planting will help to capture a huge amount of CO_2. They calculated that over several decades these new trees could suck up almost 750 billion tonnes of heat-trapping CO_2 from the atmosphere. That's nearly as much carbon pollution as humans have emitted in the last 25 years.[13]

I am a member of an organisation called Population Matters which highlights the fact that as population grows so does the demand on finite resources.[13] If we slow population growth the impact of climate change is lessened. An estimated 1.2 billion people rely on forests for their livelihood, including about 60 million indigenous people who are almost entirely dependent on them, the International Union of Forest Research Organizations has stated.[15]

Expanding agriculture accounts for nearly three-quarters of the world's forest loss, the report, released at the United Nations Forum on Forests, has stated.[16] Some of this forest loss is just subsistence farming to support a growing population. Other clearances of tropical forests are down to the high meat diet of developed countries, which requires the growing of soya to feed animals. I shall expand on this in the chapter on species loss/biodiversity.

Other Greenhouse Gases

Water vapour is an important gas and tends to trap heat from the sun and prevent it from radiating back into space. Its presence in the atmosphere results in a feedback loop that amplifies more warming. A warmer planet holds more moisture in the atmosphere which leads to more warming, leading to more atmospheric moisture and so on. The increase in water vapour also amplifies strong weather events because it adds buoyancy to the air flowing into storms, promoting them so they become more intense and their impacts even more severe.[17]

Nitrous oxide (N_2O) is also naturally present in the atmosphere as part of the Earth's nitrogen cycle, and has a variety of natural sources. Globally, about 40% of total N_2O emissions come from human activities. N_2O contributes 6% of greenhouse gas emissions. It remains in the atmosphere for 114 years and it absorbs 300 times the heat of a similar amount of carbon dioxide. It is produced by agricultural and industrial activities. It is also a by-product of fossil fuel and solid waste combustion. More than two-thirds results from its use in fertiliser. According to the IPCC report of 2013, fertiliser application has increased 9 fold since 1961. Farmers can reduce nitrous oxide emissions by reducing nitrogen-based fertiliser use.[18]

Another greenhouse gas is methane (CH_4). Globally, 50-65% of total CH_4 emissions come from human activities. Methane traps 25 times more heat than an equal amount of carbon dioxide. But it dissipates after 10 to 12 years. CH_4 concentration in the atmosphere has increased approximately 150% since pre-industrial times. Other top sources of methane come from the digestive process of livestock and from landfills, which emit it as the waste decomposes. As meat consumption increases so does the amount of methane emitted from livestock production. There is more information on this in the chapter on food production.

A significant source of human-made methane emissions is fossil fuel production. For example, methane is a key by-product of the rapidly rising global extraction and processing of natural gas. Fracking, the process of shale gas extraction, has boomed in the USA and has caused a sudden spike in methane emissions globally.[19] I was part of the first anti-fracking camp in the U.K. and thank goodness the UK government has stopped its development for the time being. As the world warms, future methane sources will come from the melting of the tundra, which will release methane hydrates. There are trillions of tons of methane embedded in a kind of ice slurry called methane hydrate or methane clathrate crystals in the Arctic and in the seas around the continental shelves in the polar regions. The Canadian Arctic is raising alarm bells for climate scientists. The permafrost there is thawing 70 years earlier than expected, a research team discovered. It is the latest indication that the global climate crisis is ramping up faster than predicted.[20]

The final source of greenhouse gases are chlorofluorocarbons (CFCs), hydrochlorofluorocarbons (HCFCs), hydrofluorocarbons (HFCs), perfluorocarbons (PFCs), and sulphur hexafluoride (SF_6), together called F-gases or Fluorinated gases. They are often used in coolants, foaming agents, fire extinguishers, solvents, pesticides, and aerosol propellants. They are thousands of times more potent than an equal amount of carbon dioxide. F-gases have a long atmospheric lifetime, and some of these emissions will affect the climate for many decades or centuries.[21]

THE SPIRITUAL CAUSES OF CLIMATE CHANGE

As previously mentioned, the underlying causes of climate change are spiritual in nature. Some aspects of this are discussed below, grouped under the following headings: Greed and Materialism, Karma (Cause and Effect), Maintaining a Balance, and Losing our Connection with Nature. Within each section, there are quotations from the world's religions which are relevant to the aspect under discussion.

GREED AND MATERIALISM

Christopher Wright and Daniel Nyberg, in their book about climate change and capitalism, describe our current economic system very succinctly and accurately: "Our economic system is now engaged in ever more inventive ways to consume the very life-support systems upon which we rely as a species; moreover, the irrational activity is reinvented as perfectly normal and sensible processes to which we can all contribute and from which we all benefit."[19] They postulate that capitalism is reliant on the destruction of nature for its further development. David Orr in his book on climate change as a "threat multiplier" compares capitalism to cancer, saying: "Perpetual growth is the ideology of the cancer cell." [23] Jonathon Porritt, in his new book "Hope in Hell", states we need to ask questions of ourselves when he says "In fact climate change is a civilisation issue, rather than an environmental issue, going right to the heart of today's growth-obsessed economy, challenging our very understanding of what we mean by progress." [24]

This insatiable appetite by humankind is well illustrated by the Earth Overshoot Day. This marks the date when humanity's demand for ecological resources (fish and forests, for instance) and services in a given year exceeds what Earth can regenerate in that year.[21] Pope Francis made this comment on Overshoot Day for 2019, "By July 29th, we used up all the regenerative resources of 2019. From July 30 we started to consume more resources than the planet can regenerate in a year. It's very serious. It's a global emergency." All consumption leaves a carbon footprint and adds to greenhouse gas emissions. We should reflect upon the values which give rise to our drastically increasing consumption, thereby altering the world's climate. The developed world has evolved a lifestyle driven ultimately by ownership, consumption, status and greed, not real need. These values have rubbed off on us all to varying degrees. Cunning advertisers exploit man's base nature, creating in us a dissatisfaction that compels us to consume more and more. Misguided, we have come to equate happiness with having rather than with being. Like an addict, the consummate consumer is constantly looking for the next fix.

Apparently, our consumption provides us relief from the "pain of being" - of facing uncomfortable personal issues. Worse - and for the advertiser "best" - what little relief we do find doesn't last: we just keep on searching in the vain hope of finding the thing - or service or partner or holiday or second home - that gives lasting relief from the dreaded "pain of being". In the final analysis, as Dieter Helm states in his book *Net Zero*, we all have to cut back on our consumption in order to bring greenhouse emissions down, whether the consumer goods are made in our country or more likely in China.[27]

However, my contention is that the only way we can really find satisfaction is in having a spiritual dimension to our lives – recognising that we are primarily and ultimately spiritual beings. The great spiritual teachers have all told us that we should avoid materialism and concentrate on the development of our spiritual lives. The quotations which follow illustrate this.

Christianity

Christianity arose from the teachings of Jesus Christ. Jesus was the model non-materialist. He concentrated on his relationship with God, not on the accumulation of wealth. He spent his days on walkabout preaching: he totally depended on God for his material needs. In terms of being carbon-aware, treading lightly on the planet, his life was exemplary. The warnings about greed are permeated throughout the New Testament as many of these extracts show:

"What good will it do for a man if he gains the whole world, yet forfeits his soul."
Jesus (Matthew 16:26)
"If you want to be perfect, go, sell your possessions and give to the poor and you will have treasure in heaven. Then come, follow me."
Jesus (Matthew 19:21)
"The love of money is the root of all evils and there are some who, pursuing it, have wandered away from the faith and so given their souls any number of fatal wounds." St. Paul (Timothy 6:10)
"No one can be a slave to two masters: he will hate one and love the other; he will be loyal to one and despise the other. You cannot serve both God and money." Jesus (Matthew 6:24)
"Watch out! Be on your guard against all kinds of greed; a man's life does not consist in the abundance of his possessions."
Jesus (Luke 12:15)
"Do not save riches here on Earth, where moths and rust destroy and robbers break in and steal. Instead save riches in heaven, where moths and rust cannot destroy and robbers cannot break in and steal."
Jesus (Matthew 6:19-20)
"May the relationship between man and nature not be driven by greed, to manipulate and exploit, but may the divine harmony between beings and creation be conserved in the logic of respect and care."
Pope Francis
"This planet is a life-giving organism, which is more than plentiful for those who know and practise moderation."
Ecumenical Patriarch Bartholomew

Judaism

Judaism, rooted in the Old Testament of the Bible, has many teachings about greed, as you can see from these extracts from the teachings of Moses:

"You shall not set your heart on your neighbour's house. You shall not set your heart on your neighbour's spouse, or servant, man or woman, or ox, or donkey, or any of your neighbour's possessions." Ten Commandments (Exodus 20:17)

"You shall have no other gods to rival me." Ten Commandments (Exodus 20:3).

Islam

Islam is based on the teachings of Muhammad. Muhammad was the "perfect man" who lived frugally and gave all his wealth away to the poor. Like Christ, he led a life that in our terms was non-materialistic and consumed a minimum of the Earth's resources. This quotation enlightens us to the teachings of Islam:

"Happy is the man who is content with what he has." Muhammad.

Hinduism

Hinduism is based on the teachings of Rama and Krishna plus a large number of traditions, many of which point to the need to give up material attachment in order to help spiritual growth.

The ideal of the Hindu in later life is to become a *sannyasin* or holy wandering man. The Naga type of *sannyasin* does not have any clothes let alone any possessions! Their lifestyle involves walking from place to place, often sleeping outside and depending on people to give them food; therefore their energy demands are very low. The *sannyasin* learns from the guru, who also practises non-attachment to the material world. He or she lives a non-materialistic lifestyle focussing on God consciousness, and in consequence uses very little energy. These quotations illustrate this:

"If one is a slave to his passions and desires, one cannot feel the joy of real freedom."
Swami Vivekananda

"Man has to turn inside knowing that this makes him contented, peaceful and satisfied." Swami Chidanand Saraswati, Head of Parmarth Niketan Ashram, Rishikesh, Uttarakhand, India.

"The human being is greedy - after all, if there is no peace in their heart, they will be." Swami Jivanmukhtananda, Rishikesh, Uttarakhand, India.

"Everybody has the seeds of happiness in them but this happiness is not found in the body comforts, it is in the state of mind." Swami Swatantranand Ashram, Rishikesh, Uttarakhand, India.

"Earth provides enough to satisfy every man's need but not every man's greed." Gandhi

Buddhism

Buddhism was founded by the Buddha. The Buddha was non-materialistic. His focus was on achieving enlightenment. Even when he achieved that, he spent his life teaching people how to achieve it for themselves. Buddhism teaches that the cause of our suffering is rooted in desire. One reason that energy use is so high in developed countries is that people desire more and more material comfort and this material prosperity is founded on using vast amounts of cheap energy. Buddhism reminds us that it is wisest to live in the "middle way" between extremes of wealth and poverty. Acting on this wisdom would significantly reduce our energy use, and enhancing our self-awareness would help us recognise in our lives the consumption we could easily do without. These quotations illustrate his philosophy:

"End greed, hatred and delusion." Buddha

"Not to do any evil, cultivate good, to purify one's mind, this is the teaching of the Buddhas." Buddha

"The more we possess, the more we want." Buddha

"Follow the middle path. Neither extreme will make you happy." Buddha

"Desire does not create problems. Our attachments to desire do." Buddha

"I truly feel that contentment is the greatest wealth. Anyone can claim it for themselves. Anyone can own it. Contentment is an incredible wealth that we don't have to pay for, or seek anywhere outside ourselves. The natural resources to create this wealth are the inner riches of our own mind. Contentment is a wealth." 17th Karmapa Lama

11

"Greed keeps us focused on what we do not have, and blinds us to all that we already have. Greed guarantees that no matter how much we acquire, it will never be enough. Building a society or a life based on greed is a recipe for dissatisfaction, plain and simple." 17th Karmapa Lama
"Physical comforts cannot subdue mental suffering, and if we look closely, we can see that those who have many possessions are not necessarily happy. In fact, being wealthy often brings even more anxiety." Dalai Lama

Jainism

Jainism was founded by the great spiritual leader Mahavira at the time of the Buddha. Jainism teaches seventeen types of internal restraint that can enhance personal serenity. The ideal way of life in Jainism is that of the Jain monk and nun. I have myself witnessed that, following ancient Jain teachings, they possess no more than they themselves can carry. Theirs is a life of minimal consumption and energy use. This restraint is an embodiment of the attitude of non-attachment, to which Jains commit when they take the vow of *apagraha* or non-possession. The restraint of this vow serves to interpose a pause to think twice before indulging in the acquisition of material goods - one of the root causes of our climate crisis. Since fewer goods are bought, fewer goods are made, use of finite resources and pollution are reduced. There are limits on the amount of furniture one has and the number of clothes, ornaments, soaps, food, creams and powders possessed. Even the number of baths taken is limited. Jains are encouraged to give up luxuries, which of course helps the environment. These are quotations from Jain spiritual leaders:
"On the aggravation of one's greed, a person fails to distinguish between what should be done and what should not be done. He is dare-devil who can commit any offence even at the cost of his own life." Mahavira (Bhagavati Aradhana, 857)
"Let me give up attachment through unattachment. My soul will be my only support (in this practice of unattachment). (Hence) let me give up everything else".
 Mahavira (Mulachara 2/44)
"To abandon attachment is the art of living as it is also the art of dying." Acharya Shri Mahaprajna, Head of the Jain Terapanth Sect
"The first rule of ecology is limitation." Acharya Shri Mahaprajna

"The instinct of getting more and more is one of the biggest causes of environmental problems." Saddavi Pramukha Kanak Pharbhaji, Chief Nun of the Jain Terapanth Sect, India.

Sikhism

With a global community perhaps 30 million strong, Sikhism is the world's fifth largest religion. Sikhism was founded by Guru Nanak, the first Sikh guru. The Sikh gurus lived simple and frugal lives; they focused on their relationship with God. They saw the gaining of riches as a distraction from the process of God-realisation. They gave an example of a non-materialist lifestyle, which was focused on God.
"Riches cannot be gathered without sin." Guru Nanak
"Lust and wealth are poisons - heavy and hard."
(Guru Granth Sahib p.1187)
"Then why get attached to what you will leave behind. Having wealth, you indulge in pleasures but, from that, tell me, who will bail you out?"
(Guru Granth Sahib)
"The world is consumed by ego and selfishness; see this, lest you lose your own self as well."
(Guru Granth Sahib, 441).

Taoism

Taoism was founded by the great sage Lao Tzu in China. Taoism is a spiritual philosophy of life based on Nature, originally practised by the ancient Chinese more than 8,000 years ago. Taoism can be simply translated as "the teaching of the way". It means to follow the Tao or the Way (or Path), which means living in harmony with the eternal essential principles underlying existence: ultimate reality. Today, Taoism has some 20 million followers, mainly in Taiwan. There are about 30,000 Taoists in North America and it enjoys a rising following in China. Taoism idealises the sage, a man who lives a frugal, simple life and who therefore consumes minimal energy. Being, rather than possessing, is the key to the Tao. There is a warning in the *Tao Te Ching* of the corruptions of greed and materialism when it states, "Great conflict arises from wanting too much."
The following quotations illustrate this:

"When a man seeks for external things, he is going away from the Great Tao, which is also a process of going away from his inner nature, or Virtue. The wisest person trusts the process, without seeking control; takes everything as it comes; lives not to achieve or possess but simply to be all he or she can be." Lao Tzu

"Seek simplicity, grasp the essential." Lao Tzu

"If you want to be given everything, give everything up." Lao Tzu

"Lessen selfishness and restrain desires." (Tao Te Ching Chapter 19)

"Be content with what you have; rejoice in the way things are. When you realise there is nothing lacking, the whole world belongs to you." Lao Tzu

"The Master has no possessions. The more he does for others, the happier he is. The more he gives to others, the wealthier he is." Lao Tzu

"There is no greater misfortune than greed." (Tao Te Ching Chapter 46|)

"Those who know when they have enough are rich." (Tao Te Ching Chapter 33)

Shamanism

Shamanism is founded on the leadership of the shaman and dates back at least 40,000 years. The shaman remains the ideal spiritual person. As specialists in the sacredness of the elemental forces of earth, wind, fire, water, they never did accumulate things but valued the imponderable such as visions and connection with the supernatural world. For instance, one measure of wealth for the Navajo tribe was in how many songs a person knew by heart.

"The role of religion and spirituality (in environmental activism) is to hold up the values that go beyond the value of profit and the value of somebody winning and somebody losing, to say... there are things that are more important than money or gain. The value of generosity, the value of putting the good of the community and the good of the whole before your own personal gain - those are things that every religion at its core has always stood for." Star Hawk

Bahá'í Faith

One of the most modern religions is the international Bahá'í Faith, which has now grown to be the seventh largest religion in the world. The largest number of Bahá'ís live in Asia (3.6 million), and there are 150,000 members in the USA. The Bahá'í Faith originated in the nineteenth century in Persia (modern day Iran). Its Founder, Bahá'u'lláh, was born into a very wealthy family but gave it all up in order to spread his message. He lived in poverty and exile for the rest of his life. The main purpose of the Bahá'í Faith is to serve humanity. This means practising the teachings of Bahá'u'lláh and spreading his message - which is replete with Earth wisdom - rather than accumulating material possessions. `Abdu'l-Bahá, the Son of its Founder, defined a Bahá'í very succinctly, saying, "To be a Bahá'í simply means to love all the world; to love humanity and try to serve it."

These quotations enlighten us as to the Bahá'í attitude:

"Man is, in reality, a spiritual being, and only when he lives in the spirit is he truly happy." 'Abdu'l-Bahá (Paris Talks)

"Verily, the most necessary thing is contentment under all circumstances." Bahá'u'lláh (quoted in "Bahá'u'lláh and the New Era")

"Take from this world only to the measure of your needs, and forego that which exceedeth them." Bahá'u'lláh (The Summons of the Lord of Hosts, p. 194).

"If carried to excess, civilisation will prove as prolific a source of evil as it had been of goodness when kept within the restraints of moderation." Bahá'u'lláh (Gleanings, CLXIV)

KARMA

Karma is simple to define but immense in its implications. It simply means cause and effect. If we want to accumulate good karma, we have to be more aware of the results of our actions. For around 25 years scientists have been clear that burning fossil fuels is the major cause of climate change, in other words creating bad karma for all of humanity. Despite their having warned us about this, world emissions have risen - along with rates of consumption - ever faster and continue their upward spiral. The way we have as a global community avoided awareness of our actions looks like denial by unspoken consensus. This principle of cause and effect, or karma, is common to many spiritual teachings. They powerfully underscore our innate sense of good balance which industrialisation and materialism have disturbed.

Christianity

"Do not be deceived: God cannot be mocked. A man reaps what he sows." St. Paul (Galatians 6:7)

Islam

"Act in your life as though you are living forever." Muhammad
"And truly the Lord will repay everyone according to their works for He is well aware of what they do." (Quran 11:113)
"Corruption doth appear on land and sea because of (the evil) which men's hands have done, that He may make them taste a part of that which they have done, in order that they may return." (Quran 30:41)
"Believe in Allah and His messenger, and spend of that whereof He hath made you trustees; and such of you as believe and spend (aright), theirs will be a great reward." (Quran 57:7)
"And do good as Allah has been good to you. And do not seek to cause corruption in the earth. Allah does not love the corrupters." (Qur'an 28:77)

Judaism

"When one loves righteousness and justice, the earth is full of the loving-kindness of the Eternal." (Psalms 33:5).
"There is no dark place, no deep shadow, where evildoers can hide." (Job 34:22)
"As ye sow, so shall ye reap." (Jeremiah 1–19)

Buddhism

In Buddhism the need to be fully aware of karma - or cause and effect - is paramount.
"If you should speak or act with mind defiled, suffering will follow just as a wheel follows the hoof of a drawing ox." The Buddha (Dhammapada)
"Avoid doing wicked actions, practise most perfect virtue, and thoroughly subdue your mind." The Buddha (Dhammapada)
"The universe we inhabit and our shared perception of it are the results of a common karma. Likewise, the places that we will experience in future rebirths will be the outcome of the karma that we share with other beings

16

living there. The actions of each of us, human or non-human, have contributed to the world in which we live. We all have a common responsibility for our world and are connected with everything in it." Tenzin Gyatso, 14ᵗʰ Dalai Lama.

Hinduism

Hinduism shares the same philosophy about karma as Buddhism.
"There is nothing mightier in the world than karma: karma tramples down all powers as an elephant tramples down lotuses."
(Hindu Scriptures)
"The world is like a river and our acts are like its ripples." (Hindu Scriptures)
"Persons of demoniac nature cannot understand actions in their best spiritual interests and actions in their worst spiritual interests; there is never purity, nor good conduct nor even truth in them." (Bhagavad Gita 16.7)

Sikhism

"According to one's own actions and deeds, they will get near to God or they will get far away from him." (Jaap Ji Sahib-Salok, Guru Granth Sahib.)
"If we do good or bad all our actions are narrated before Dharam Raj and those that have done good will be sent to Heaven and others to Hell." (Jaap Ji Sahib-Salok, Guru Granth Sahib.)
"As are one's deeds, so will one become." (Dhansari Mahalla I p.662.)
"The soul knows, that as one sows, so will one reap."
(Guru Granth Sahib p1243)

Jainism

"A person of right world-view reflects on karma and its results." (Bhasyam Sutra 53.)
"All unenlightened persons produce sufferings. Having become deluded, they produce and reproduce sufferings, in this endless world." Mahavira (Uttaradhyayana, 6/1)

Taoism

"Never take over the world to tamper with it. Those who want to tamper with it are not fit to take over the world." (Tao Te Ching Chapter 48)

Shamanism

"In our every deliberation, we must consider the impact of our decisions on the next seven generations". (Iroquois saying)

Bahá'í Faith

"If a man eats too much, he ruins his digestion; if he takes poison he becomes ill or dies. If a person gambles he will lose his money; if he drinks too much he will lose his equilibrium. All these sufferings are caused by the man himself, it is quite clear therefore that certain sorrows are the result of our own deeds." 'Abdu'l-Bahá (Paris Talks, p. 51)
"Co-operation and reciprocity are essential properties which are inherent in the unified system of the world of existence, and without which the entire creation would be reduced to nothingness." 'Abdu'l-Bahá (quoted in compilation on Huquq'u'llah)

MAINTAINING A BALANCE

Balance is the state of stability towards which nature always restores things. Like karma, we ignore it at our peril. Over and over again, we humans have disturbed the balance of nature by our exploitative attitude towards it. We lack respect for nature. The lack of balance and harmony within ourselves is reflected in our behaviour towards the planet, causing imbalances in natural systems, and now we are paying the price. These spiritual teachings remind us of the need for balance in all that we do.

Islam

"And the firmament He has raised high and He has set up the balance; in order that ye may not transgress balance." (Qur'an 55:7-8)
"Verily, all things have we created in proportion and measure." (Qur'an 54:49)

"Do no mischief on the earth, after it has been set in order, but call on Him with fear and longing (in your hearts): for the Mercy of God is (always) near to those who do good." (Qur'an 7:56).

"This world is a universal guest house given to us by God. We have to live here like a guest and not disturb the house." Mr Maulana Wahiduddin Khan, Delhi, India, Mullah and published scholar on Islam.

Buddhism

"The environment is irreplaceable. All life forms on earth coexist in delicate balance. Although some habitats are naturally more abundant than others, we are degrading the environment by exploiting and polluting it, affecting the entire world irrespective of borders. For everyone's sake, let's stop polluting the environment. How foolish to destroy our planet." 17th Karmapa Lama

Hinduism

Hinduism describes a Universal Order in the cosmos called *rita*. Its laws of being and of nature contain and govern all forms, functions and processes in the earth. In disturbing these processes we humans are breaking "Universal Law."

"God has made the balance of Nature perfect." (Hindu scriptures)

"The world is a living whole, an interconnectedness of cosmic harmony." (Hindu scriptures)

"A large number of man's activities are polluting the physical environment around him and creating an imbalance in the ecological situation, which is difficult to restore or cannot be restored at all." Swami Smarananda, General Secretary of the Ramakrishna Mission, Kolkata, India

Christianity

According to the book of Genesis, God made the world for mankind to inhabit and that world was in balance.

"There are limits to which we can make use of the resources of Nature." Archbishop Vincent Concessao of Delhi, India

Jainism

"If we free ourselves from the notions of uselessness and instead try and understand the concept of usefulness, ecological balance would automatically be maintained." Acharya Shri Mahaprajna, Head of the Jain Terapanth Sect

Taoism

The ideal of Taoism is the sage who lives in harmony with the Tao by not interfering with the natural order. In this way the balance of nature is not disturbed. Nature ensures that the essential balance be maintained between the pairs of opposite forces of yin and yang, male and female, light and dark, hot and cold etc. Yin and yang being out of balance is considered an unstable situation that nature will already be restoring to balance. The task of mankind is to accept the balance of yin and yang and to recognise the inescapable inter-dependence of all things. Heaven, Earth and Mankind must be in balance. This is particularly poignant when we think of the causes of the climate crisis.
"When you know Nature is part of yourself, you will act in harmony." Lao Tzu
"Fill your bowl to the brim and it will spill. Keep sharpening your knife and it will blunt." Lao Tzu

Bahá'í Faith

"… even as the human body in this world, which is outwardly composed of different limbs and organs, is in reality a closely integrated, coherent entity, similarly the structure of the physical world is like unto a single being whose limbs and members are inseparably linked together." 'Abdu'l-Bahá (quoted in compilation on Huququ'u'llah)
"For every part of the universe is connected with every other part by ties that are very powerful and admit to no imbalance." 'Abdu'l-Bahá (Selections from the Writings of 'Abdu'l-Bahá, p157)
"This nature is subject to a sound organisation, to inviolable laws, to a perfect order, and to a consummate design, from which it never departs." 'Abdu'l-Bahá (Some Answered Questions, Chap. 1, p. 3)

Judaism

Redressing the vast accumulated imbalances which mankind has heaped upon nature will of course not easily, if ever, be "put right". Even if we severely curbed carbon emissions tomorrow, because carbon dioxide gas has a 50 to 1,000 year life, its effects will last for centuries. From a Judaic perspective this suggests that mankind's covenant with God has definitely been broken.

Joel was a prophet of nature who warned if the Lord's way was not followed there would be dire consequences, with fields being devastated, granaries failing and animals searching vainly for fresh pasture. But if the way of God is followed there would be vats full of oil, trees bearing fruit and animals having plenty of pasture. The Jewish rules were introduced to train souls to love that which is good, useful and creative and refrain from all destructive activities. (see Book of Joel)

"Look at my creations. See how beautiful and perfect they are. Do not desecrate or corrupt my world. For if you corrupt it, there will be no one to set it right for you." (Talmud)

LOSING OUR CONNECTION WITH NATURE

In the developed world it has taken only about five generations - the Industrial Revolution heralding the advent of materialism and consumerism - for people to have largely lost their connection with the natural world. Such is the disconnect from nature created with our urban lifestyles, some people believe food is manufactured in a supermarket and milk in a carton. From this loss of connection stems our blindness to how nature actually works, to its delicate networks and interdependencies and to just how dependent on nature mankind remains. What emerges is alienation from nature, a loss of respect for it, our brutish exploitation of it. However, many spiritual traditions originated in natural settings. So to reflect on what they say about how we are intrinsically connected with nature is at once poignant, humbling and illuminating.

Hinduism

An attitude of respect for creation is reflected in Hinduism as all beings are seen to emanate from God. Also, because of their belief in the transmigration of souls, many Hindus believe that human beings have taken animal and plant forms in previous lives. Their belief that all living things in nature are connected is mirrored in the new understanding of nature's web of life that is emerging with our growing understanding of her subtle ways, such as the miracles of symbiosis.

"For the world is a living whole, a vast interconnectedness of cosmic harmony, inspired and sustained by the One Supreme." (Bhagavad Gita 10.20.)

"He on whom the sky, the earth and the atmosphere are woven and the wind, together with all life-breaths, know Him to be the one Soul." (Mundaka Upanishad 2.2.5)

"Hinduism teaches us to understand the laws of Nature and respect them."

Swami Dharammanda, Rishikesh, India

Jainism

The principle of interdependence is an ancient Jain principle which teaches that all of nature is bound together, and says that if one does not care for nature one does not care for oneself. A famous Jain aphorism states, "All life is bound together by mutual support and interdependence."

Buddhism

The Buddhist view of nature is helpful in terms of ecology and sustainability. Buddhism teaches that the idea of separateness is an illusion. The health of the whole is inseparably linked to the health of the parts and the health of the parts is inseparably linked to the health of the whole. Buddhist practice makes one feel one's own existence has no greater importance than another's.

"Our Planet is our house and we must keep it in order and take care of it if we are genuinely concerned about happiness for ourselves, our children, our friends and other sentient beings who share this great house with us."
Tenzin Gyatso 14th Dalai Lama

"All parties are changed by being in relationship. Just being connected to someone or something means we are each forming part of the other. This is true in all forms of interdependence, from those that form planetary systems to our most intimate and personal relationships." 17th Karmapa Lama

"Recognising our intimate dependence on the natural environment allows us to see its true value and treasure it." 17th Karmapa Lama

Paganism

Ancient Pagans were very connected with nature. They saw spirits, gods and goddesses in their immediate natural environment. Their festivals expressed their connection with nature throughout the year. Today, Paganism has been revived from its ancient roots and my Pagan friends are deeply committed to the Green movement. Rather than seek dominance over the environment, modern Pagans work to live as a part of nature, finding a balance between the self, the biosphere and society. Paganism emphasises connectedness between mankind and the immediate environment via spiritual forces.

"The Earth's biosphere may be understood as a single ecosystem and that all life on Earth is interconnected." (A Pagan Community Statement)

"If you submit to the ocean, you drown. If you try to control the ocean, then you're deluded. You learn how to live with the ocean. You learn how to float, to swim, to be a part of it, to be with it. That is the nature of the Pagan's relationship with nature." Emma Restall Orr

"This planet is our home. Our life and hers are interdependent." Doreen Valiente

Bahá'í Faith

The Bahá'í scriptures explain that, from one viewpoint, the components of nature are all different. But from another viewpoint, they are all the same because they all emanate from God.

"Every man of discernment, while walking upon the earth, feeleth indeed abashed, inasmuch as he is fully aware that the thing which is the source of his prosperity, his wealth, his might, his exaltation, his advancement and power is, as ordained by God, the very earth which is trodden beneath the feet of all men." Bahá'u'lláh (Epistle to the Son of the Wolf, p. 44)

"By nature is meant those inherent properties and necessary relations derived from the realities of things. And these realities of things, though

23

in the utmost diversity, are yet intimately connected one with the other."
'Abdu'l-Bahá (Tablet to Dr. Forel, in The Bahá'í Revelation, p. 223)
"We cannot segregate the human heart from the environment outside us
and say that once one of these is reformed everything will be improved.
Man is organic with the world. His inner life moulds the environment and
is itself also deeply affected by it. The one acts upon the other and every
abiding change in the life of man is the result of these mutual reactions."
Shoghi Effendi (Compilation on Social and Economic Development, p. 4)

Shamanism

Shamanism stands out as a spiritual tradition both for its ancient origins
but also because of its deep connection with the natural world.
Shamanism is perhaps unique in its attitude of sacredness towards all life,
which is born out of its intimate relationship with the untamed universe.
"With all beings and all things we shall be relatives." Black Elk
"We are all flowers in the Great Spirit's Garden; we share a common root,
and the root is Mother Earth." Grandfather David Monogye
"The whole universe is enhanced with the same breath, rocks, trees, grass,
earth, all animals and men." Intiwa, Hopi.
"The earth does not belong to us. We belong to the earth." Chief Seattle.
"Nature is not our enemy, to be raped and conquered. Nature is
ourselves, to be cherished and explored." Terence McKenna
"We are not separate - rather we are connected to one source and to a
web of life." Sandra Ingerman
"Man's heart away from nature becomes hard." Standing Bear
"The Great Spirit is in all things, he is in the air we breathe. The Great
Spirit is our Father, but the Earth is our Mother. She nourishes us, that
which we put into the ground she returns to us…." Big Thunder
"Regard Heaven as your Father, Earth as your Mother, and All That Lives
as your Brother and Sister." (Native Wisdom)

Sikhism

Sikh gurus exemplified how to stay in contact with nature. The whole of
Sikh spiritual literature is imbued with descriptions of nature as an
expression of God.

"By divine prompting, look upon all existence as one and undifferentiated." (Guru Granth Sahib)

"I perceive Thy form in all life and light; I perceive Thy power in all spheres and sight." (Guru Granth Sahib p 464)

Christianity

"Whether you like it or not, whether you know it or not, secretly all Nature seeks God and works toward Him." Meister Eckhart (Christian mystic)

"As stewards of God's creation, we are called to make the earth a beautiful garden for the human family. When we destroy our forests, ravage our soil and pollute our seas, we betray that noble calling." Pope Francis

"There can be no renewal of our relationship with nature without a renewal of humanity itself." Pope Francis

"A truly human intimacy with the earth and with the entire natural world is needed."
 Thomas Berry

Taoism

"Man is ruled by Earth. Earth is ruled by Heaven. Heaven is ruled by the Way. The Way is ruled by itself." (Tao Te Ching Chapter 25)

CONCLUSION

If all humanity had been following the spiritual guidance shown here, climate change would not have appeared. If we follow the guidance now, then we should be able to avoid the worst of its effects.

Chapter 2:

EXTREME WEATHER EVENTS

By ignoring the teachings of all spiritual traditions on the need for harmony and balance with nature, humanity incurs the blight of extreme weather. We are out of harmony with nature. We are pumping more and more greenhouse gases into the atmosphere, causing an imbalance in that atmosphere and in our climate. In consequence the temperatures rise ever higher. Over the past decade, global emissions have risen by 15%. The analysis undertaken by the National Oceanic and Atmospheric Administration (NOAA) found that 2019's average global temperature was 0.95 degrees Celsius above the 20th century average. The last decade was the hottest since record-keeping began 150 years ago, according to the latest data from the U.S. National Aeronautics and Space Administration (NASA) and the NOAA. 2019 was only a fraction of a degree cooler than the warmest year on record, which was 2016.[1]

The past five years have also been the warmest for the oceans since reliable measurements began in the 1950s. This is according to Lijing Cheng at the International Center for Climate and Environmental Sciences at the Institute of Atmospheric Physics of the Chinese Academy of Sciences.[2] Warmer seas generate more extreme storms.

Using climate models and statistical analysis of global temperature data, scientists have concluded that temperature increase has been driven mostly by increased emissions into the atmosphere - of carbon dioxide and other greenhouse gases - produced by human activities. According to the World Meteorological Organization (WMO)'s annual *Greenhouse Gas Bulletin*, which collects data from 54 countries, the average concentrations of CO^2 reached 407.8 parts per million in 2018, up from 405.5 ppm in 2017. Methane is the second most important long-lived greenhouse gas. According to the WMO, atmospheric methane reached a new high of about 259% of the pre-industrial levels. Levels of nitrous oxide were 123% of pre-industrial levels.[3]

SPIRITUAL PERSPECTIVES ON BALANCE AND HARMONY WITH NATURE

Taoism

Taoism starts and ends with observation of nature. In this way, it is just like science, but it is different in that science observes nature objectively, separate from the observer, whereas Taoism observes nature subjectively, seeing the observer and the observed as one entire system. This is the first principle of Taoism: Oneness. There is not "just us," or "just nature," but both. Taoism always stresses the importance of harmony between human beings and nature, as well as the protection of nature. Taoism is always opposed to the violation of natural laws. As described in the first chapter, Taoism is all about keeping the balance in nature. This is particularly poignant when we think of the causes of the climate crisis being an imbalance in the weather system due to greenhouse gases which we release.[4] The following quotations illustrate the Taoist way:

"Humanity follows the earth. Earth follows Heaven. Heaven follows the Tao. The Tao follows Nature." (Tao Te Ching, Verse 25)

"Mastery of the world is achieved by letting things take their natural course. If you interfere with the way of Nature, you can never master the world." (Tao Te Ching, Verse 48)

Islam

Islam teaches that God created the world to be in perfect harmony and balance and that mankind's role is to keep it like that by living in harmony and balance with nature through practising moderation.

In the Qur'an, God speaks of creating everything in balance, and warns that transgression of the balance will have disastrous consequences. Islam teaches that we should be moderate and balanced in all aspects of life, whether it is religion, worship, relationships, ideas, or daily activities. Principled moderation is one of the defining characteristics of good

27

character in Islam. Muslims say that Islam is the middle path. We will be answerable for how we have walked this path and how we have maintained balance and harmony in the whole of creation around us. So there is an emphasis on the avoidance of any type of extremism - pleasing to Satan - that leads away from the straight path. This path means we live in harmony with this natural order, take only what we need, and do not waste resources.

Climate change is a sign that increasing the proportion of carbon dioxide in the atmosphere has disturbed the *mizan* or balance that has been established.[5]

The following quotations show the Islamic attitude to balance and harmony:

"Behold, everything have We created in due measure and proportion." (Qur'an Ch 67 v 3, 4).

"And the sky has He raised high, and has devised (for all things) a balance, so that you (too, O men) might never transgress the balance: weigh, therefore, (your deeds) with equity, and do not upset the balance!" (Qur'an Ch 55 v 7-9).

"He is raised high and set up the measure, that ye may not exceed the measure." (Qur'an, Ch 55 v 8-10)

"And the earth We have spread out (like a carpet); set thereon mountains firm and immovable; and produced therein all kinds of things in due balance. And We have provided therein means of subsistence – for you and for those for whose sustenance ye are not responsible." (Qur'an Ch 15, v 19-20)

"But waste not by excess for God loveth not the wasters." (Qur'an Ch 6 v 141)

"Verily, everything has two ends and a middle. If you hold one of the ends, the other will be skewed. If you hold the middle, the two ends will be balanced. You must seek the middle ground in all things." (Hilyat Al-Awliya 4818)

"And We have willed you to be a community of the middle path (umatan wasatan)" (Quran Ch 2 v 143).

"So set thou thy face steadily truly to the faith: establish Allah's handiwork according to the pattern on which He has made mankind: no change let there be in the work wrought by Allah: that is the standard religion: but most among mankind understand not." (Quran Ch 30 v 30)

"Do no mischief on the earth, after it hath been set in order." (Quran Ch 7 v 56).

"Make not your own hands contribute to your destruction; but do good; for Allah loveth those who do good." (Quran Ch 2 v 195)

Hinduism

Hinduism has always been an environmentally sensitive philosophy. The Hindu scriptures of the Vedas, Upanishads, Ramayana, Mahabharata, Bhagavad Gita, Puranas and Smriti contain the earliest messages for preservation of environment and ecological balance. Nature, or Earth, has never been considered a hostile element to be conquered or dominated. In fact, man is forbidden from exploiting nature. Mankind is taught to live in harmony with nature and recognise that divinity prevails in all elements, including plants and animals. The *rishis* or holy men of the past have always had a great respect for nature. Maintaining balance in nature and harmony with nature have always been emphasised by Hinduism. Hinduism describes a Universal Order in the cosmos called *rita*. Its laws of being and nature contain and govern all forms, functions and processes in the earth. In disturbing these processes we humans are breaking 'Universal Law'.[6]

These quotations explain the Hindu view of harmony:

"God has made the balance of Nature perfect." (Hindu scriptures)

"The world is a living whole, an interconnectedness of cosmic harmony." (Hindu scriptures)

"By living in harmony with Nature one gains a healthy mind and body." Mata Amritanandamayi

"Happiness is what you think. What you say and what you do are in harmony." Mahatma Ghandi

"Harmony in nature will bring you happiness known to few city dwellers. In the company of other truth seekers it will be easier for you to meditate and think of God." Parahmahansa Yogananda

"In the universal sense, love is the divine power of attraction in creation that harmonises, unites, binds together....Those who live in tune with the attractive force of love achieve harmony with nature and their fellow beings, and are attracted to blissful reunion with God." Parahmahansa Yogananda

29

"Live in complete harmony with nature, experience the grace of God in the splendour of the universe." (Yajur Veda 34.37)

Buddhism

In the Buddha's time, explicit care for the environment was not really an issue. Fragile pockets of human civilisation existed dotted in the midst of vast tracts of wilderness. Today the situation is reversed as fragile remnants of wilderness struggle to exist under the growing demands of a vast human population. Although there may not be explicit guidance in Buddhist scriptures relating to care for the environment, the Buddhist path or way of life lends itself especially well to living in balance with Nature and to focussing on our needs rather than on greed. The Buddhist path is about growing mindfulness through meditation and awareness based on experience, of acknowledging and understanding the interconnectivity of all life. Individual responsibility is one of the strongest ethics promoted by Buddhism in support of positive action to address the current environmental crisis.[7]

"Because we all share this planet earth, we have to learn to live in harmony and peace with each other and with nature. This is not just a dream, but a necessity." H.H. Dalai Lama

Bahá'í Faith

Bahá'ís see all creation as interconnected. Our purpose in life to is to progress as spiritual beings through our interactions within the material world. Therefore we should not be attached to the material world, but we should have great respect for it as God's creation.[8]

The following extracts illustrate the Bahá'í view of moderation and interdependence of all things:

"Every man of discernment, while walking upon the earth, feeleth indeed abashed, inasmuch as he is fully aware that the thing which is the source of his prosperity, his wealth, his might, his exaltation, his advancement and power is, as ordained by God, the very earth which is trodden beneath the feet of all men." Bahá'u'lláh (Epistle to the Son of the Wolf, p. 44)

"In all matters moderation is desirable. If a thing is carried to excess, it will prove a source of evil." Bahá'u'lláh (Tablets of Bahá'u'lláh, p. 68)

"Whoso cleaveth to justice, can, under no circumstances, transgress the limits of moderation... The civilisation, so often vaunted by the learned exponents of arts and sciences, will, if allowed to overleap the bounds of moderation, bring great evil upon men... If carried to excess, civilisation will prove as prolific a source of evil as it had been of goodness when kept within the restraints of moderation. Meditate on this, O people, and be not of them that wander distraught in the wilderness of error. The day is approaching when its flame will devour the cities..."

Bahá'u'lláh (Gleanings from the Writings of Bahá'u'lláh, p. 342)

"Reflect upon the inner realities of the universe, the secret wisdoms involved, the enigmas, the inter-relationships, the rules that govern all. For every part of the universe is connected with every other part by ties that are very powerful and admit of no imbalance, nor any slackening whatever."

'Abdu'l-Bahá (Selections from the Writings of 'Abdu'l-Bahá, p. 156)

"...cooperation and reciprocity are essential properties which are inherent in the unified system of the world of existence, and without which the entire creation would be reduced to nothingness."

'Abdu'l-Bahá (Compilations, Huqúqu'lláh)

"The Lord of all mankind hath fashioned this human realm to be a Garden of Eden, an earthly paradise. If, as it must, it findeth the way to harmony and peace, to love and mutual trust, it will become a true abode of bliss, a place of manifold blessings and unending delights. Therein shall be revealed the excellence of humankind..."

'Abdu'l-Bahá (Selections from the Writings of 'Abdu'l-Bahá, p. 275)

THE CONSEQUENCES OF IGNORING THIS ANCIENT WISDOM

EXAMPLES OF TROPICAL STORMS AROUND THE WORLD

Since warm air can hold more water vapour than cold, it's not surprising that the atmosphere is 4% more moist than it was 40 years ago. Warmer sea surfaces provide more energy for storms to grow stronger.

Tropical storms in different parts of the world have been given different names. If they occur in the north-west Pacific they are referred to as typhoons. If they form in the North Atlantic or off the other side of North America they are called hurricanes. Those forming in the Indian Ocean, the South Pacific and South Atlantic are called cyclones. However, they are essentially the same phenomenon.

Typhoons

Typhoons are formed in the Pacific, near the equator. They depend on higher temperatures to form. Logically the higher temperatures we are currently experiencing mean that they are more likely to occur and also when they happen they might well be more destructive. A tropical storm needs two main ingredients: a cluster of thunderstorms and a warm body of water - at least 27°C - from which the storm gathers its energy. Water from the warm tropical ocean under a developing storm first evaporates, then condenses to form clouds, releasing heat throughout the process. The heat energy, combined with the rotation of the Earth, gets the cyclone spinning and propels it forward.[9]

We can look at the Philippines as an example of how the intensity of tropical storms has increased. In 2012 Typhoon Bhopa was the strongest tropical storm to ever hit the southern Philippine island of Mindanao, making landfall as a Category 5 super typhoon with winds of 175 mph, killing 1,900 people and leaving 300,000 homeless, in great need of fresh water, food and shelter.[10] In 2013 it was followed by Super Typhoon Haiyan at speeds of 195mph, killing 6,000, and displacing 4 million.[11] Then in 2014 there was Typhoon Rammasun which killed some 100 people in the Philippines and Vietnam, destroyed more than 100,000 houses and damaged 400,000 others. Half a million people were displaced.[12]

Hurricanes

The U.N. Intergovernmental Panel on Climate Change has run computer simulations suggesting that global temperatures could rise by between 2° and 6° C by the end of the century. The extreme storms are highly sensitive to temperature changes, and the number of events of the magnitude of hurricane Katrina in 2005 could double due to the increase in global temperatures that occurred in the 20th century, according to research reported in the journal *Proceedings of the National Academy of Sciences*.

If temperatures continue to warm in the 21st century, as many climate scientists project, the number of Katrina-strength hurricanes could at least double, and possibly rise much more. Every Atlantic hurricane season would also get longer, at a rate of 5 to 10 days per degree C rise in global temperatures, according to researchers.[13]

I remember Hurricane Katrina, which hit New Orleans, because I wrote a song about it to perform with my band the Eco Worriers. Besides the death toll of nearly 2,000 people, hurricane Katrina left many people homeless as more than 800,000 housing units were destroyed or damaged in the storm. Much of the damage from Hurricane Katrina was caused by high storm surges across a wide area of the Gulf of Mexico coast, according to the NOAA. A storm surge is an abnormal rise in water, over and above the normal high tide, pushed towards the shore by the winds whipping around the centre of the storm.[14] Then came Hurricane Sandy in 2012, which hit the north-eastern United States, Cuba and Haiti. At least 233 people were killed along the path of the storm, which made 200,000 people homeless in Haiti alone. The storm became the largest Atlantic hurricane on record as measured by diameter, spanning 1,100 miles. Ironically, New York was flooded by a storm surge and the capitalist icon of the New York stock exchange had to close for two days! [15] In 2015 came Hurricane Patricia which was the most intense tropical hurricane ever recorded in the Western Hemisphere. This affected both Texas and Mexico.[16]

2017 was a very bad year for destruction caused by hurricanes, starting with Hurricane Harvey which affected southern US states, Nicaragua and Honduras. In the US 13 million people from Texas through to Louisiana, Mississippi, Tennessee and Kentucky were badly affected. Flooding damage was extensive and total rainfall hit 51.88 inches in Cedar Bayou on the outskirts of Houston. That's a record for a single storm in the continental United States.[17] In 2017, Hurricane Irma affected Florida, Cuba, Puerto Rico, and many small islands in the Caribbean. It killed 134 people. This was the most powerful Atlantic hurricane in recorded history. Irma held 7 trillion watts of energy. That's twice as much as all the bombs used in World War II. Its force was so powerful that earthquake seismometers recorded it. There was by now a growing awareness that the frequency of more intense hurricanes was taking shape, as for the first time in 100 years two storms of Category 4 or above (the highest category is 5) had hit the U.S. mainland in the same year. Hurricane Harvey had already devastated Houston on August 25, 2017.[18] This was swiftly followed by Hurricane Maria which gravely affected Puerto Rico. According to the Washington Post, a Harvard study published in the *New England Journal of Medicine* estimated that 4,645 deaths could be linked to the hurricane and its immediate aftermath. Official estimates had placed the number of dead at 64.[19]

In 2018 there was another category 5 hurricane in the form of Hurricane Michael, which hit the Florida panhandle and Central America. Michael produced massively high tides along the coast, causing a lot of damage.[20] Also in 2018, Hurricane Willa became the third Category 5 hurricane of the Pacific hurricane season, thus adding evidence that the frequency of hurricanes had not changed but their strength and intensity had.[21] In 2019 Hurricane Dorian was the most intense hurricane on record to strike the Bahamas, and is regarded as the worst natural disaster in the country's history. It was also one of the most powerful hurricanes recorded in the Atlantic Ocean in terms of 1-minute sustained winds, with these winds peaking at 185 mph. Dorian also surpassed Hurricane Irma, becoming the most powerful hurricane on record in the open Atlantic region, outside of the Caribbean Sea and the Gulf of Mexico.[22]

According to the Union of Concerned Scientists, records show that between 1924 and 2019 there have been only 35 category 5 hurricanes in the North Atlantic. That's about one every 3 years. Having five such storms form in just four hurricane seasons is way beyond the average occurrence rate. Over the past half century, the ocean has absorbed more than 90% of the excess warming caused by burning fossil fuels and the overloading of the atmosphere with carbon. Research has confirmed that 2019 had the highest recorded sea surface temperatures, and warm waters are known to fuel hurricanes. What is clear is that there have been rapid intensifications with recent Atlantic hurricanes and a tendency toward slow-moving storms which means more property destruction and loss of human life. According to Kristy Dahl, Senior Climate Scientist with the Union of Concerned Scientists, the projected increase in intense hurricanes will be substantial - a doubling or more in the frequency of category 4 and 5 storms by the end of the century - with the western North Atlantic experiencing the largest increase.[23] We have to stop fuelling our economies with fossil fuels now if we wish to start to deal with the causes of extreme weather events such as hurricanes.

EXAMPLES OF HEATWAVES AROUND THE WORLD

Global warming over the last century means that heat extremes which previously only occurred once every 1,000 days are happening four to five times more often, according to a study published in *Nature Climate Change*.[24] Currently, nearly twice as many record hot days as record cold days are being observed both in the United States and Australia; the length of summer heat waves in western Europe has almost doubled, and the frequency of hot days has almost tripled over the period from 1880 to 2005. Extremely hot summers are now observed in about 10% of the global land area, compared with only about 0.1 - 0.2% for the period 1951 to 1980. The research found that just under a third of the global population is currently exposed to heat extremes. Up to three quarters of the world's population could be at risk from deadly heat extremes by the end of the century. This is particularly a problem in urban areas, where the majority of the population lives, as temperature increases can exacerbate what is known as the "heat-island" effect, in which densely built-up areas tend to be hotter than nearby rural areas.[25] The year 2015 was also the first year in which global temperatures were more than 1°C above the pre-industrial era.

Extreme heat has a detrimental effect on human health. If the core body temperature rises to 38°C for several hours, heat exhaustion occurs, and mental and physical capacity becomes impaired. If the core temperature goes above 42°C, even for just a few hours, heat stroke and death can result.[26]

The risk to human health is even greater than it may appear. Frank Landis, in his book *"Hot Earth Dreams"*, predicts the future for climate change up to 400,000 years from now. He quotes some researchers as suggesting that when temperature and humidity are high you can reach a "wet bulb temperature" as a threat to human life. This is the temperature that is usually thought of as air temperature, and it is the true thermodynamic temperature (the lowest temperature which may be achieved by evaporative cooling). At a wet bulb temperature of 35°C humans stop being able to shed heat from their bodies by sweating. The Marine Corps call this "black flag" weather. According to Landis, in the next 200 years we could see episodes of this type of weather occurring over much of the Middle East, the Australian outback, much of India, much of China, central Brazil and the south-eastern USA.[27] According to research by Sherwood and Huber this type of extreme weather could displace more people than rises in sea level.[28]

Europe

There are many present day examples of extreme heat-related deaths. The 2003 European heat wave led to the hottest summer on record in Europe since at least 1540. France was hit especially hard with 15,000 deaths. The heat wave led to health crises in several countries and combined with drought to create a crop shortfall in parts of Southern Europe. Peer-reviewed analysis places the overall European death toll at more than 70,000.[29]

Russia has also experienced heat waves. From late July until the second week in August 2010, record heat was recorded in Russia and Eastern Europe, causing the worst drought in nearly 40 years, and resulting in the loss of at least 9 million hectares of crops. A combination of smoke from wildfires - producing heavy smog which blanketed large urban regions - and the record-breaking heat wave put stress on the Russian healthcare system, resulting in an estimated 56,000 deaths.[30] According to research in 2011, experiencing mega-heat waves like that of 2010 will increase by a factor of 5 to 10 within the next 40 years.[31]

The 2018 European heat wave was a period of unusually hot weather that led to record-breaking temperatures and wildfires in many parts of Europe during the spring and summer of 2018. According to the World Meteorological Organization, the severe heat waves across the northern hemisphere in the summer of 2018 were linked to climate change, as were events of extreme precipitation. It was estimated there were 250 heat deaths in Denmark and also a few in Spain and Portugal.[32] It continued with the June 2019 European heat wave, which was a period of unusually hot weather affecting south western to central Europe, starting in late June and resulting in the hottest June ever recorded in Europe. An estimated 567 people died. But by July there was an even more intense heat wave. The deaths of 868 people in France and one person in Belgium were reported, along with thousands of animals.[33]

North America

North America has had its share of heat waves. The best example of the effect of "heat islands" was the heat wave deaths in Chicago in 1995, which led to an estimated 739 heat-related deaths over 5 days.[34] The 2006 North American heat wave affected a wide area of the United States and parts of neighbouring Canada during July and August 2006. Over 220 deaths were reported.[35] This was followed by the summer 2012 heat wave, which was one of the most severe in modern North American history. It resulted in 104 heat-related deaths across the United States and Canada.[36] The 2018 North American heat wave affected regions of Canada, where at least 70 deaths in Quebec were heat-related. There was also severe disruption and wild fires in California.[37] This was followed by another heat wave in North America in 2019. In Anchorage, Alaska, which is just 370 miles from the Arctic Circle, a record 32 degrees Celsius was recorded – this was hotter than New York city![38]

India

Developing countries are not immune. In India more than 1 billion people lack access to electricity and reliable sources of clean water. Such resources are particularly important to protecting those most vulnerable to heat-related illness - the very young, the elderly, and those with underlying medical conditions. Eleven of India's 15 warmest years have occurred since 2004. More than 6,000 heat-related deaths have been reported in India since 2010, according to the *Times of India*.[39] Heat waves killed 1,300 people there in 2010.[40] In 2015 more than 2,200 people died in India's different geographical regions and in Karachi, Pakistan, 2,500 died.[41] In early 2019, an intense heat wave scorched northern India. 65% of India's population was exposed to temperatures of over 40°C between May and June. 184 died in Bihar state but accurate numbers of deaths overall are not available at the time of publication.[42]

Australia

Australia is the driest and hottest continent. From 1844 to 2010, extreme heat events killed at least 5,332 people in Australia.[43] The 2009 heat wave that hit Victoria and South Australia killed 432 people, which is two and a half times the number of people killed in the Black Saturday bushfires that followed.[44] In 2014 a report by Australia's Climate Council found that climate change is causing more intense and frequent heat waves in Australia. Since 1950, the annual number of record hot days across Australia has more than doubled, the report found.[45] The Bureau of Meteorology of Australia released its biennial *"State of the Climate Report"* in 2016, which highlighted the impact climate change is having on the continent. According to an Australian Government report of the same year there will be more than 2,000 heat-related fatalities in 2050, compared with about 500 recorded in 2011.[46] 2019 produced record-breaking temperatures. In some areas the temperature was so hot that fruit on fruit trees cooked from the inside out![47]

WILDFIRES

With great heat comes the likelihood of further deaths from wildfires. You would expect wildfires in Australia. Australia's deadliest wildfire, and arguably the nation's worst natural disaster, was the "Black Saturday Fire" of February 7 - March 14, 2009. A swarm of fires burned 1.1 million acres and killed 180 people.[48] In 2013 came New South Wales bushfires: 208 houses lost, 2 fatalities, and 210,000 acres burned.[49] In 2014 there were more bushfires, burning 190,000 acres and killing 3 people.[50] In the 2015-2016 fire season there were 780,000 acres burnt, 400 houses destroyed and 9 people killed.[51] The catastrophic 2019–20 Australian bushfire season has burned an estimated 15.6 million acres, destroyed over 1,400 homes, and killed at least 24 people and an estimated 1 billion animals.[52] Meanwhile Australia is one of the main exporters of coal in the world!

More broadly, according to the IPCC report, almost all of North America and most of Europe will see an increase in wildfires by the year 2100. In the USA, the Southwest (Arizona, New Mexico and western Texas) is the fastest-warming region, and this warming trend will worsen wildfire risk.[53] In 2011 wildfires across this region burnt 3 million acres of land and killed 5 people.[54] This was followed in 2012 with western wildfires burning 9.2 million acres and killing 8 people.[55] The year 2015 was the worst year to date for wildfires in the long-term record, and was marked by intense drought across much of the western U.S. Dry conditions from drought likely contributed to the high levels of wildfire activity. The Alaskan and western wildfires together burnt 10 million acres. Of these, the most extensive wildfires occurred in Alaska where over 5 million acres burned. There was also much loss of property in California.[56] In 2017 California was again hit by extensive wildfires burning 220,000 acres, destroying 8,400 buildings and killing 47 people - almost surpassing the previous 10 years combined.[57] In 2018 North America experienced more wildfires and it was even worse in California where 103 people died and a state of emergency was declared.[58]

In Europe, in June 2017, Portugal experienced devastating wildfires which killed 64 people and 111,000 acres of land were burned.[59] In 2018 Greece suffered from wild fires with an estimated 102 people confirmed dead. The fires were the second-deadliest wildfire event in the 21st century, after the 2009 Black Saturday bushfires in Australia.[60]

DROUGHT

Drought is the *absence* of water. It is a creeping phenomenon that slowly sneaks up and impacts many sectors of the economy, and operates on many different time scales. Precipitation has declined in the tropics and subtropics since 1970. At the same time, increased heating due to climate change leads to greater evaporation of moisture from land, thereby increasing the intensity and duration of drought.

Southern Africa, the Sahel region of Africa, southern Asia, the Mediterranean, U.S. Southwest, eastern Australia, northern South America, most of Alaska, and western Canada are showing a long-term drying trend.[61]

Australia

Australia is already the driest of the habitable continents. It is no surprise that Australia was the first to see such climate change-driven decadal drought. Australia's "Millennium" drought began in 1995 and continued country-wide until late 2009. By 2009, most of the south of the country was gripped by an unprecedented 12-year drought. Between 2017 and 2019, severe drought developed once more across much of eastern and inland Australia including Queensland, New South Wales and Victoria, also extending into parts of South and Western Australia. The state of New South Wales was declared to be 100% in drought by August 2018, remaining at 98.6% into May 2019. Australia's national science research agency, the Commonwealth Scientific and Industrial Research Organisation (CSIRO), states that on account of projected future climate change, hot days will become more frequent and hotter (very high confidence), and the time in drought is projected to increase over southern Australia (high confidence).[62]

Africa

The poor will be inheritors of the worst hell of climate change. Drought in Africa illustrates this point perfectly. The Sahel is a 1000-mile wide strip of land between the Sahara and the start of the tropical rain forests. Droughts have been happening in the Sahel for the past 12,000 years but due to climate change they have become more regular and intense. The basic cause is that evaporation is occurring at a higher rate due to the change in sea surface temperature brought on by climate change. This then impacts the amount of rain the Sahel region receives. There was a drought in 2005 but in 2010 more than 10 million people in the Sahel region experienced major food shortages after drought destroyed crops and cattle. A massive aid operation prevented all-out famine. In Niger some 7 million people, or nearly half the population, experienced food shortages in 2010. Of those, more than 3 million faced severe shortages.[63] In 2011 this was followed by a drought in the horn of Africa: in Somalia, Djibouti, Ethiopia, Kenya, Uganda and neighbouring countries. On 20 July, the United Nations officially declared famine, the first time a famine had been declared in the region by the UN in nearly thirty years. The Food Programme said that it expected 10 million people across the Horn of Africa region to need food aid. Total deaths were estimated between 50,000 and 260,000 people.[64] In 2012 there was yet another drought in the Sahel. Over 18 million people across nine countries were affected, and more than one million children's lives were at risk because households could not obtain enough food.[65]

Brazil

Brazil is home to the largest equatorial forest in the world and is a carbon sink taking a great deal of carbon dioxide out of the atmosphere. In an average year, the Amazon basin absorbs about 1.5 billion tonnes of CO_2 from the atmosphere. There were droughts in 2005 and 2010. The 2010 drought stretched over 1.1 million square miles. The causes of both these droughts may have been high surface temperatures in the Atlantic Ocean from global warming resulting in decreased rainfall over the Amazon region. Basically the 2010 drought killed trees, and this may release a further 5 billion metric tons of carbon dioxide into the atmosphere over the coming years once the trees that are killed by the new drought rot away. The horror story is that if these droughts occur more frequently the Amazon basin will be a source of carbon emissions rather than a sink for them![66]

China

Although China is the powerhouse of the world economy it has problems with drought. The 2010–2011 drought impacted eight provinces in the northern part of the People's Republic of China. It was the worst drought to hit the country in 60 years, and it affected most of the wheat-producing regions. By February 2011, the drought had hit a total of up to 19 million acres. According to government estimates, 18 million people and 11 million farm animals were short of water.[67]

USA

So we come to the USA, with the richest economy in the world, and the only country to withdraw from the United Nations Climate Change agreement of 2015 (until a change of president). Drought has a long history in the USA and now its more frequent occurrence is connected to climate change. The Southern Plains and the South West of the United States were hit by a drought in 2011, across Texas, Oklahoma, New Mexico, Arizona, southern Kansas, and western Louisiana. A research report in the American Meteorological Society magazine in May 2012 found a direct correlation between climate change and the Texas drought.[68] This was swiftly followed by the 2012 drought as the most extensive drought to affect the U.S. since the 1930s. Moderate to extreme drought conditions affected more than half the country for the majority of 2012. Drought across the central agricultural states resulted in widespread harvest failure for corn, sorghum and soybean crops.[69] The period between late 2011 and 2014 was the driest in California since record-keeping began. The 2012-15 period was the driest in at least 1,200 years,

41

following which (in 2015), California experienced its lowest snowpack in at least 500 years. The drought ended in 2016. California's 9.3 million acres of irrigated crops help grow over a third of the country's vegetables and two-thirds of the country's fruits and nuts. If drought becomes more consistent how will America make up the food deficit?[70]

FLOODING

If it is not dry then it is very wet! Peter Stott, head of climate monitoring and attribution at the U.K. Meteorological Office's Hadley Centre for Climate Change has said, "The upshot is that overall rainfall increases only 2 to 3% per degree of warming, whereas extreme rainfall increases by 6 to 7%." Geoffrey Maslen in his pessimistic book on climate change describes extreme rainfall as "rain bombs", where 20-30cms (8-12ins) of water is dumped in an hour. Basically what has happened during the past 25 years is that satellites have measured a 4% average rise in water vapour in the air column. The more water vapour, the greater the potential for intense rainfalls. Sudden rainfall leads to flooding because the infrastructure cannot cope, especially in poorer countries.[71] Colin McFarlane, a Durham University urban geographer, has stated, "It's now estimated that about one in four residents living in cities in the global south are in informal settlements", and these are characterised by lack of planned development to deal with possible flooding. Floods are the most common natural disaster and the leading cause of natural disaster fatalities worldwide.[72] According to the U.N. about 90% of all natural disasters are water-related. Over the period 1995–2015, floods accounted for 43% of all documented natural disasters, affecting 2.3 billion people, killing 157,000. Globally, 2016 saw 384 flood disasters, compared with 58 in 1980.[73]

Asia

Southern Asia is already the wettest area on that continent and one of the wettest regions in the world, receiving an average of at least 1,000mm of rainfall a year. In the next 30 years, some research has projected that heavy rainfall events will be increasing in Asia by about 20%.[74]

On a larger scale, heavier monsoon rains and tropical storms are a result of climate change, a very complex system that is characterised by the dynamic relationships between land and bodies of water. The monsoon is the major factor in flooding in South East Asia. This area is particularly vulnerable to the impacts of climate change due to its fast growing population, the majority of whom are living in poverty, as well as poor food security and dwindling natural resources.

The floods in Pakistan began in late July 2010, resulting from heavy monsoon rains. Approximately one-fifth of Pakistan's total land area was affected by floods. According to Pakistani government data, the floods directly affected about 20 million people, mostly by destruction of property, livelihood and infrastructure, with a death toll of close to 2,000.[75]

This was followed in 2011 by catastrophic floods across S.E. Asia in the monsoon season. According to the United Nations Office for the Coordination of Humanitarian Affairs it was estimated that 9.6 million people were affected by the flooding. All told, well over 2,828 lost their lives to a series of flooding events of varying origins in the Southeast Asian countries of Thailand, Cambodia, Myanmar, Malaysia, Vietnam, Laos and the Philippines.[76]

Then came the floods of Northern India in 2013, which were a classic example of less frequent, but more intense, rainfall. In this case it was about 375% more than the benchmark rainfall during a normal monsoon. A study by Utah University connected the increase of rainfall in North India to climate change. According to figures provided by the Uttarakhand state government, more than 5,700 people were presumed dead.[77]

This was rapidly followed in 2017 by further flooding in India, Nepal and Bangladesh, leaving 1,200 dead. According to UNICEF, 45 million people were affected. Bangladesh was the worst affected country with nearly 700,000 homes damaged or destroyed, 11 million acres of farmland inundated, and thousands of miles of damaged roads. One third of Bangladesh was under water and this precipitated food shortages and the danger of water-borne diseases.[78]

2018 saw the severe flooding in Kerala, in southern India, with the worst flood in nearly a century. Over 600 people were estimated to have died and about a million people were evacuated.[79]

Most Indian scientists now acknowledge that the increasing rainfall from monsoons is caused by climate change. There were more floods in India in 2019, with Kerala being flooded again. There was a series of floods that affected over thirteen states in late July and early August 2019, due to incessant rains. At least 200 people died and about a million people were displaced. Karnataka and Maharashtra were the most severely affected states.[80]

China

China is deeply involved in the need to combat climate change, which is not surprising since it has been devastated by floods for years. This is a country which has suffered from the increase in intensity of rainfall due to climate change which means that the existing infrastructure cannot cope. In 2010, floods, heavy rains and landslides left more than 4,000 people dead or missing, affected 230 million people, and caused 15 million to evacuate their homes.[81] Again in 2011, flooding occurred in central and southern parts of China. This caused 355 deaths and affected 36 million people.[82] In 2016, areas along the Yangtze River and Huai River flooded due to sudden extreme rainfall. An estimated 32 million people across 26 provinces were affected and more than 200 people were killed. 80,000 hectares of cropland were destroyed.[83] This was rapidly followed in 2017 when more than 60 rivers were close to overflowing their banks, flooding killed more than 50 people and forced more than 1.2 million people to evacuate their homes.[84]

Europe

Europe has had its fair share of floods caused by climate change. The 2010 Central European floods were caused by extreme rainfall across several central European countries during May and June. Poland was the worst affected, with two months' worth of rain pouring down over a 24-hour period. Austria, the Czech Republic, Germany, Hungary, Slovakia, Serbia and Ukraine were also affected. At least 37 people died in the floods and approximately 23,000 people were evacuated.[85]

In my own country flooding is becoming more devastating as rainfall becomes more intense over shorter periods of time. Even our modern infrastructure cannot cope. In 2012 Britain had the wettest April in a hundred years, followed by the wettest early June in 150 years. It turned out that 2012 was the second wettest year on record for the UK. The worst hit areas were Wales, Yorkshire, South West England and North East England.[86] In 2013-2014 there was the greatest January rainfall in southern England at least since yearly records began in 1910. The worst affected areas were Somerset, Devon, Dorset and Cornwall in the south west and the Thames Valley in the south-east.[87] This was followed by the winter of 2015-2016, when a study, carried out by scientists from the Centre for Ecology & Hydrology, in collaboration with the British Hydrological Society, concluded that this episode ranked alongside the floods of 1947 as one of the two largest flood events of the last 100 years at least. There was extensive river flooding in northern England, Scotland, Northern Ireland and parts of Wales over a three month period. There were at least nine deaths.[88] In November 2019, Yorkshire and the Humber, the East Midlands, and the West Midlands, as well as parts of South-east England and Gloucestershire were struck by serious river and surface water flooding.[89] Climate change has ensured that the UK faces the possibility of severe flooding every year with a great human and economic cost.

USA

The 2014 *National Climate Assessment* reported that downpours from storms are dumping more water across the nation than ever before, with the Midwest, Pacific Northwest and the Upper Plains receiving the greatest increase in heavy rainfall. The Environmental Protection Agency notes that heavy rainfall events have increased by 70% in the Pacific Northwest over the past six decades or so, more than any other region in the United States. The Mid West is particularly vulnerable with one report finding that the number of extreme rainstorms - deluges that dump 3 inches of rain or more in a day - doubled in the region over the last half-century. Across the Midwest the biggest storms increased by 103% from 1961 through to 2011, a study released by the Rocky Mountain Climate Organization and the Natural Resources Defense Council reported. Overall annual precipitation for the region rose 23% between 1961 and 2011. In 2008, seven of the eight Midwestern states had flooding disasters. This resulted in 16 deaths.[90] Preceded by more than a week of heavy rain, a slow-moving storm system dropped tremendous precipitation across much of Texas and Oklahoma during May 2015. This resulted in 31 deaths. A study by Utah State University implicated climate change as a main cause of the increased rainfall over the region.[91] This was followed in 2016 by extensive flooding in a large area of southern Louisiana, resulting from 20 to 30 inches of rainfall over several days in what was considered a 1 in 500 year event. This flood has been called the worst US natural disaster since Hurricane Sandy in 2012. The result was that over 50,000 homes were destroyed and 13 people died.[92] In 2017 California was devastated by floods. Northern California saw its wettest winter in almost a century, breaking the previous record set in the winter of 1982–83. At one point it necessitated 188,000 people being evacuated because of the Oroville Dam spillway being damaged.[93] This was followed by what the *New York Times* called "The Great Flood of 2019". The 2019 January-to-May period was the wettest on record for the U.S., with multiple severe weather outbreaks through May in the Midwest, High Plains, and south exacerbating the flooding and causing additional damage. Nearly 14 million people in the mid-western and southern states were affected. At least 1 million acres of U.S. farmland, in nine major grain-producing states, flooded.[94]

CONCLUSION

What the spiritual teachings at the opening of the chapter are telling us is that we have to find balance and harmony in ourselves. If this is achieved then we will create harmony and balance in the environment. The way that we do this is simply by adopting spiritual values and acting upon them in our lives. We have ignored spiritual guidance on the values to live by and the consequences are dire. Extreme weather is just a manifestation of the general population's lack of awareness that there are better values to guide the way we live.

Chapter 3: WATER SHORTAGES

First let us look at water from a spiritual perspective to see how it is valued by some spiritual traditions. They have not forgotten that water is a fundamental necessity for life. Then we will go into how this precious resource has been affected by our ignoring and forgetting these values, causing climate change which has resulted in water shortages.

THE IDEAL - OUR RELATIONSHIP WITH WATER FROM A SPIRITUAL PERSPECTIVE

Judaism and Christianity

These two faiths share many of their scriptures so are considered here together. The Bible and water are very much connected. Water is mentioned 722 times in the scriptures. Jeremiah describes God as "the fountain of living waters". (Jeremiah 2:13, 17:13) In day five of creation we find in Genesis 1:20 God said, "Let the waters bring forth abundantly the moving creatures that have life..." This passage shows us that life comes out of the water. In Job 5:10 "He bestows rain on the earth; he sends water upon the countryside." There is a quote by Moses in Deuteronomy 8:7, "For the Lord our God is bringing you into a good country, a land with streams of water, with springs and fountains welling up in the hills and valleys."

Water is seen as coming from God and therefore sacred. The scarceness of water was very serious and drought was often viewed as a result of the wrath of God. The prophets Elijah, Jeremiah and Haggai all predict drought as punishment from God (1 Kings 17:1, Jeremiah 14: 1-6 and Haggai 1: 10-11 respectively). Conversely rainfall is a sign of God's favour and goodness.

In the New Testament water is a symbol of the gift of eternal life. Some examples are John 4:14: "But whosoever drinketh of the water that I shall give him shall never thirst; but the water that I shall give him shall be in him a well of water springing up into everlasting life." Also Revelation 21:6: "I am Alpha and Omega, the beginning and the end. I will give unto him that is athirst of the fountain of the water of life freely."

Water is used in the baptism ceremony, whereby a person becomes a member of the Christian Church. Baptism is seen as a form of cleansing for the forgiveness of sins, as in Hebrews 10:22: "Let us draw near with a true heart in full assurance of faith, having our hearts sprinkled from an evil conscience, and our bodies washed with pure water." In this ceremony the baby or adult is immersed in water and their re-emergence from water has an extremely powerful meaning. Indeed it symbolises death and rebirth, the elimination of impurity and the guarantee of eternal life. Water is also one of the symbols used to represent the Holy Spirit. Jesus informed us of this when he said, "Unless one is born of water and the Spirit, you cannot enter the kingdom of God." (John 3 1-13)

The purifying properties of water are clearly recognised by St. Francis of Assisi, a beacon of Christian ecology when he stated: "Be praised, my Lord, through Sister Water; she is very useful and humble and precious and pure." Christian sanctuaries are found by water springs which are held to have potent healing powers. Among the principal sanctuaries are the Marian shrines to the Virgin Mary: Lourdes in France, Loreto in Italy, Fatima in Portugal, Santiago de Compostela in Spain and Medjugorje in Bosnia-Herzegovina.

Jainism

The Jains see water as sacred as it is full of living beings as part of the eternal self or *Jiva Tattva*. The *anarth dand tyag* vow in Jainism prohibits unnecessary or excessive violence and therefore water has to be used in a respectful way. As their scriptures say, "Water itself has been propounded as a living being." (Bhasyam Sutra 53). There are two types of *jeevs* or lifeforms in water. Firstly there is *Apkaay Jeev* - Infinitely small organisms that make up the water itself. Secondly there are microorganisms.

Islam

Muslims believe that God created the world. The Qur'an states, "We made from water every living thing. Will they not then believe?" (Qur'an 21:30). The Qur'an also states, "The whole Earth has been created as a place of worship for me, pure and clean." Accordingly, Muslims are charged with the religious duty of treating the Earth, including water, with the respect due to a place of worship and with keeping it pure and undefiled. According to Islamic teachings, no one can own or possess water since it is a divine gift.

In Islam water is important for cleansing and purifying. Muslims must be ritually pure before approaching God in prayer. Firstly, *ghusl*, the major ablution, is the washing of the whole body in pure water, after declaring the intention to do so. The second ablution is *wudu*, the minor ablution, which is performed to remove minor ritual impurity from everyday life. This must be done before each of the five daily prayers and involves washing the face with pure water, rubbing the head with water, washing the hands and arms up to the elbows and the feet up to the ankles. This comes from the verse "O you who believe, when you prepare for prayer, wash your faces and your hand to the elbows; rub your head and your feet to the ankles." (Qur'an 5: 7/8) Every Mosque has running water for the performance of *wudu*.

To desert people, water is life. There are 900 references to water in the Qur'an. Muhammad said, "People share three things: water, pasture and fire." Extravagance in using water was forbidden; this applied to private use as well as public and whether the water was scarce or abundant. It is related that the Prophet passed by his companion Sa'd, who was washing for prayer and said, "What is this wastage, O Sa'd?" "Is there wastage even in washing for prayer?" asked Sa'd; and He said, "Yes, even if you are by a flowing river!" Water conservation was practised in the Prophet's time in that large rivers were decreed for use by all; and with local rivers, the rights of people living upstream were more restricted than the rights of those downstream. With naturally-occurring springs, ownership was deemed to be held in common. If a person discovered a spring, then the water rights of that person would be assured. Yet, significantly, even when a spring was someone's property, the owner was expected to allow others to use it to water their livestock. Wells were also carefully managed. Generally the priority of usage was granted to those with livestock and crops. If a person dug a well then they had the right to the water but it was expected that any surplus would be available to the livestock of others. If a well was of a temporary nature then the person who dug it had the right to the water, but if they abandoned the well then anybody had access to it. The Qur'an also prohibited the misuse and pollution of water, declaring that those who did so would suffer on the day of judgement. The Prophet forbade that a person relieve himself in a water source or on a path, or in a place of shade, or in the burrow of a living creature.

Paganism

From prehistoric times, humans venerated gods and goddesses of water, both agricultural and funerary, often with characteristics in common. For early humans the source of all life was the Mother Goddess from whose underground womb all living creatures were born. This Goddess was the goddess of the Earth or Nature itself, she who could give or take life and renew herself in the eternal cycle of seasons and water, from death to rebirth. The first evidence we have of this belief system goes back to the Middle Palaeolithic, which began about 100,000 years ago, when humans started using triangular tombstone symbols in stone (symbol of the female reproductive organs) and dug little cups into the stone to collect rainwater, life-giving fluid. From the upper Palaeolithic onwards, or from 40,000 years ago, humans produced stone sculptures and rock engravings of animals and female figures. Whole vases or fragments found by archaeologists near to water sources in areas that are not easily accessible are evidence that these waters were probably considered sacred or magic, or that they had healing properties, if drunk *in loco*, perhaps also due to the mirror effect they produced. During the Neolithic period, alongside circular ditches found in caves, there is archaeological evidence of rituals in the presence of water. These finds are located in particular near underground water, springs, or caves containing stalagmites. Later, during the Bronze Age, men tended not to consider still waters sacred so much as running water, a common symbol of purity.

The Celts revered all kinds of water habitats - rivers, springs, lakes and seas - and so they would never despoil them. Among their numerous riverside deities, Coventina was the water nymph at the sacred spring at the Roman fort on Hadrian's Wall near Carrawburgh, Northumberland in England. Thirteen altars discovered there, along with some 13,000 Roman coins, attest to her popularity. Springs were thought to be places of spiritual power, especially hot springs. At the spa town of Buxton in Derbyshire, England, they found evidence of a whole healing cult, with people immersing themselves in the water and drinking it. There are few written records, but the clear archaeological evidence of offerings near springs and rivers suggests that water's life-giving qualities were not just recognised but actively honoured and water held as sacred.

Shamanism

For thousands of years, Native American tribes across north America developed their own methods of living with the natural world and its limited water supply. They also learned from their religious ideas, passed on from generation to generation in the form of stories. You can see from the following that they thought water was sacred:

"We call upon the waters that rim the Earth, horizon to horizon, that flow in our rivers and streams, that fall upon our gardens and fields and we ask that they teach us and show us the way." (Chinook Indian Blessing.)

"We should be as water, which is lower than all things yet stronger even than the rocks." (Oglala Sioux Proverb)

"This shining water that moves in the streams and rivers is not just water but the blood of our ancestors. The rivers are our brothers, they quench our thirst and feed our children." Chief Seattle of the Suquamish and Duwamish Native American tribes.

"They shall offer thanks to the Earth where all people dwell - to the streams of water, the pools, the springs and the lakes." (Iroquois saying.)

"Water sustains all life. Her songs begin in the tiniest of raindrops, transform to flowing rivers, and travel to majestic oceans and thundering clouds and back to earth again. When water is threatened, all living things are threatened." (Indigenous Declaration on Water, 2001)

The Blackfeet tribe viewed water as a distinct place – a sacred place. It was the home of divine beings and divine animals who taught the Blackfeet religious rituals and moral restrictions on human behaviour. The Blackfeet believed that in addition to the divine beings, about which they learned from their stories, there were divine animals, such as the beaver. The divine beaver, who could talk to humans, taught the Blackfeet their most important religious ceremony.

51

The Pueblo Indians saw all water as sacred, especially their Blue Lake, and to be the source of all life - as well as the home for all deceased souls. Pueblos had a reverence for the Blue Lake that included yearly pilgrimages to the site and also recognised the waters and area surrounding the lake as sacred lands.

According to Cheyenne theology, all things in the universe have spirits. This includes people, plants, and animals, all types of water (rivers, creeks, springs, ground water and swamps). Rivers, streams, and springs are a central feature of Cheyenne ceremonies. Sacred waters are used in sweat lodge ceremonies, in medicine, and to wash off sacred earth paints. Springs were seen as the homes of spirits. Offerings are commonly left at springs today.

Hualapai religious ceremonies revolve around water, and they believe water from the mountain peaks near the Grand Canyon is sacred. This sacred water is used in their sweat lodge purification ceremony, as they pour the sacred water onto heated rocks to make steam. In a healing ceremony, people seeking treatment drink from the water used to produce the steam and are cleansed by brushing the water on their bodies with feathers. At the conclusion of the healing ceremony, the other people present also drink the water.

The Cherokee saw water as having healing properties. One ritual, called "going to water," was performed on many occasions - at the new moon, before special dances, after bad dreams, or during illnesses. Going to water cleansed the spirit as well as the body. The ritual was performed at sunrise. Cherokee men, women, and children would face the east, step into a river or creek, and dip under the water seven times. When they emerged, they would be rid of bad feelings and ready to begin anew, with a clear mind.

Hinduism

Water in Hinduism has a special place because it is believed to have spiritually cleansing powers. To Hindus all water is sacred, especially rivers, and there are seven sacred rivers, namely the Ganges, Yamuna, Godavari, Sarasvati, Narmada, Sindhu and Kaveri. The Ganges River is the most important of the sacred rivers. The ancient scriptures mention that the water of Ganges carries the blessings of Lord Vishnu's feet; hence Mother Ganges is also known as Vishnupadi, which means "Emanating from the Lotus feet of Supreme Lord Sri Vishnu." Its waters are used in *puja* (worship) and if possible a sip is given to the dying. It is believed that those who bathe in the Ganges and those who leave some part of themselves on the left bank will attain *Svarga* (the paradise of Indra).

Water was considered to be sacred and vital to the ecosystem. As the Rig Veda states, "Water in the sky, water in the rivers, water in the well, whose source is the ocean; may all these sacred waters protect me". (Rig Veda 7, 49.2) Water is described as the foundation of the whole world, the essence of plant life and the elixir of immortality. (Satapatha Brahmana VI 8, 2.2; III 6, 1.7) Water is seen as giving vigour, potency and vitality. (Yajurveda 29, 53) "May the Water bring us well-being!" (Atharva Veda II, 3.6.) "The rivers are the veins of the cosmic person; trees are the hairs of His body." (Bhagavad Gita II.1.33-34)

"Hail, Water, ye bring health and bliss: ye help us to energy, that we may look on great delight!" (Sama Veda 9:2:10)

During all purification rites water is sprinkled on the objects which are to be purified. Water used to be sprinkled on any offerings to the deities. Water is very important for all the rituals in Hinduism. For example, water is essential as a cleaning agent, cleaning the vessels used for the rituals, and for Abhishekas or bathing of Deities. Water offered to the Deity and the water collected after bathing the Deities is considered very sacred. This water is offered as "Theertha" or blessed offering to the devotees.

Sikhism

According to the Holy Scripture of the Sikhs, Sri Guru Granth Sahib, water is considered to be the most important thing for the origin of life. The entire universe was created from water and the light of the Lord exists in everything. As life cannot exist without water, it has been called the father of the world in the Guru Granth Sahib. As it says in the Guru Granth Sahib, "Air, water, earth and sky - the Lord has made these His home and temple." (p723) Also "Air is the Guru, water is the Father and Earth is the Great Mother of all." (Japji Sahib Prayer in the Guru Granth Sahib.)

The sacredness of water for the Sikhs is confirmed in the *amrit* ceremony whereby a person becomes initiated as a Sikh. *Amrit* is prepared. *Amrit* is a mixture of sugar and water that has been stirred with a double-edged sword. The candidates for initiation drink some of the *amrit* from the same bowl, and have it sprinkled on their eyes and hair. Each then recites the *Mool Mantra* (the fundamentals of Sikhism). There are then readings from the Guru Granth Sahib and an explanation of the rules of Sikhism.

THE ACTUAL – WHAT CLIMATE CHANGE HAS DONE TO OUR WATER

Demand For Water

Water makes up 81% of our bodies and so for us, fresh uncontaminated water is the single most important resource on Earth. Only 3% of the world's water is fresh water, and two-thirds of that is tucked away in frozen glaciers or otherwise unavailable for our use. It is predicted that global warming will alter precipitation patterns around the world, melt mountain glaciers, and worsen the extremes of droughts and floods.

Globally 70% of water used goes to agriculture, 20% to industry and 10% to households. Our water footprint is the amount of water we use in and around our home throughout the day. It includes the water we use directly (i.e. from a tap) and the water that is used to produce the food we eat, the products we buy, the energy we consume. We may not drink, feel or see this virtual water, but it makes up the majority of our water footprint. Dr. Chenoweth of Surrey University estimates that for a high quality of life every person requires approximately 135 litres (over 35 gallons) a day. His estimate includes cooking, drinking, hygiene, as well as industry, agriculture, and service sectors. Currently the largest water guzzlers in the developed world - Canada and New Zealand - consume 700 litres of water per person per day.[1]

Global warming is expected to account for about 20% of the global increase in water scarcity this century. At present, according to the U.N., over 2 billion people live in countries experiencing high water stress. This means about a third of the world has water scarcity, and, according to the researchers, climate change can make this even worse. Currently 4 billion people live under conditions of severe water shortages at least one month of the year, according to new research. Nearly half of these people live in India and China. Other populations facing severe water scarcity live in Bangladesh, the United States (mostly in western states), Pakistan and Nigeria. Of the total figure half a billion people experience water shortages all year round, with the highest number affected in India and Pakistan.[2]

The food we eat makes up more than two thirds of our total water footprint. Around 70% of freshwater withdrawal is used by agriculture across the world. The irrigated area of the world increased dramatically during the early and middle parts of the twentieth century, driven by rapid population growth and the resulting demand for food. Irrigation provides approximately 40% of the world's food, including most of its horticultural output.[3] The average water footprint per calorie for beef is 20 times larger than that for cereals and starchy roots. When we look at the water requirements for protein, it has been found that the water footprint per gram of protein for milk, eggs and chicken meat is about 1.5 times larger than for pulses. For beef, the water footprint per gram of protein is 6 times larger than for pulses. According to the Food and Agriculture Organisation (FAO), it is estimated that the livestock sector uses 10% of the annual global water flows. Often, more than 90% of the water consumption in livestock and poultry production is associated with the production of feed.[4]

In the modern materialist economy there is no shortage of demand for water. At the same time we have an ever-growing population in developing countries which will demand water just for drinking and for growing food. The expected increase in world population up to 10 billion people means that by 2050 there will be only half the amount of water available per person than there is today. The world population is currently growing by approximately 83 million people each year. More than 90% of this growth will be in the least developed countries, which are generally overpopulated. In the next 40 years, population growth will be absorbed by urban areas, particularly in less developed regions. Urbanisation leads to increased pressure on water sources as individuals become more concentrated in one area. An emerging middle class could clamour for more water-intensive food production and electricity generation.[5]

By 2050, demand for water will increase by 20 to 30%, due to higher demand from a larger global population. One study from 2014 in the academic journal *Agricultural Economics* stated that food demand might increase by 59% - 98% between 2005 and 2050. [6] Climate change will significantly impact agriculture by increasing water demand, limiting crop productivity and by reducing water availability in areas where irrigation is most needed.

Water Scarcity From Climate Change

Global atmospheric temperature is predicted to rise by approximately 4°C by 2080, consistent with a doubling of atmospheric CO_2. The maximum sustainable water vapour concentration increases by about 7% per degree Celsius. In response to global warming, the hydrological cycle is expected to accelerate as rising temperatures increase the rate of evaporation from land and sea. Thus rainfall is predicted to rise in the tropics and higher latitudes, but decrease in the already dry semi-arid to arid mid-latitudes and in the interior of large continents. Water-scarce areas will generally become drier and hotter. [7]

More than 5 billion people could suffer water shortages by 2050 due to climate change, increased demand and polluted supplies, according to a UN report on the state of the world's water. The number of people living in river basins under severe water stress is projected to reach 3.9 billion by 2050, totalling over 40% of the world's population. According to research by the Water Footprint Network, some 52% of the world's projected 9.7 billion people will live in water-stressed regions by 2050. [8]

Let's look at some examples in the developing and the developed world.

The Effect On Developed Countries

USA

The richer countries, which have caused climate change, will not escape the consequences of a dire shortage of water. Although the burden of climate change water scarcity will fall on the poorer countries, the very country which withdrew for a time from the Paris agreement will be one of the most affected by shortages of water from climate change.

California is a great example of water shortages increasing as temperatures rise. What this does is to increase the rate at which plants transpire water into the air to keep cool, and thereby more water is needed to grow them. Most of the fruits, vegetables and nuts are grown on irrigated farmland. About 90% of crops harvested in California are grown on farms that are entirely irrigated, so a sustained decrease in the amount of water available for irrigation would force farmers to either reduce the acreage under cultivation or shift away from the most water-intensive crops. Less water is likely to be available, because precipitation has not increased as much as evaporation. The result is that soils are likely to be drier, and periods without rain are likely to become longer, making droughts more severe.

Roughly 75% of California's precipitation falls in the winter, north of Sacramento. However, the greatest demand for water comes during the spring and summer from users south of Sacramento. California relies on snowpack in the Sierra Nevada Mountains for water supply during these dry months. The Sierra Nevada snowpack, which provides 60% of the state's water via a vast network of dams and reservoirs, has already been diminished by human-induced climate change and, if emissions levels aren't reduced, the snowpack could largely disappear during droughts, according to findings in the study published in the journal *Geophysical Research Letters*. Hall and Berg found that the Sierra Nevada snowpack during the 2011 to 2015 drought was 25% below what it would have been without human-induced warming. If humans continue emitting greenhouse gases in a business-as-usual scenario, average temperatures in the Sierras are projected to rise, causing the snowpack to decrease during drought periods by a massive 85%. Over the past 50 years, snowpack has been melting earlier in the year. As global warming continues, decreasing snowmelt and spring stream flows, coupled with increasing demand for water resulting from a growing population and a hotter climate, will likely lead to more water shortages.[9]

For much of the arid south-western United States, the Colorado River is the only major water supply and provides water to nearly 30 million people. It irrigates more than one and a half million hectares of farmland in Wyoming, Colorado, Utah, New Mexico, Arizona and Nevada, as well as California. Research in 2017 by Bradley Udall and Jonathon Overpeck found that between 2000 and 2014, annual Colorado River flows averaged 19% below that of 1906 - 1999. Approximately one-third of the flow loss was due to high temperatures - a result of human-caused climate change. These losses may exceed 20% at mid-century and 35% at the end of the century.[10] President Trump's actions in exiting the Paris agreement increased the chances of these scenarios becoming reality.

Europe

The Europeans have at least started to address climate change but even so the Mediterranean countries face an uncertain future in terms of water supply and food production. The 2013 IPCC report highlights the Mediterranean as one of the most vulnerable regions in the world to the impacts of global warming. It indicates that there may be an increase in temperature of between 2.2 and 5.1°C for the period 2080 - 2100. As regards rainfall regime changes in the Mediterranean, they estimate that precipitation over land might vary between -4% and -27%.[11] In 2018, the Helmholtz Centre for Environmental Research carried out a study and found negative consequences can be expected for the Mediterranean region, where the drought regions could expand from 28% of the area to 49% of the area compared to the 1971 to 2000 baseline in the worst case scenario. The number of drought months per year will also increase significantly in Southern Europe.[12]

A study in 2016 by Guiot and Cramer, from the European Centre for Geoscience Research, suggests that temperatures could rise by over 4°C by 2100 over many inland areas. Over the same period, annual precipitation is projected to decline by 10 to 40% over much of Africa and south-eastern Spain. The researchers warned that southern Spain will be reduced to desert by the end of the century if the current rate of greenhouse gas emissions continues unchecked.[13]

The European Commission (of the European Union) has estimated that at least 11% of Europe's population and 17% of its territory have been affected by water scarcity to date. Over the past thirty years, droughts have dramatically increased in number and intensity in the EU. The number of areas and people affected by droughts went up by almost 20% between 1976 and 2006.[14]

There have been recent droughts in Europe. Parts of the continent were affected by a severe drought in June and July 2015, as a consequence of the combination of rain shortages and very high temperatures. France, Benelux, Germany, Hungary, the Czech Republic, northern Italy and northern Spain experienced particularly exceptional conditions.[15] In 2018 there was another drought, and the main countries affected by this were Denmark, England, the Netherlands, Belgium, France, Germany, Norway, Sweden, Estonia and Latvia. The Deputy Secretary-General of the World Meteorological Organization, Elena Manaenkova, said of the event that "The heat waves and extreme heat we are experiencing are consistent with what we expect as a result of climate change caused by greenhouse gas emissions. This is not a future scenario. It is happening now."[16] So it goes on. We ask where the food that is lost is going to come from? Where will the displaced people go? These are consequences of not really understanding the spiritual teachings in relation to our need for reliable water resources.

The Effect On Developing Countries

Within Africa

Of all the areas where water scarcity is felt, the worst is on the continent of Africa. This is ironic because Africa has contributed least to the build-up of greenhouse gases in the atmosphere. The continent, which is home to 14% of the world's population, contributes only 3 - 4 % of total greenhouse gas emissions.[17] The IPCC has reported that land surface temperatures across most of Africa have increased by 0.5°C or more during the last 50 - 100 years. Part of that vulnerability is simply down to geography. It is already the hottest continent, and its warming is expected to be up to 1.5 times faster than the global average, according to the IPCC.[18]

East Africa affords a good example of the effect of climate on water shortages. Seven of the last ten years have seen chronic droughts in East Africa, due to poor or failed rains. Sub-Saharan Africa generally faces water shortages because of climate change, and droughts cause the most deaths because they can initiate malnutrition and deny the community a water supply. Two thirds of the people dwelling in sub-Saharan Africa live in areas of little to no rainfall, which often results in failed vegetation and agricultural efforts. It is estimated that by 2030 between 75 and 250 million people in sub-Saharan Africa will not be able to meet their water needs, if warming in the atmosphere continues; and these numbers could increase to 350 - 600 million by 2050. This is likely to displace anywhere between 24 million and 700 million people as food shortages increase.[19]

In southern Africa the IPCC predicts that temperatures in the region will be up to 3°C hotter than pre-industrial levels by 2050. Rainfall will increasingly come in short and violent storms, evaporating or running off quickly rather than sinking into the ground.[20] As an example: in 2016 five countries in the region – Swaziland, Lesotho, Malawi, Namibia and Zimbabwe – declared national drought disasters. There was the worst drought in South Africa for 30 years. There was also a severe drought in Ethiopia, where 10 million people needed food aid. Massive crop failures were experienced across these regions. The UN estimated that about 49 million people needed humanitarian assistance.[21]

Drought continued in East Africa in 2017. In Somaliland, 6 million people were affected by the drought. In Kenya, the drought left 2.7 million people in need of humanitarian assistance and in Ethiopia, five and a half million people needed food aid. In South Sudan, a famine was officially declared in 2017, with 4.6 million people in urgent need of food. Rain is usually expected in the East African region between April and June, but in 2019 it was recorded as one of the driest seasons in 35 years. Prolonged dry conditions across the region led to farmland and pastures failing, loss of livestock, increased food prices, and reduction of the availability of water. By September 2019 it was found by Action Aid that 21.5 million people needed humanitarian assistance across South Sudan, Somalia, Kenya and Ethiopia. Also in Somalia and Somaliland, it was found 2.2 million people were at risk of hunger. There are now fears that Somalia could see a repeat of the famine that struck in 2010-2011, and which killed over 250,000 people.[22]

Southern Africa's low level of economic development and its reliance on agriculture -namely cereal crops and livestock - leaves the region highly susceptible to droughts. The worst drought in decades affected 45 million people in 14 countries across Southern Africa in 2019. According to the International Federation of Red Cross and Red Crescent (IFRC), at least 11 million people faced food shortages due to drought in Namibia, Botswana, Lesotho, South Africa, Zimbabwe and Zambia. Grain production was down 30% across the region.[23]

India

The agrarian economy in South Asia supports nearly 1.2 billion people, and it is currently critically dependent on the use of groundwater. South Asia is hit particularly badly by drought because there have recently been massive losses of groundwater, which has been pumped up with reckless lack of control over the past decade. This affects 600 million people who live in Pakistan, northern India and into Bangladesh. This land is the most intensely irrigated in the world. Up to 75% of farmers rely on pumped groundwater to water their crops.[24]

Before long, India will become the most populated country on earth. By 2050, the population is expected to reach 1.6 billion people, surpassing

China. Having travelled around India in 2002 to do research for my previous book, I can testify that the poverty of the people is everywhere. With water shortages predicted in the next century, this situation will get worse.

India has 18% of the global population and only 4% of the global water resources. Nearly two-thirds of its agriculture – the mainstay of its economy – depends on the monsoon. The startling fact is that India only stores 6% of water in such facilities as reservoirs. The monsoon helps to replenish the ground water used in irrigation: as much as 55% of India's total water supply comes from groundwater resources. Today, groundwater irrigates over half of India's crops. The Indian government subsidises the farmers' electric pumps and places no limits on the volumes of groundwater they extract, creating a widespread pattern of excessive water use. The water table has fallen on average by 0.3 metres and by as much as 4 metres in some places. There has been a 61% decline in groundwater level in wells in India between 2007 and 2017, according to the Central Ground Water Board (CGWB), under the Ministry of Water Resources. This over-use of groundwater has come at a time when India's rainfall has decreased since the 1950s - some scientists say because of climate change. When rainfall decreases, so does the water table.[25]

Now, a new study by the Indian Institute of Technology (IIT) in the city of Gandhinagar, published in *Nature Geoscience*, shows that variable monsoon precipitation, linked to climate change, is likely to be the key reason for declining levels of groundwater. In India, warmer air over the Indian Ocean has altered the path of monsoons. Changes in monsoon patterns due to increased temperatures would make droughts and floods more common in many parts of India.[26]

India has experienced widespread drought every year since 2015, with the exception of 2017. In 2016 the states of Karnataka, Tamil Nadu and Kerala missed out on monsoon rains. Indian scientists are reporting increasingly erratic monsoon rains, with more frequent and intense extreme events such as drought, cyclones and floods. The 2015-16 drought has been categorised as one of the worst droughts in the history of India, and affected more than 330 million people in more than 11 states. State surveys revealed that the scale of damage done by drought was huge; the proportion of farmers who reported crop loss ranged from 60% to 94%.[27] The southwest monsoon of 2018-19, responsible for 80% of India's rainfall, was delayed and below normal in both northern and southern India. The north-east monsoon - also known as 'post-monsoon rainfall' (October - December) - that provides 10 - 20% of India's rainfall, was deficient by 44% in 2018. The state of Maharashtra declared drought in 42% of its area. In 2019 the drought continued and almost half of India - an area home to more than 500 million people – faced drought-like conditions. 8.2 million farmers in Karnataka and Maharashtra were affected by the drought. Chennai, India's sixth largest city, ran out of water.[28] So it goes on.

CONCLUSION

It is clear that all spiritual traditions see water as sacred, and value it as essential for life. Those close to the land, such as the Native Americans, see it as a vital resource to be conserved to ensure their survival. This is in contrast to the thoughtless and blatant disregard for the conservation of water by "modern" man, driven by a set of values based on greed and materialism. Climate change, as you have seen from this chapter, has meant that water is now going to be in short supply both in the developed and in developing countries. It is time that we listened to the spiritual wisdom in relation to water and started to reverse the current climate change trends of producing a world of widespread drought and untold suffering. We can change our vision and change our values so that water shortages in the future will be less devastating to humanity.

Chapter 4: FOOD SUPPLY

THE IDEAL SITUATION

First let us look at different spiritual traditions and see how they value land and growing food. If we had followed these values in the first place we would not have allowed climate change to have such a devastating effect on land and the growing of food.

Judaism and Christianity

Jewish and Christian values towards the land and hence towards growing food are explained very early in the Bible. Firstly, Jews and Christians believe that land belongs to God: the Bible implies that the Earth is not man's, but God's. "The land must not be sold permanently, because the land is mine and you are but aliens and my tenants." (Lev 25:23) and "...the Earth is the Lord's and everything in it." (Psalms: 24)

Secondly, according to Scripture, God created humans to "serve and keep" the land (Gen. 2:15) - they were to be the stewards of God's creation. The word "steward" and "stewardship" is used throughout the Old and New Testaments of the Bible (Genesis 15:2; Genesis 44:1; 1 Chronicles 28:1; Matthew 20:8; 1 Corinthians 4:2; Luke 12:42; Luke 16:1-2) The word used for steward in the Bible can also be interpreted as manager or servant. The proper model for the caretaking of nature from a Biblical perspective is the Judeo-Christian stewardship model. (Genesis 2; Luke 12:16)

Thirdly it is implied in the Bible that if humans live in accordance with spiritual values, as is God's will, God will provide in abundance. "It shall come about, if you listen obediently to my commandments which I am commanding you today, to love the Lord your God and to serve Him with all your heart and all your soul, that He will give the rain for your land in its season, the early and late rain, that you may gather in your grain and your new wine and your oil. He will give grass in your fields for your cattle, and you will eat and be satisfied." (Deuteronomy 11:8-15) It is stated further, "He causeth the grass to grow for the cattle, and herb for the service of man: that he may bring forth food out of the earth" (Psalm 104:14); also, "Now he who supplies seed to the sower and bread for food will also supply and increase your store of seed and will enlarge the harvest of your righteousness." (Corinthians 2:9-10)

What is clear from Biblical history is that God intended that the land should be looked after and made sustainable. There is clear recognition of the need for biodiversity in the environment as well as thought for the poor. Even after harvest some of the crop was left in the corners of a field, allowing wild flowers to grow. This is advised here: "When you reap the harvest of your land, you shall not reap all the way to the edges of your field... you shall leave them for the poor and the stranger." (Leviticus 23:22) Fertility and sustainability of the soil was also practised by not growing any crops or fruit on land in the seventh year and therefore allowing it to rest and replenish nutrients. "You may plant your land for six years and gather its crops. But during the seventh year, you must leave it alone and withdraw from it. The needy among you will then be able to eat just as you do, and whatever is left over can be eaten by wild animals. This also applies to your vineyard and your olive grove." (Exodus 23:10–11) It will become clear from information to be presented later that a fertile soil with good soil structure is much more robust when threatened with the effects of climate change.

Islam

Land was recognised as a primary resource. It is mentioned 485 times in the Qur'an and was carefully and wisely controlled in Islamic law. God created the earth for the benefit of mankind, as you can see in this statement: "He it is Who has spread out the earth for His creatures. Therein is fruit, and date palms, with sheaths, and husked corn, and scented herbs. Then which of the favours of your Lord will you deny?" (Qur'an 55:10-13). Muslims are required to follow the will of God and His commandments but also to show gratitude so that the abundance of the land will be forthcoming. "O ye who believe! Eat of the good things wherewith we have provided you, and render thanks to Allah if it is (indeed) He whom ye worship." (Qur'an 2:172)

The Qur'an states that God has granted human beings the responsibility of stewardship (*khilafah*) of the Earth as "It is He who appointed you viceroys of the Earth." (Qur'an 6:165) "The world is sweet and verdant green and Allah appoints you to be His regents in it and will see how you acquit yourselves…" (Sunnah of the Prophet) "It is He Who has made you His agents, inheritors of the Earth: He hath raised you in ranks some above others: that he may try you in the gifts He hath given you." From these words it is clear that mankind represents the interests of God on Earth. Man is thus entrusted with its maintenance and care and, as a trustee, he must care for it within the limits dictated by God.

There should be good farming practice to conserve soil, and attention should be given to making land sustainable for the long term. As with Judaism and Christianity, good soil husbandry means that the effects of climate change on food production are less extreme. In early Islam, land reclamation or revival was encouraged in Islamic law. Any person who brought life to un-owned land by undertaking its cultivation or reclamation acquired it as his private property and according to Muhammad would be rewarded in heaven. Only those actions that brought new life to the land conferred ownership; mere exploitation did not constitute revival. Thus this law gave people a powerful incentive to invest in the sustainable use of the land and avoid desertification and so provide for their own welfare and the welfare of their families and descendants.

Hinduism

In Hinduism the earth itself has divine meaning, as it is the abode of the earth goddess Bhumi. She is described as being dependable, patient and conscious of human activity and can easily be offended by destructive and disrespectful activities. These quotes from Hindu scriptures describe how Hindus see earth as divine and as the fountain of all abundance:
"Impart to us those vitalising forces that come, O Earth, from deep within your body, your central point, your navel; purify us wholly. The Earth is the mother; I am the son of Earth." (Rig Veda)
"Mother of plants and begetter of all things, firm far-flung Earth, sustained by Heavenly Law, kindly and pleasant is she. May we ever dwell

on her bosom, passing to and fro." (The Hymn to the Earth, Atharva Veda)

"May she, the ruling Mistress of what has been and what will come to us, spread wide a limitless domain." (Rig Veda)

It follows that agriculture is carried out with respect for the land. The agricultural practices talked about in the Rig Veda, Krishiprasara, Manusmriti, Agni Purana and Vriksha Ayurveda are also known as the Vedic Agriculture, and were assiduously followed by early Hindus. These Agriculture methods were devised to pursue the exclusive belief of "harmony" with nature to put emphasis on *saha-astitva*, co-existence and co-relation with living and non-living entities, and to never follow the line of dominance or exploitation. The farming methods were often ecologically benign, such as growing organically. This type of agriculture is still practised by the farms established by Maharishi Mahesh Yogi, and organic growing is expanding in India with Sikkim state declared fully organic in 2016.

Hinduism does not require a vegetarian diet, but many Hindus avoid eating meat because of their belief that it minimises hurting other life forms. Lacto-vegetarianism is favoured, which includes milk-based foods and all other non-animal derived foods, but it excludes meat and eggs. In Hinduism, many food items represent the various gods and goddesses of the religion's pantheon, for example, rice and grains represent Lord Brahma, or the Creator. Most sacred, however, are dairy products. The cow is revered in Hinduism because it represents a divine mother, who provides milk. Meanwhile, *sattvic* is the Hindu term for a diet of vegetables, fruits, nuts and whole grains. A *sattvic* diet is supposed to purify the person and calm the soul; and as such, it is dictated by the Vedas as highly desirable. It is because they are not generally a meat-eating society that there is less stress on the agricultural system and they do not contribute large quantities of methane, a potent gas which accelerates climate change.

Sikhism

The Sikh view is that spirit and matter are not antagonistic. Guru Nanak declared that the spirit was the only reality and matter is only a form of spirit. Spirit takes on many forms and names under various conditions. "When I saw truly, I knew that all was primeval. Nanak, the subtle (spirit) and the gross (material) are, in fact, identical." (Guru Granth Sahib, page 281)

According to Sikhs the world is divine because it is created by God as a place where mankind can practise spirituality:
"Creating the world, God has made it a place to practise spirituality." (Guru Granth Sahib, 1035) In Sikhism the scriptures say that the Earth should be seen as the Mother and provider of life and therefore should be held in deepest respect:
"The air is the Guru, Water the Father, and Earth the Great Mother." (Jap Ji Sahib-Salok, Guru Granth Sahib)
"The Earth teaches us patience and love."
(Guru Granth Sahib.)

The Gurus used the language of the people to communicate how to live a harmonious life in this world. While speaking to farmers, the fifth Guru, Guru Arjan, used the metaphor of cultivating land with one's own hands to describe union with the Beloved: "By Your Command, the month of Saawan (monsoon season) has come. I have hooked up the plough of Truth, and I plant the seed of the Name in hope that the Lord, in His Generosity, will bestow a bountiful harvest." (Guru Granth Sahib, 73)

Becoming one and being in harmony with God implies that humans endeavour to live in harmony with all of God's creation. God is "seated in Nature, and watches with delight what he creates." Guru Nanak ('Adi Granth' Asa-di-Var-1:3). A benevolent God provides Nature for the sustenance of man. The inference is that man must take care of Nature and not destroy it or seek to control it.

Food is part of the spiritual life of every Sikh, and is commonly referred to as *rijak*, divine sustenance, or *giras*, nourishment. According to Sikh thought, after creating the Creation, the Divine continuously nourishes it and sustains it through breath and food. Sikhs are unique in that they share what food they have to anyone for free via a communal kitchen which is always part of their place of worship, the Gurdwara. I myself have eaten at the kitchen of the Golden Temple, which feeds more than 100,000 people every day of the year. They are now committed to serving organic vegetarian food, which makes them significant leaders in promoting organic farming throughout India in general, and in the Punjab in particular.

Jainism

From its inception 2,600 years ago, Jainism has remained faithful in its commitment to nonviolence and vegetarianism. There remain today some 4 million Jains in India. Jainism centres on the teachings of twenty-four spiritual leaders called *tirthankaras*, from the idea that they form a *tirth* or a ford across the ocean of existence. The first *tirthankara* was Rishabh in the 9th century BCE, or even earlier. He is credited with introducing agriculture and he told farmers to sow more seeds than they needed because there would then be some left over for mice, birds and ants. Many of the staunch followers of Lord Mahavira, the last *tirthankar*, including Anand Shrawak, were engaged in agriculture. The guiding principle of how Jains relate to the land and growing food is that of *Ahimsa*, which means the practice of non-violence in all situations. It applies equally to the environment and to all beings within it - Mahavira said "There is no quality of soul more subtle than non-violence and no virtue of spirit greater than reverence for life." Another quote, from the Acaranga Sutra, states: "I so pronounce that all the omniscient of all times state, speak, propagate, and elaborate that nothing which breathes, which exists, which lives, and which has any essence or potential of life, should be destroyed or ruled over, or subjugated, or harmed, or denied of its essence or potential. . . . The result of actions by you has to be borne by you, so do not destroy anything." Jains are required to be vegetarians - which of course is more benign to the environment, as growing vegetables does not produce greenhouse gases. So the method of producing food is in the way which is least detrimental to all life forms. As Mahavira said that everything has a soul, therefore people should take as little as possible from nature and live in harmony with it.

Jains believe that all aspects of reality have *jivas* or souls. There are animate entities such as living beings called *jeevs*. Jains classify the life-quality of all living entities according to the number of senses they possess. The lowest forms of life have only one sense: touch. This group includes plants. The highest life forms - including humans and most animals - have all five senses: touch, taste, smell, sight and hearing. Generally, vegetables that grow underground are prohibited, because harvesting them usually means pulling them up by their roots, which destroys the entire plant, as well as all the microorganisms living around the roots.

Among the central tenets of Jainism, the Tatwarth Sutra affirms that all forms of life are mutually supportive. Clearly, Jains see the biosphere as an integrated whole and they discipline themselves to act in accord with life and Nature. Mahavira said "All life is bound together by mutual support and interdependence." He also stated, "One who neglects or disregards the existence of earth, air, fire, water and vegetation disregards his own existence which is entwined with them."

Taoism

The Tao Te Ching is the main scripture of Taoism, and it says: "Humanity follows the Earth The Earth follows Heaven. Heaven follows the Tao. The Tao follows Nature." Taoists therefore obey the Earth. In Taoism, Nature is symbolised by Mother Earth from which all things are born and to which all things return. With a philosophy of this kind respect for the land is given and maintaining it in a sustainable way is the practical outcome.

The Taoist universe is governed by a set of natural and unalterable laws, which manifest themselves as a flow of continuous change. This natural order and flow is what is referred to as the Tao, or the Way. By recognising and aligning ourselves with these laws, we can attain a state of being which combines the experience of total freedom with one of complete connectedness to life's processes - being at one with the Tao. Taoism always stresses the importance of harmony between human beings and Nature as a key aspect of the protection of Nature. Taoism is always opposed to the violation of natural laws. It denies any human right to conquer Nature, or wage a war against Nature. Taoist scriptures make constant reference to Nature. It is taken as an expression of the spiritual dimension of existence.

To most Taoists, living in harmony with all the natural forces, creatures and living beings here on earth is a key spiritual goal, alongside practising these other important spiritual virtues: simplicity of thought, causing no harm to oneself or others, avoiding extremes, maintaining balanced emotions and practising non-attachment, having physical discipline and practising self-restraint. Lao Tzu, the wise sage who founded Taoism, expressed it perfectly in these two quotes:

"When you know that Nature is part of yourself, you will act in harmony."
Lao Tzu

"Realise that we live in Nature. But we cannot possess it. We can guide and serve, but never control. This is the highest Wisdom." Lao Tzu

The core philosophy of Taoism primarily teaches the universal principle of Tai-Chi which essentially is the art of balancing opposite and complementary forces. But, another equally important teaching of Taoism is to always remember that all things and people are connected and share the same ONE spiritual essence; so, if you cause harm to other people, animals or things you are essentially causing harm to yourself. Taoism's central principle is that all life, all manifestation, is part of an inseparable whole, an interconnected organic unity that arises from a deep, mysterious and essentially unexplainable source, which is the Tao itself. Putting this into practice means that producing food from the land is carried out in a harmonious way with deep respect for all biodiversity.

Bahá'í Faith

Bahá'ís see the world as created by God with the responsibility of men to be stewards of it. Bahá'u'lláh stated, "Nature in its essence is the embodiment of My Name, the Maker, the Creator. Its Manifestations are diversified by varying causes, and in this diversity there are signs for men of discernment. Nature is God's Will and is its expression in and through the contingent world. It is a dispensation of Providence ordained by the Ordainer, the All-Wise."

Bahá'u'lláh, the founder, recognised that growing food was one of the most important occupations in a society and he gave farmers high status. One of the central principles of the Bahá'í Faith - spiritual solutions to the world's economic problems - begins with agriculture. Bahá'ís see the land and people as an integrated whole - the Bahá'í writings say, "We cannot segregate the human heart from the environment outside us and say that once one of these is reformed everything will be improved. Man is organic with the world. His inner life moulds the environment and is itself also deeply affected by it. The one acts upon the other and every abiding change in the life of man is the result of these mutual reactions." The farming principles described, if followed, would not contribute to climate change. In fact, Bahá'u'lláh's son, Abdu'l-Bahá, outlined a remarkable, unique Bahá'í economic model for agriculture, based at the village level and locally-controlled to maximise the welfare of all people and the quality and quantity of the harvest, since so many people around the world cultivate and grow food to feed their families. There is an example of this Bahá'í farming practice in Haiti where there are organic and smallholder farms run by Bahá'ís. Hugh Locke is President of the Smallholder Farmers Alliance in Haiti, which has organised small holdings so that they retain agricultural revenue, are locally-managed and provide their income. They also have a system of planting trees in order to reverse damaging deforestation. Since farmers generate the sustenance for all of humanity, the Bahá'í teachings on the economy focus first on the impact of agriculture and its primary importance to every person. Bahá'ís believe that restructuring agriculture will assist in the emergence of a sustainable, just and prosperous world civilisation that will exist on this planet for half a million years.

Shamanism

Native Americans lived off the land. Native Americans thought that the 'Great Spirit' had given each creature a "piece of his heart". Respect for all of creation was so important to them that they recognised Nature as the source of deepest wisdom and guidance for their ways. This quote illustrates this: "We thank our Mother Earth who we claim as Mother because the Earth carries us and everything we need." - prayer of the shaman of the Delaware tribe. They saw mankind as part of nature as you can see from this quote: "We are part of the Earth and the Earth is part of us. The Earth does not belong to man, man belongs to Earth. Whatever befalls the Earth befalls the sons of Earth. Man did not weave the web of life; he is merely a strand in it." Chief Seattle, of the Suquamish and Duwamish people. They saw everything as interrelated. They sought to co-operate with the spiritual forces of nature to ensure a successful harvest. This often entailed having special ceremonies.

Pueblo
The Pueblo People are a diverse group of Native American inhabitants of New Mexico, Texas, and Arizona in the USA, who traditionally subsisted on agriculture.

The religion and beliefs of the Pueblo tribe were based on Animism, encompassing the spiritual or religious idea that the universe and all natural objects - animals, plants, trees, rivers, mountains, rocks etc - have souls or spirits. Pueblos have many ceremonies throughout the year. The

71

dances and songs vary from Pueblo to Pueblo. The dance and song are prayers to the soil, the plants, the pollinators, and gratitude for the harvest. The season starts in the spring with ceremonies for preparing the soil and starting seeds. The ceremonies also bless the land with songs and dances. Then throughout the summer, there are many dances that bless the field and crops, bring in the pollinators like the butterflies, and for a good harvest. The traditions and ceremonies of Acoma Pueblo Indians testify that to the Acomas all life is interrelated, balanced and inter-dependent. Mankind is in a partnership with nature and they sustain a reciprocal relationship. Mankind must perform certain rites and ceremonies and, in turn, nature responds by providing the essentials of human survival. An example of this is worship of the *kachina*, a spirit being, by "*kachina* dancers", masked members of the tribe who dress up as *kachinas* for religious ceremonies, and *kachina* dolls, wooden dolls representing *kachinas* which are given as gifts to children. In order to determine the proper times for planting, cultivating, and harvesting, the early Pueblo peoples studied the patterns of nature and the movements of the sun, moon, clouds, and wind. The Pueblo today practise dry farming, a method which conserves water. They also practise companion planting of the "Three Sisters", maize, pole beans and winter squash, which are planted together, along with biodiversity techniques.

Navajo

The Navajo are the second-largest nation of native Americans, and live in the states of Utah, Arizona and New Mexico. The Navajo religion explains the universe as ordered, beautiful, and harmonious. Navajo religion emphasises rituals to restore the harmony, balance, and order expressed by the word "*hozho*". Harmony and balance are disrupted by death, violence, and evil. The Navajo believe that the Yei Spirit mediates between humans and the Great Spirit which created everything, and is believed to control elements such as the rain, snow, wind and sun as well as controlling night and day. Navajos believe they were created from a perfect ear of corn, white corn for male and yellow corn for females. Different coloured corn is planted to honour deities by using it as an offering. Navajo plant in accordance with certain positions of the constellations. The Pleiades played an important role in determining the timing for planting and harvesting. The Navajo farm is often small scale and has diverse crops, with a range of healthy fruits, vegetables, and beans. The Navajo practised numerous cultivation and soil revitalisation techniques to ensure the continued quality and productivity of the land. They also practise "dry farming" to conserve as much soil moisture as possible.

Iroquois

The Iroquois are native American people who lived in the north-eastern United States. The area is also referred to as the Eastern Woodlands region and encompasses New York State and the immediate surrounding areas. They had deep respect for their surrounding environment. The Iroquois believed in a supreme spirit, Orenda, the "Great Spirit" from whom all other spirits were derived. According to the legend, corn, beans and squash are inseparable sisters that were given to the people by the "Great Spirit." The Oki is the personification of the life-force of the Iroquois, as well as the name of the life force itself. The Iroquois were very spiritual people. They believed that everything took place for a reason and everything, living and non-living, had a spirit. Stories were passed down verbally from generation to generation. The older tribe members would customarily sit around longhouse fires on cold winter nights and tell stories of how things came to be to the younger Iroquois. Like other tribes, their whole agricultural year was centred around ceremonies. Life revolved around the seasons and was integrated with nature which was cherished as a gift from the "Great Spirit". Spirituality infused Iroquois culture. Shamans were seen as understanding this spirituality and using it for the good of the tribe. In the early spring there was the Maple festival when the sap started flowing. There were speeches of thanks and repentance for past sins, and dances. In the late spring there was the Planting Festival asking for a good crop of corn, beans and squash. This was followed in the summer by a Strawberry festival giving thanks for the crop. Maize or corn was a very important crop. The Green Corn Festival held in the late summer exemplifies this (also called the Green Corn Dance or Ceremony). The dance was held each year. The festival typically lasted for three days. During the festival, members of the tribe gave thanks for the corn, rain, sun, and a good harvest. There was a special Feather Dance. At the end of every day, the people feasted together. The last festival was held in the autumn and called the Harvest Festival. This was characterised by speeches of gratitude from tribal leaders, by dancing and feasting. Altogether the festivals provided structure for the year, created social bonding and reinforced common values about respecting nature.

THE ACTUAL SITUATION

Climate Change Caused by Poor Agricultural Methods

Far more land is used for livestock than for growing crops. If we combine pastures used for grazing with land used to grow crops for animal feed, livestock accounts for 77% of global farming land. While livestock takes up most of the world's agricultural land it only produces 18% of the world's calories and 37% of total protein. Land which is only used for growing crops uses 7% of the total land area.[1] The FAO estimates that agricultural production must rise by about 60% by 2050 in order to feed a larger and generally richer population.[2]

The indictment of modern agriculture is that it generates more climate change. In 2014 the FAO estimated that greenhouse gas data showed that emissions from agriculture, forestry and fisheries have nearly doubled over the past fifty years and could increase by an additional 30% by 2050 if the right actions over climate change are not taken. The FAO has calculated that, globally, agriculture generates 30% of the total man-made emissions of greenhouse gases, including half of methane emissions and more than half of the emissions of nitrous oxide.[3] Historically, land-use conversion and soil cultivation have been an important source of adding greenhouse gases to the atmosphere. Recognition of the vital role played by soil carbon could mark an important if subtle shift in the discussion about global warming, which has been heavily focused on curbing emissions of fossil fuels. Carbon dioxide emissions from agriculture are mainly attributable to losses of above and below ground organic matter, through changes in land use, such as conversion of forests to pasture or cropland, and land degradation such as that caused by over-grazing. We do not look after the very thing that we need in order to grow food, the soil! It is estimated that up to 80 percent of the total organic carbon in the terrestrial biosphere, excluding fossil fuels, is stored in soils, while about 20 percent is stored in vegetation. Soils represent the Earth's second largest carbon pool, after oceans, and small changes in the stock of soil organic carbon may result in large changes in levels of atmospheric CO_2. It has been estimated that 25 to 40% of the current excess of CO_2 in the atmosphere comes from the destruction of soil and its organic matter.[4]

In 2009, the Chair of the 36th FAO Conference called for an elevated role for organic agriculture within FAO's work. The long-term objective of the FAO Organic Agriculture Programme is to enhance food security, rural development, sustainable livelihoods and soil fertility by building capacities of member countries in organic production, processing, certification and marketing. In 2013 a UN report advocated that small scale organic farming was the only logical solution to the world's food needs. There was a call to move away from industrial agriculture with high inputs, monoculture and destruction of soils. The major reason for FAO support for organic farming is that organic farming recycles wastes as nutrients, using nitrogen-fixing plants in rotational farming systems that include livestock and do not over-work and degrade soils through year-on-year monoculture. This means that more carbon is stored in the soil.[5]

The Role of Livestock Farming

The bulk of direct emissions of methane and nitrous oxide, two potent greenhouse gases, are the result of enteric fermentation in livestock, of rice production in flooded fields and the application of nitrogen fertiliser and manure, all of which can be reduced through the implementation of better management practices based on natural systems. The biggest source of agricultural methane emissions is enteric fermentation, about two thirds of the total. This is the digestive process by which microbes in the guts of ruminant livestock break down plant matter and produce methane as a by-product. Methane is an important greenhouse gas, second only to carbon dioxide, in terms of its overall contribution to human-driven climate change. Methane from agriculture accounts for around 7% of total global emissions and is thought to have roughly the same impact on climate change as the transport sector.[6]

Meat and dairy production has a huge impact on climate change. It is estimated to be responsible for about 15% of global emissions. Since livestock require so much food, meat production is a leading cause of deforestation, which takes away trees that will filter out greenhouse gas emissions. According to the *Guardian* newspaper in 2016, the top 20 meat and dairy companies emitted more greenhouse gases in 2016 than all of

Germany, Europe's biggest climate polluter by far. If these companies were a country, they would be the world's seventh largest greenhouse gas emitter.[7] One third of all the cereals eaten are fed to animals: enough to feed 3 billion people. Yet 70% of the food fed to animals is lost in the conversion process.[8]

Humans exacerbate the problem by not even eating all the food produced. Between 30 and 40% of food produced around the world is never eaten, because it is spoiled after harvest and during transportation, or thrown away by shops and consumers. Food waste makes up 8% of greenhouse gas emissions worldwide, according to the UN's Food and Agriculture Organisation and the World Resources Institute. According to the FAO, the land devoted to producing wasted food is roughly 5.4 million square miles, which would make it the second largest country in the world behind Russia. All the world's nearly one billion hungry people could be fed on less than a quarter of the food that is wasted in the US, UK and Europe.[9]

Crop Reduction

As we have seen in previous chapters there is going to be a dramatic global rise in temperatures due to climate change. A warming planet leads to less food. Crops are adapted to particular patterns of temperature, rainfall and the length of the growing season. When climate changes those parameters, agricultural systems are disrupted. Rising temperatures mean the grains won't germinate; rain patterns are disrupted so crops are stunted and growing seasons are altered. Another reason is that crops derived from wild grasses - that includes wheat, corn, rice, sorghum, oats, rye, and barley - cannot quickly adapt to the rise in temperatures. A report in the Royal Society journal *Biology Letters* found that climate is changing between 3,000 and 20,000 times faster than many grassland species can respond to.[10] The IPCC Report 5th Assessment results show that by 2050, relative to a world with no climate change, global average crop yields will decline by between 5 and 7 percent, depending on the type of actions taken on climate change.

According to the IPCC's report from 2014, every decade of warming that happens decreases the amount of food the world can produce by 2%. The yields of many crops can be drastically reduced by temperatures above 32°C during the flowering stage - especially crops derived from grasses. Humans gain at least 49% of their calories directly from the cereals developed from wild grasses. Wheat is the first big staple crop to be affected by climate change, because it is sensitive to heat and is grown around the world, from Pakistan to Russia to Canada. Projections suggest that wheat yields could drop 2% a decade, according to the 2014 IPCC report.[11]

Professor Challinor is one of a team of more than 60 scientists who reported in the *Nature Climate Change* journal that with just 1°C global temperature increase, wheat yields are expected to fall by between 4.1% and 6.4%. Maize is also a staple crop and warmer temperatures are bad news for corn: in fact, a global rise in temperatures of just 1°C would slow the rate of growth by 7%. Global corn production, in particular, has already been nearly 4% lower than it would have been if the climate were not warming.[12]

The Effect of Rising Sea Levels

Melting ice caps and glaciers point to a world where sea level rises are inevitable. More precise data gathered from satellite radar measurements reveal an accelerating rise of 7.5 cm (3 ins) from 1993 to 2017. If sea encroaches on land, the area covered by sea is lost for growing crops and even some distance inland, agricultural production is impossible as salt intrudes into the soil. Food shortages and the displacement of people inevitably follow. The IPCC's report stated that by the end of the century there would be between 18 and 59 centimetres sea level rise. In Asia and North Africa - where the most vulnerable people live in the river deltas of Myanmar, Bangladesh, India, Pakistan and Egypt - farming areas in the coastal regions are exposed to sea-level rise. It is really unfair that poor countries like Bangladesh who contributed little to climate change bear the brunt of it and countries like the U.K. get off lightly.[13]

Increasing Acidity of the Seas

Food from the oceans is a vital source of protein. Fish provide 20% of the animal protein for around 3 billion people. In general, fish tend to live near their tolerance limits of a range of factors, particularly temperature and acidity. Right now there is the fastest acidification rate in 300 million years. The rising ocean acidity makes it more difficult for marine organisms such as shrimp, oysters or corals to form their shells – a process known as calcification. Many important animals, such as some zooplankton, which form the base of the marine food chain, have calcium shells. Some fish species are already migrating towards the poles because water is becoming too warm for them. Models based on predicted changes in environmental conditions, habitat types and phytoplankton primary production forecast a large-scale redistribution of global marine fish catch potential, with an significant increase in the high-latitude regions and a decrease in the tropics.[14]

Malnutrition Caused by Climate Change

All the above examples of the effects of climate change could quite possibly lead to the most widespread starvation and death the world has ever seen. As food prices rise, hunger follows. By mid-century, increasing food prices will reduce dietary diversity, which reduces dietary quality and hence increases malnutrition. According to the most recent UN Food and Agriculture Organisation data of 2019, more than 820 million people in the world are still hungry today. Another disturbing fact is that about 2 billion people in the world experience moderate or severe food insecurity. Their report showed that the decline in hunger the world had enjoyed for over a decade had come to an end, and that hunger was again on the rise. In 2018, 49.5 million children under five were affected by acute malnutrition or wasting with malnutrition, this being the underlying cause of 2.5 million childhood deaths per year.[15]

An Oxford University Study, in conjunction with the *Lancet*, on the *Future of Food* estimated that more than half a million people worldwide are likely to die annually by 2050 because of the impact on agriculture of changing climate. The study suggests 248,000 people will die each year in China by 2050 because of climate-linked decreases in food production. India faces a yearly loss of 160,000 people. What will shock many Americans is that America came 5th in the number of deaths. Marco Springmann, lead author in the department of population health at the Oxford Martin Programme on the Future of Food, explained "The US comes in fifth because of its high population and its vulnerability to climate shocks."[16]

Examples of Developing Nations

Within Africa

African economies are heavily dependent on agriculture. The industry employs 65% of Africa's labour force and accounts for 32% of the continent's overall GDP. The impact of climate change on food security will be greatest in African nations. Much of African agriculture's vulnerability to climate change lies in the fact that its agricultural systems remain largely rain-fed and underdeveloped, as the majority of Africa's farmers are small-scale farmers with few financial resources, limited access to infrastructure, and often little access to information. The IPCC are projecting an increase of about 4 degrees Celsius by the end of the century, though there is little agreement on how that change will impact precipitation as there is incomplete data. What does seem certain is that variability in timing and quantity of rainfall will increase, with significant social consequences. Subtropical southern and northern Africa have seen temperature rises of the order of twice the global rate of temperature increase - with the most significant warming in southern Africa having been experienced in the last two decades. 650 million people are dependent on rain-fed agriculture in environments that are affected by water scarcity, land degradation, recurrent droughts and floods, and this trend is expected to exacerbate with climate change and population growth. According to the IPCC, climate change is very likely to have an overall negative effect on yields of major cereal crops across Africa, with strong regional variability in the degree of yield reduction. Estimated yield losses at mid-century range from 18% for southern Africa to 22% aggregated across sub-Saharan Africa, with yield losses for South Africa and Zimbabwe in excess of 30%. There could be a 35% decline in wheat production by 2050.[17]

Declining food production leads to malnutrition and famine. Africa has the largest number of malnourished people, the fewest resources to adapt and the fastest growing population to deal with. One in four undernourished people in the world live in Africa: Africa is the only continent where the absolute number of undernourished people has increased over the last 30 years. At present, under-nutrition causes 1.7 million deaths per year in Africa and is currently estimated to be the largest contributor to climate change-related mortality. Children often are the first to suffer: for instance, the IPCC reports that in Mali, by 2025, 250,000 children are expected to suffer stunting, or chronic malnutrition, and that "climate change will cause a statistically significant proportion" of these cases.[18]

India

With the growing population, the imminent challenge for India is to increase food production in order to feed the population that will have reached 1.3 billion by the year 2020. As mentioned in the previous chapter, India has 18% of the world population but only has 4% of the water resources. About 65 percent of India's cropped area is rain-fed. Farmers will have to produce 50% more grains by 2050 to meet the current growing demand. In 2013, a World Bank report predicted that unusual and unprecedented spells of hot weather were expected to occur far more frequently and cover much larger areas. A 2°C rise in the world's average temperatures will make India's summer monsoon highly unpredictable. An abrupt change in the monsoon could precipitate a major crisis, triggering more frequent droughts as well as greater flooding in large parts of India. Under 4°C warming, the west coast and southern India are projected to shift to new, high-temperature climatic regimes with significant impacts on agriculture. Also, droughts will pose an increasing risk in the north-western part of India while southern India will experience an increase in wetness from monsoons. Crop yields are expected to fall significantly because of extreme heat by the 2040s. Already research has suggested that without climate change, average rice yields could have been almost 6% higher. Wheat yields peaked in India and Bangladesh around 2001 and have not increased since. The situation could get worse as temperatures in northern India are now sometimes above 34 degrees centigrade. At that temperature, wheat finds it difficult to grow.[19] According to one study, for each degree rise in temperature, wheat production is thought to reduce by 6%.[20] Another study found that each degree Celsius increase in global mean temperature would, on average, reduce global yields of rice by 3.2%, maize by 7.4%, and soybean by 3.1%.[21] For example the Indo-Gangetic Plains could become significantly heat stressed by the 2050s. Here, by 2050, variability in growing conditions due to climate change is projected to lower crop yields by 10 to 40% and total crop failure will become more common.[22]

China

The Chinese government is acutely aware that it has to feed 19% of the world's population using just 9% of its arable land and 6% of its renewable water resources. Agriculture employs about 40 percent of China's population.[23] The climatic shocks to agriculture will not only threaten the food security of the world's largest population, but also have a ripple effect on the global food market. China already has to import grain in an attempt to meet its food needs, and the gap between those needs and national food production is likely to increase as climate change proceeds. Mean near-surface air temperatures across China rose by 0.5–0.8°C during the 20th century and there is evidence that this process is accelerating. Extreme heat waves could make the north China plain uninhabitable in places if climate change is not curbed - it is home to 400 million people and vital to China's food production. New scientific research shows that humid heat waves, that can kill even healthy people within hours, will strike the area repeatedly towards the end of the century, thanks to climate change, unless there are heavy cuts in carbon emissions. This will mean that farm workers cannot go outside to work for long periods and hence a decline in food production would result.[24]

China's agricultural core is in the north, but its water resources are in the south. 80% of the water is in the south but 64% of the farmland and more than 50% of the people are in the north. Since 1970, groundwater usage has doubled and in 2013 made up 20% of water usage. The supply of water for crops could be a problem as groundwater is over exploited as it is used to irrigate more than 40% of China's farmland. Investment in improving irrigation is important, because agriculture consumes 62.5% of all water - and wastes half of that. In northern China, water tables are dropping at a rate of up to 10 feet (3m) a year. With the water crisis in North China, overall grain production and hence food security in China will be challenged.[25]

Rice, maize and wheat are the three major crops which account for more than 90% of China's total food production. In 2016 a study published by the *Bulletin of the World Health Organization* found that by the 2040s, climate change could reduce China's per-capita cereal production by 18%, compared with 2000 levels. The report went on to say that for the North China Plain, it was projected that compared to the yields achieved in 1961–1990, maize yields would reduce by 9–10% during the

2020s, by 16–19% during the 2050s and 25–26% in the 2080s.[26] The urban area in China has increased about four-fold since the 1970s. This is one of the reasons for the decline in food production, as by 2030–2050, loss of cropland resulting from further urbanisation and soil degradation could lead to a 13–18% decrease in China's food production capacity – compared with that recorded in 2005.[26]

A report released by China's State Oceanic Administration (SOA) has warned that the average sea level along the country's coast is rising. Between 1980 and 2017, the sea level around China's coastal regions rose by an average of 3.3 millimetres per year, hitting a record high in 2016. 45 million Chinese people will be flooded by swelling seawaters if average global temperatures rise by 2 degrees Celsius, according to a Climate Central study. And a 4 degree warming will be enough to submerge land inhabited by 145 million Chinese. There would be many landless people to feed, as it has been estimated that by 2050, 40 to 200 million people could be internally displaced within China due to climate change.[27]

CONCLUSION

The right to have access to food is a fundamental human right. Through adopting our current world values we have engineered a possible future scenario where that right will not be met. It is also clear that the lack of food will affect disproportionally the poorer countries of the world, most of which did not cause the problem in the first place. There is a need for a rescue operation led by the developed countries to stop emissions so that in the future there may be a chance that everyone will have something to eat. I for one, in the rich west, do not want to witness on my television screen famines such as I have seen in the past in Nigeria, Ethiopia and Somalia. I have helped cause the suffering and I should be part of the solution. It seems pretty clear that ancient and modern food-growing systems based on deep spiritual values are a very viable alternative to the world's current approach to farming. A natural way of producing food works in harmony with nature so that ecosystems can be relied upon to perform sustainably into the future. The most important point to me is that the types of agriculture I have described which are found in the different spiritual traditions do not add to climate change but help to prevent it.

Chapter 5: LOSS OF BIODIVERSITY

First let us reflect on some of the spiritual teachings on this issue from world spiritual traditions. All of these traditions have respect for nature. This is the ideal approach to other species.

THE IDEAL: SPIRITUAL GUIDANCE ON HOW TO LIVE WITH OTHER SPECIES

Islam

Islam shares roots in the Old Testament with Judaism and therefore sees all species as God's creation. The Qur'an sees all creatures as living beings in their own right. Islam teaches that human beings are the caretakers of the earth on behalf of God who created it. "He it is that has made you vice-regent (inheritors) in the earth." (Qur'an 35:39). The teachings of Islam imply that the absolute destruction of any species of animals or plant by man can in no way be justified; hunting and fishing, forestry and woodcutting for timber and fuel, grazing and all other utilisation of living resources should be kept to within the capacity of nature to regenerate. The Qur'an states, "The merciful are shown mercy by the All-Merciful. Show mercy to those on Earth and He who is in Heaven will show mercy unto you," and "There is no creature on earth but that upon Allah is its provision, and He knows its place of dwelling and place of storage." (Qur'an 11:6)

It's a little known fact that the Prophet Muhammad developed the first conservation zones where wildlife could thrive. He instituted laws to create *Havin* lands, reserves set aside for wildlife. Within such reserves, development, woodcutting, grazing and hunting were prohibited or restricted in accordance with the special purposes of each reserve. The

Prophet Muhammad had declared a 30 km area around his city of Medina to be a protected grove, prohibiting the cutting down of trees within its borders. He forbade the cutting of cedar trees in the desert that provided shade and shelter to animals. Muhammad encouraged the creation of habitats for wildlife by stating "Whosoever plants a tree and looks after it will be rewarded in the hereafter," and "Even if the Day of Judgment should arrive and you are holding a sapling in your hand, plant it."

Animals were considered Allah's children and cruelty towards them of any kind was illegal. Muhammad said, "There is a reward in doing good to every living thing." We are to respect animals: "There is not an animal on Earth, nor any being that wings its flight but is as people like unto you", and "Whosoever is kind to creatures is kind to God" and "A good deed done to an animal is as meritorious as a good deed done to a human being, while an act of cruelty to an animal is as bad as an act of cruelty to a human being." There were specific laws about animal protection: animals are not to be worked too long, should be given sufficient water and food, and camels are not allowed to have rings put round their necks. It is forbidden to use them for fighting or target practice; they are not to be eaten whilst still alive and only be slaughtered with sharp knives. God punishes with the fires of hell any person who causes an animal to die of starvation or thirst. In his own life the Prophet actively demonstrated the importance of all creatures. He once forbade that a fire be lit upon an anthill. He related that an ant once stung one of the prophets, who then ordered that the whole colony of ants be burned. God addressed him in rebuke, "Because an ant stung you, you have destroyed a whole nation that celebrates God's glory." He once ordered a man who had taken some nestlings to return them to their nest where the mother was trying to protect them. Muhammad also forbade the killing of bees and any captured livestock.

Jainism

In Jainism all animate and inanimate objects have consciousness or *jiva*. Progress towards enlightenment consists in reincarnating in many souls. Not only this, but since all souls are interchangeable it is wise to minimise violence towards them. This is why all Jains take the vow of *ahimsa* or non-violence. In fact the *anarth dand tyag* vow prohibits unnecessary violence and participation in occupations that involve violence. For observing Jains, to hurt any being results in the thickening of one's karma, obstructing advancement toward liberation. The destruction of one form of life or another as food is essential for life. However, Jain belief states that a living being with a greater number of senses feels more pain than lower lifeforms such as vegetables. Therefore, the destruction of higher sense lifeforms - exploiting or killing of animals, birds and fish - for food is considered to be a crueller act because it inflicts more pain on them. It also causes greater destruction to the environment. Jains believe that vegetarianism is the first essential feature of the culture of non-violence. Vegetarianism not only helps eliminate intentional and avoidable physical violence of animals but also the violence of self. These quotes illustrate the teachings:

"All things living, all things breathing, all things whatsoever should not be slain or treated with violence, or insulted, or injured, or tortured, or driven away." Mahavira

"Let not anyone injure life, but be as assiduous in cherishing the life of another as his own. For Ahimsa is the highest religion." Mahavira

"Knowing the equality of all beings of the world, one should desist from the weapon of violence."
(Bhasyam Sutra 3)

"The non-violent person does not kill living beings, nor does he get them killed, nor does he approve of the killer."
(Bhasyam Sutra 46)

Judaism and Christianity

The Bible begins with Genesis, in which the creation of all species is described as the 'work of God'. This being so, then surely by implication Jews and Christians are meant to take care of these species. Those who see this as a form of stewardship on behalf of God cite Bible verses to support the case that we are duty bound to care for God's creation.

"Do not destroy trees by taking an axe to them." (Deut: 20:19)

"A righteous man cares for the needs of animals." (Proverbs: 12:10)

"If you come across a bird's nest beside the road, either in a tree or on the ground and the mother is sitting on the young or on the eggs, do not take the mother with the young. You may take the young, but be sure to let the mother go, so that it may go well with you and you may have a long life." (Deut 22:6-7)

"Whoever destroys a single life is as guilty as though he had destroyed the entire world and whoever rescues a single life earns as much merit as though he had rescued the entire world." (Talmud)

"But ask the animals, and they will teach you; the birds of the air, and they will tell you; ask the plants of the earth, and they will teach you; and the fish of sea will declare to you. In his hand is the life of every living thing and the breath of every human being." (Job 12:7-10)

This continues in the New Testament when Jesus says, "Are not five sparrows sold for two pennies? Yet not one of them is forgotten in God's sight." This has been a long tradition as can be seen from the following: St Isaac the Syrian, who lived in the 7th century CE, wrote passionately about love for animals: "What is a merciful [compassionate] heart? It is a heart on fire for the whole of creation, for humanity, for the birds, for the animals... As a result of His deep mercy or compassion the heart shrinks and cannot bear to look upon any injury or the slightest suffering of anything in creation." There have been more recent Christians who are concerned about our relationship with living beings. The Christian theologian and missionary Albert Schweitzer developed a philosophy which he called "Reverence for Life", for which he received the 1952 Nobel Peace Prize. He wrote: "Only by means of reverence for life can we establish a spiritual and humane relationship with both people and all living creatures within our reach. Only in this fashion can we avoid harming others, and, within the limits of our capacity, go to their aid whenever they need us." In 2018 the Pope presented his ecological credentials in the text "*Laudato Is*" on care for our common home in which he proposes an "ecological conversion", based on "attitudes which together foster a spirit of generous care, full of tenderness" and which "entails a loving awareness that we are not disconnected from the rest of creatures, but joined in a splendid universal communion."

Hinduism

The world is considered by Hindus to be divine in all its aspects, being the work of Brahma, the supreme creator. "You are the supreme Brahman, Infinite, yet hidden in the hearts of all creatures. You pervade everything. Realising you, we attain immortality." (Shvetashvatara Upanishad 3.7) Hindus see animals as fellow beings in different bodies. Krishna modelled the attitude to be adopted towards animals when he cared for the cows.

Cows are considered holy because higher souls are supposed to be reincarnated in them. Here is the key: because of reincarnation, every beast may be reborn a human and therefore must be respected. Indeed the Vedic Holy Scriptures forbid the killing of animals. (Yajurveda 13-47) Trees were considered the abodes of deities and it was forbidden to cut them down. The Vedas state that the "Earth belongs to all" and there needs to be a deep respect for all creation." (Atharvaveda 12 1-45). Further: "In this cosmos, whatever exists - living and non-living, all that is - is pervaded by one divine consciousness". (Isa Upanishad 1) These further quotes illustrate this theme:

"The Reality behind all these things of the universe is Brahman, which is pure consciousness. All things are established in consciousness, work through consciousness and their foundation is consciousness." (Aitareya Upanishad)

"The wise see the same (reality) in a Brahmin endowed with learning and culture, a cow, an elephant, a dog and an outcast." (Bhagavad Gita V.18)

"He whose self is harmonised by yoga seeth the Self-abiding in all beings and all beings in the self; everywhere he sees the same." (Bhagavad Gita VI.29)

"Those noble souls who practise meditation and other yogic ways, who are ever careful about all beings, who protect all animals, are the ones who are actually serious about spiritual practices." (Atharva Veda 19.48.5).

"Look upon deer, camels, monkeys, donkeys, rats, reptiles, birds and flies as though they are your own children." (Srimad Bhagavatam 7, 14-19)

"The wicked person who kills animals which are protected has to live in Ghora Naraka (Hell) for the days equal to the number of hairs on the animal killed."

(Yajyavalkyasmrti Acardhyagasth, 180)

"Let your love be all-embracing, like the sky." (Hindu Scriptures.)

"Trees are our friends. Protect them and ensure their proper growth." (Rig Veda 8.11.13)

"As the tree of the forest, just so, surely, is man. His hairs are leaves, His skin the outer bark. From his skin blood, sap from the bark flows forth a stream, as from the tree when struck. His pieces of flesh are under layers of wood. The fibre is muscle-like, strong. The bones are wood within. The marrow is made resembling pith." (Brhadaranyaka)

Buddhism

Buddhism can be thought of as the religion of compassion and non-violence. The Buddha always implored his followers to practice *metta* or loving kindness towards all beings. This attitude rests on the awareness that all fellow creatures are like us suffering in *samsara*, caught on the wheel of life. It is wise to be compassionate towards them. Many Buddhists believe that all life is interconnected because all beings undergo reincarnation and any form of violence is, after all, the ultimate denial of our interconnectedness, the furthest remove from acting in harmony with reality.

Buddha was so concerned about life in all forms that he forbade his monks to travel in the rainy season in case they inadvertently stepped on insects. One of the rules of the monks was to refrain from taking life as much as possible. Today, most Buddhists are vegetarian. Buddha was an outspoken critic of Hindu Brahmins who made animal sacrifices. He instructed that cows should never be milked dry. He encouraged the practice of letting go those wild animals caught in traps. Monks were forbidden to eat wild game or cut down any trees. In one story from his life he admonished some travellers who, having sat down under the shade of a banyan tree, proceeded to try and cut it down when leaving.

These quotes illustrate the teachings:

"Let everyone cultivate boundless love for all beings. Let him cultivate this towards the whole world, above, below, around a heart of love unstained; standing, walking, sitting or lying let him devote himself to this mind." (Buddhist scriptures)

"A person of great wisdom does not intend harm to the self, harm to others or harm to both self and others. Thinking in this way, such a person intends benefit for self, benefit for others, benefit for both and benefit for the whole world." (Buddhist scriptures)

"Life is dear to all living things. You should think of others as yourself and neither kill nor allow killing." (Buddhist scriptures)

"Abstain from injury to seed life and plant life." Buddha

"Why should we cherish all sentient beings? Because sentient beings are the roots of the tree-of-awakening. The Bodhisattvas and the Buddhas are the flowers and fruits. Compassion is the water for the roots." (Avantamsaka Sutra)

"Even as a mother protects with her life her child, her only child, so with a boundless heart should one cherish all living beings, radiating kindness over the entire world, spreading upwards to the skies, and downwards to the depths." (Karaniya Metta Sutta)

"All beings tremble before violence. All fear death, all love life. Then whom can you hurt? What harm can you do?" (Dhammapada 129-30).

"Just as each one of us wants to live and does not wish to die, so it is with all other creatures in the universe." His Holiness Tenzin Gyatso 14th Dalai Lama

"Destruction of Nature and natural resources results from ignorance, greed and a lack of respect for the Earth's living things." 14th Dalai Lama

"Many of the Earth's habitats, animals, plants, insects and even micro-organisms that we know as rare may not be known at all by future generations. We have the capability and the responsibility. We must act before it is too late." 14th Dalai Lama

"When we respect the environment, then nature will be good to us. When our hearts are good, then the sky will be good to us. The trees are like our mother and father, they feed us, nourish us, and provide us with everything; the fruit, leaves, the branches, the trunk. They give us food and satisfy many of our needs. So we spread the dharma (truth) of protecting ourselves and protecting our environment, which is the dharma of Buddha." Maha Ghosananda

Sikhism

Sikhism sees Nature as sacrosanct as it is an expression of the divine and therefore to be respected and treasured. According to Sikh metaphysics, Sikhs are related to the whole universe. So God is seen as caring for all creatures. This belief requires that Sikhs avoid harming all creatures as it is against God's will. *Daya* or compassion is regarded as the highest virtue in Sikhism. The Sikh Holy Book and ultimate teacher, the Guru Granth Sahib, says: "The merit of pilgrimages to the sixty-eight holy places, and that of other virtues besides, do not equal having compassion for other living beings." (Guru Granth, 136) Guru Hari Rai ran an animal clinic caring for sick animals and he even sent out hunting parties to collect sick animals in the wild so he could treat them. He also planted trees and flowers, purposefully creating habitats for wildlife. These quotes illustrate the Sikh beliefs:

"He is omnipresent, pervades the universe." (Guru Granth Sahib)

"With His blessings all creatures of the universe may prosper." (Guru Granth Sahib)

"That which is inside a person, the same is outside; nothing else exists; By divine prompting look upon all existence as one and undifferentiated; The same light penetrates all existence." (Guru Granth Sahib, page 599)

"The Creator created himself.... And created all creation in which He is manifest. You yourself, the bumble-bee, flower, fruit and the tree. You yourself, the water, desert, ocean and the pond. You yourself are the big fish, tortoise and the Cause of causes. Your form can not be known." (Guru Granth Sahib page 1016)

Bahá'í Faith

Bahá'ís have great respect for all beings and see all life as interconnected, as witnessed in the following extracts:

"It is not only their fellow human beings that the beloved of God must treat with mercy and compassion, rather must they show forth the utmost loving-kindness to every living creature." 'Abdu'l-Bahá (Selections from the Writings of 'Abdu'l-Bahá, p. 158)

"Train your children from their earliest days to be infinitely tender and loving to animals." 'Abdu'l-Bahá (Selections from the Writings of 'Abdu'l-Bahá, p. 158)

"Were one to observe with an eye that discovereth the realities of all things, it would become clear that the greatest relationship that bindeth the world of being together lieth in the range of created things themselves, and that co-operation, mutual aid and reciprocity are essential characteristics in the unified body of the world of being, inasmuch as all created things are closely related together and each is influenced by the other or deriveth benefit therefrom, either directly or indirectly." 'Abdu'l-Bahá (Compilations, Huquq'u'llah)

Shamanism

Shamanic traditions assert that the natural world is permeated with supernatural power; it is a source of visions and all kinds of spiritual experiences. This attitude breeds the highest respect for the natural world. Native Americans thought that the "Great Spirit" had given each creature a "piece of his heart". Even before killing a single animal, they would go through elaborate ceremonies to appease the spirit of the animal. Since the shaman works with animal spirits, within the culture there is an unwritten rule not to destroy animals unnecessarily. Certain animals such as eagles, grizzly bears, buffalo and hawks were seen as sacred. It is interesting to note that, despite the Plains Indians being largely reliant on the buffalo, the numbers they took did not impact buffalo populations. It was Europeans, with their rifles, that decimated the buffalo. Respect for animals was and remained inherent in the life of shamanic peoples. These quotes illustrate this:

"The whole universe is enhanced with the same breath, rocks, trees, grass, earth, all animals and men." Intiwa, Hopi tribe

"We are part of the Earth and the Earth is part of us. The Earth does not belong to man, man belongs to Earth. Whatever befalls the Earth befalls the sons of Earth. Man did not weave the web of life; he is merely a strand in it." Chief Seattle, of the Suquamish and Duwamish people

"One thing to remember is to talk to the animals. If you do, they will talk back to you. But if you don't talk to the animals, they won't talk back to you, then you won't understand, and when you don't understand you will fear, and when you fear you will destroy the animals, and if you destroy the animals, you will destroy yourself." Chief Dan George, Tsleil-Waututh

"We must protect the forests for our children, grandchildren and children yet to be born. We must protect the forests for those who can't speak for themselves such as the birds, animals, fish and trees." Chief Edward Moody, Nuxalk Nation

"When we show our respect for other living things, they respond with respect for us." (Arapaho nation)

"Every seed is awakened and so is all animal life. It is through this mysterious power that we too have our being and we therefore yield to our animal neighbours the same right as ourselves, to inhabit this land." Sitting Bull, Lakota tribe

"If all the beasts were gone, men would die from a great loneliness of Spirit, for whatever happens to the beast also happens to the man. All things are connected." Chief Seattle

"All things are our relatives; what we do to everything, we do to ourselves. All is really One". Black Elk

"Kinship with all creatures of the earth, sky and water was a real and active principle. In the animal and bird world there existed a brotherly feeling that kept the Lakota safe among them. And so close did some of the Lakotas come to their feathered and furred friends that in true brotherhood they spoke a common tongue." Luther Standing Bear

"All plants are our brothers and sisters. They talk to us and if we listen, we can hear them." (Arapaho)

"With all things and in all things, we are relatives." (Sioux Indian Proverb)

"In an eagle there is all the wisdom of the world." Lame Deer, Minnicoujou

THE ACTUAL: WHAT WE ARE DOING TO OUR FELLOW SPECIES THROUGH CLIMATE CHANGE

Climate change in combination with habitat destruction is accelerating species loss on Earth, and by the end of this century, as many as one in six species could be at risk of extinction. Humans contribute most to habitat loss according to a report by The Intergovernmental Science-Policy Platform on Biodiversity and Ecosystem Services (IPBES) on loss of biodiversity and ecosystem services. Human activities affect three-quarters of land, two-thirds of the oceans and three-quarters of fresh water leaving little room for anything else. The alarming rate of extinction is 100 – 1,000 times greater than the expected natural rate. A new report by the International Union for Conservation of Nature (IUCN) has added more than 9,000 to its Red List of threatened species, pushing the total number of species on the list to more than 105,000 for the first time. The IUCN estimates that 35% of bird species, 52% of amphibians and 71% of reef-building corals will be particularly vulnerable to the effects of climate change. Almost half of plant and animal species have experienced local extinctions due to climate change, research reveals, with the tropics suffering the most pronounced loss.[1]

The Intergovernmental Panel on Climate Change (IPCC) indicated that if the global average temperature rises by 1.5 to 2.5 degrees Celsius, around 20 to 30% of global species will face extinction. Today, warming is set to take place 10 times faster than any change recorded in the past 65 million years. There are an estimated 8 million animal and plant species on Earth (including 5.5 million insect species). A 2019 U.N. Report concluded that around 1 million animal and plant species are now threatened with extinction, many within decades, more than ever before in human history. More than 40% of amphibian species, almost 33% of reef-forming corals, more than a third of all marine mammals and a quarter of land mammals are currently threatened with extinction. 25% is also the average proportion of species threatened with extinction across the total terrestrial, freshwater and marine vertebrate, invertebrate and plant groups that have been studied in sufficient detail.[2]

Insects make up 70% of earth's creatures. Insects are essential as pollinators, food sources for animals and nutrient recyclers in many ecosystems. Yet a third of insects are now endangered species, and they are going extinct at a rate eight times that of birds, mammals and reptiles. According to research by Sánchez Bayo of Sydney and Queensland University, "In 10 years you will have a quarter less, in 50 years only half left and in 100 years you will have none."[3]

Climate is important in determining where a species can live – its range. Species are adapted to particular climatic conditions, but as global temperatures rise, the conditions they actually experience are changing. Climate change forces three fates on a species: adapt, flee or die. Some species may tolerate the change at their location, by rapid adaptation. However, given the unprecedented pace of current climate change, many species will need to move in order to track the conditions suitable for them. Evolution would have to occur 10,000 times faster than it typically does in order for most species to adapt and avoid extinction. One study found that even if we hold the temperature rise to the recommended 1.5 degrees, then two-thirds of insects and half of plants and vertebrates are projected to lose 50% of their geographical range.[4]

Due to global warming, ecosystems are generally shifting away from the equator or upward in altitude, but in some cases they will run out of space, as a 1°C change in temperature corresponds to 100 kilometres change in latitude. Hence, average shift in habitat condition by the year 2100 will be in the order of 140 to 580 km (87 – 360 miles). For example, one study found that whole ecosystems in the Great Plains of North America are shifting dramatically north. The northernmost ecosystem boundary has shifted more than 365 miles north, with the southernmost boundary moving about 160 miles from the 1970 baseline.[5]

Because the climate is changing this leads to changes to life cycle events such as having young, earlier starts of seasonal growth, and the time birds choose to migrate. The Intergovernmental Panel on Climate Change, in a 2007 report, estimated that spring arrived earlier by 2.3 to 5.2

days per decade over the previous 30 years.[6] There are now mismatches in the timing of migration, breeding, pest avoidance, and food availability. Growth and survival are reduced when migrants arrive at a location before or after their usual food sources are present. These timing shifts are a threat when they force birds' life cycles out of synchrony with the plants and insects upon which they depend. Dr Luis Cadahía of the University of Oslo found in a study that some populations of pied flycatchers, which are long-distance migratory birds, have suffered a 90% decline in numbers over the past two decades.[7] Also, changing seasons have altered the birth cycle of many species, such as the caribou. Their birth season normally takes place at peak food availability, but global warming has caused the timing to be off, thereby endangering them because the necessary food supply is not present.[8]

Another factor that exacerbates the effect of climate change centres on our activities as the dominant species on earth. Calculated by numbers of individuals, humans comprise just 0.01% of living beings. Since 1800, the global human population has grown sevenfold, surpassing 7.6 billion, and the global economy has grown 30-fold.[9] The great modern human enterprise was built on exploitation of the natural environment. Today, we entirely dominate 36% of the bio-productive surface of the earth. According to Global Footprint Network we actually need 1.75 planets to support humanity's demands on eco systems.[10] In the chapter on food we saw an example of how meat consumption causes habitat loss. As our habitat expands, the habitat of wildlife contracts.

Let's take a look around the world on different continents with some examples to see how climate change is affecting our fellow creatures.

South America

This region holds almost one half of the world's tropical forests. In terms of numbers of species found in the world it has a third of the mammals, 35% of its reptilian species, 41% of its birds and half of its amphibians. Many of these are found nowhere else in the world.[11]

No other place on Earth showcases the diversity of life like the Amazon basin. It is a vast region that spans eight countries and one overseas territory: Brazil, Bolivia, Peru, Ecuador, Colombia, Venezuela, Guyana, Suriname and French Guiana. South America's Amazon contains nearly a third of all the tropical rainforests left on Earth. Despite covering only around 1% of the planet's surface, the Amazon is home to 10% of all the wildlife species we know about – and probably a lot that we don't know yet. Research by WWF has shown that, on average, a "new" species of animal or plant is being discovered in the Amazon every 3 days. The Amazon contains one of Earth's richest assortments of biodiversity; thousands of species of plants, over a million insect species, more than 700 fish species, 1,000 bird species, and more than 430 species of mammal, the majority of which are bats and rodents.[12]

The Amazon has already experienced habitat destruction through climate change. This is because of the severe droughts in the Amazon in 2005 and 2010. When drier-than-normal conditions exist, fires from the open edges encroach on the forests and burn dry and stressed trees. Under normal conditions, when the rainforests are wetter, this is far less common. About 30% of the Amazon basin's total current forest area was affected by the 2005 drought. The 2010 drought affected nearly half of the entire Amazon forest, with nearly a fifth of it experiencing severe drought. Researchers attribute the 2005 Amazonian drought to the long-term warming of tropical Atlantic sea surface temperatures and hence altering rainfall patterns. Climate change may have a devastating effect on the forest in the future. Models suggest that by the year 2050, temperatures in the Amazon will increase by 2–3°C. At the same time, a decrease in rainfall during the dry months will lead to widespread drying. Altogether, the models predict that the area affected by mild drought will double and the area affected by severe drought will triple by 2100. Research carried out under the auspices of Brazil's National Space Research Institute shows that a warmer and drier environment for the region could convert from 30% up to 60% of the Amazon rainforest into a type of dry savanna grassland. This will cause the devastation of many species and become a source of CO_2 emissions rather than a forest area which absorbs CO_2 emissions (known as a carbon sink).[13]

With the loss of forest comes the loss of species. A study, conducted by the World Wildlife Fund, the University of East Anglia and the James Cook University, warns that rising temperatures could have a disastrous impact on areas such as the Amazon. With an increase of 3.2°C, 60% of plant species and almost half of animal species in the Amazon could disappear during this century. Under the bleakest scenario, a 4.5°C increase, the Amazon could see amphibian species, which are projected to be the worst hit, to plummet by nearly 75% and plant species by almost 70% by the 2080s, according to the WWF's analysis.[14]

The loss of species is compounded by man-made causes. Since the Trans-Amazonian Highway was built through the Amazon, exploitation of the resources has been unmerciful. Mining and oil has seen the displacement of indigenous people, who have always managed the rainforest sustainably. Logging has cleared vast swathes, usually in preparation for cattle ranching - cattle are found here in their highest concentrations anywhere in the world. About 3,050 square miles of forest was cleared in the Brazilian Amazon between August 2017 and July 2018, the worst annual deforestation rate in a decade, according to government data. That's a 13.7% jump from the same period last year. This means that large areas of forest habitat are fragmented and according to Elizabeth Kolbert in her book "The Sixth Extinction", tropical rain forests lose 5,000 species per year due to this.[15]

Australia and New Zealand

Species in Australia and New Zealand are considered to be of great concern as these countries have a high level of animals that are not found anywhere else in the world – these are known as endemic species. For example, over 80% of the 2,500 species of native conifers, flowering plants and ferns are found nowhere else. And of the 245 species of birds breeding in New Zealand before human arrival, 71% were endemic. This high rate is mainly the result of the country's long isolation from other land masses.[16] With habitats ranging from desert to coral reef, via tropical and temperate rainforests, rivers and grasslands, Australia is home to many of the world's most recognisable animals, including kangaroos, koalas, emus, platypuses, wombats and goannas.[17]

Australia and New Zealand have experienced warming of 0.4°C to 0.7°C since 1950, with changed rainfall patterns and sea level rise of about 70 mm (approx 3 inches) across the region; there has also been a greater frequency and intensity of droughts and heat waves, reduced seasonal snow cover, and glacial retreat. Australian droughts are more intense. There is now less rain in southern and eastern Australia and north-eastern New Zealand. There are more heat waves and fewer frosts.[18]

In Australia and New Zealand, future climate changes are more than 90% likely to exceed the adaptive ability of many species to changing climate in terms of food supply and may lead to extinction for some. A report to the National Climate Change Adaptation Research Facility (NCCARF), showed that the climate in most of Australia is predicted to go far outside natural variability, indeed beyond the climates that most species have experienced in their entire evolutionary history. Worryingly, many of the areas predicted to have the greatest climatic change correspond to some of the most important biodiversity areas in Australia.[18]

The IPCC predicts that by 2050 under a medium emissions scenario changes would include significant loss of biodiversity in areas such as alpine regions, the Wet Tropics, east coast wet forests, the Australian southwest, the Kakadu wetlands, coral reefs, and sub-Antarctic islands.[19]

In 2019 Australia had its hottest year on record. Since the 1970s, there has been an increase in extreme fire weather and a lengthening of the fire season across large parts of Australia, particularly in southern and eastern regions, due to increases in extreme hot days and drying. The devastating bushfires of the 2019/2020 summer season actually began in the spring, when new temperature records of nearly 50 degrees were set. Heat waves are forecast to become more frequent and intense, with the number of very hot days (over 35°C) doubling by 2070. According to research highlighted by the Australian Institute, by 2020 the number of 'very high' or 'extreme' fire days could increase by 4 - 25%, and 15 - 70% by 2050.[20] In the northern part of the state of New South Wales alone, there are projected to be ten more heat wave days per year by 2030 and thirty more by 2070, according to the government's Adapt NSW website.[21] Intense heat leads to wild fires that kill wildlife. The 2019/2020 season killed an estimated 1 billion animals and some species may have been driven to extinction.[22]

One region of international importance in terms of bio-diversity is the Great Barrier Reef. This is the world's largest continuous reef system, extending more than 1,300 miles (2,100 km) through the Coral Sea off north-eastern Australia. The reef is home to a diverse array of tropical fish, birds, and reptiles. Corals die off if the temperature of sea water rises to at least 1 degree centigrade above the norm and the result is called bleaching. The reef has suffered eight mass coral bleaching events since 1979, triggered by unusually high water temperatures, believed to have been caused by climate change. For example, in the eight months after the 2015/16 event, nearly 30% of shallow water corals died. Two years later, recruitment of new coral, which leads to regrowth, has been reduced by about 90%. Research highlighted by the Climate Council has stated that by 2034, the extreme ocean temperatures that led to the mass bleaching events of 2016 and 2017 may occur every two years if emissions continue on current trends. By 2080 it has been estimated that there will be a 95% decrease in the distribution of Great Barrier Reef species.[23]

North America

All of North America is very likely to warm during this century, at a higher rate than the global average. A U.S. government report in 2017 stated that annual average temperature over the contiguous United States has increased by 1°C over the period from 1901 to 2016. Over the next few decades (2021–2050), annual average temperatures are expected to rise by another 1.4 degrees. In northern regions, warming is likely to be greatest in winter, and in the southwestern USA greatest in summer. Annual mean precipitation is very likely to increase in Canada and the northeast USA, and likely to decrease in the southwest of the USA. Snow season length and snow depth are very likely to decrease in most of North America.[24]

Based on analyses of the nation's best-studied groups of plants and animals -including birds, mammals, fish, reptiles, amphibians and plants - scientists at Nature Serve estimate that about a third of all U.S. species are at risk of extinction. Climate change will be one of the factors producing this depressing figure.[25]

As temperatures increase, the habitat ranges of many North American species are increasingly moving north and to higher elevations. While this means a range expansion for some species, for others it means movement into less hospitable habitat, increased competition, or range reduction, with some species having nowhere to go because they are already at the top of a mountain or at the northern limit of land suitable for their habitat. These factors lead to local extinctions of both plants and animals. Some climate change modelling for North America shows that 53% of species are projected to lose more than half of their current geographic range by the end of the 21st century. Noted conservation scientist David Wilcove estimates that there are 14,000 to 35,000 endangered species in the United States, which is 7% to 18% of U.S. flora and fauna.[26]

We can look, as an example, at the effect on bird species. The National Wildlife Federation reports that 177 of 305 North American bird species shifted their range further north by 35 miles in the last 40 years.[27] Audubon's 2017 *Birds and Climate Change Report* predicted that 314 of the 588 species studied will lose more than half of the geographical range they can operate in, making them climate endangered.[28]

As mentioned earlier, for many species, the climate where they live or spend part of the year influences key stages of their annual life cycle. The earlier arrival of spring means that for animals and birds there may be mismatches in the timing of migration, breeding, pest avoidance, and food availability. Earlier springs have led to earlier nesting for 28 migratory bird species on the East Coast of the United States. North-eastern birds that winter in the southern United States are returning north in the spring 13 days earlier than they did a century ago. One large-scale study showed that birds are laying eggs on average 6.6 days earlier per decade.

Ornithologists calculate that in the past 48 years, total North American bird numbers have fallen drastically. There are now 2.9 billion birds fewer compared to 1970. That is more than 1 in 4. Sparrows, warblers, blackbirds and finches are down in numbers and swallows, swifts, nightjars and other insectivores are also in decline.[29]

We can now look at an example of how climate change affects mammals. According to Carbon Brief, temperatures in the Arctic are rising at least twice as fast as the global average and sea ice cover is diminishing by nearly 4% per decade because of warming seas.[30] Declines in the duration and extent of sea ice in the Arctic leads to declines in the abundance of ice algae, which thrive in nutrient-rich pockets in the ice. These algae are eaten by zooplankton, which are in turn eaten by Arctic cod, an important food source for many marine mammals, including seals. Seals are eaten by polar bears. Hence, declines in the early melting of sea ice and of algae can contribute to declines in polar bear populations. Globally, polar bears are listed as 'vulnerable' under the IUCN Red List due primarily to sea ice loss.[31] Scientists' best estimate is that there's a high chance that the global population of polar bears will fall by more than a third within the next three generations.[32]

Africa

Africa contains about one-fifth of all known species of plants, mammals, and birds, as well as one-sixth of amphibians and reptiles. Africa boasts over 1,100 species of mammals, including herd animals like wildebeest, buffalo and impala, as well as zebras, giraffes, and elephants. It has some of the world's most diverse and biologically important ecosystems such as savannahs, tropical forests, marine coral reefs and freshwater habitats, wetlands and mountains.

Africa consumes a tiny fraction of the world's fossil fuels, yet it is predicted to suffer far more than its share of the negative impacts of climate change. With its size, range of climates and unique weather patterns, the continent is especially susceptible to the effects of rising temperatures. Unfortunately there is great difficulty in accessing accurate information about how climate is changing in Africa due to the utter lack of weather recording stations.

According to the IPCC, the historical climate record for Africa shows warming of approximately 0.7°C over most of the continent during the 20th century, a decrease in rainfall over large portions of the Sahel, and an increase in rainfall in east central Africa. Future warming across Africa is predicted to be between 0.2°C per decade to more than 0.5°C per decade, meaning that temperatures in Africa are projected to rise faster than the global average. This warming will be greatest over the semi-arid margins of the Sahara and of central southern Africa.[33]

Over time, climate change has emerged as a silent threat to African wildlife, as changing weather patterns trigger shifts in habitat composition and forage availability as well as access to water.

Thomas Smith from the Center for Tropical Research at the University of California has stated that with a 1.5 degree centigrade rise in global temperature, Africa may lose 30% of its animals and plants. He also estimated that a rise of 3 degrees in global temperatures could mean a loss of 40% of all mammal species in Africa by the end of the century.[34] The International Union for the Conservation of Nature stated in 2014 that 6,419 species of animal and 3,148 types of plant in Africa were recorded as threatened with extinction on its Red List.[35] The Worldwide Fund for Nature estimated in 2014 that the overall combined population of African vertebrate species was calculated to have already declined by around 39% since 1970.[36]

The African savannah rolls across much of central and south-eastern Africa. This tropical grassland encompasses or touches 27 countries, from Cote d' Ivoire in the northwest to Madagascar in the southeast. The savannah is home to 45 mammal species, 500 bird species and numerous plants. Climate change in combination with habitat destruction and poaching has led to the rapid decline of iconic species.

In 2018, according to the WWF, it has been estimated that only 20,000 African lions remain on the savannah - a reduction by half since the 1950s. Lion populations are most threatened by habitat loss and diseases related to climate change.[37]

Around 90% of African elephants have been wiped out in the past century – mainly due to the ivory trade, because of growing demand for ivory in China and the Far East. Around 20,000 African elephants are being killed every year for their ivory – that's around 55 every day. The situation is compounded by climate change, which causes habitat loss and diminishing food supply because of the shortage of water. Since the early 1900s, their population has decreased from about 20 million to somewhere between 450,000 and 700,000 in 2018.[38] In 2019 there was a severe drought in southern Africa. In Zimbabwe 200 elephants died due to lack of food and water and some were saved only by moving them 1,000 miles away to a more sustainable environment.[39]

According to the latest Red List by the International Union for Conservation of Nature (IUCN), the giraffe population has declined by 40% in the last three decades. There has been more emphasis on saving rhinos and elephants, while the situation of giraffes has been neglected. With the rising human population and expansion of farmland, this threatened giant is under severe pressure in its core ranges across Central, East, and West Africa. There is also illegal hunting and civil strife, but the situation is compounded further by drought caused by climate change which reduces the plant food available.[40]

Europe

According to a European Environment Agency report, annual average land temperatures over Europe are projected to continue increasing by more than the global average temperature. The largest temperature increases are projected over eastern and northern Europe in winter and over southern Europe in summer. Annual precipitation is generally projected to increase in northern Europe and to decrease in southern Europe, thereby enhancing the differences between currently wet regions and currently dry regions. The effects of climate change, particularly rising temperatures combined with habitat destruction from industrial development and pollution, are predicted to increase the number of extinctions of species in Europe.[41]

According to the world conservation union (IUCN), among Europe's 1,000 species of native mammals, birds, reptiles and amphibians, 155 are classified as threatened. Extinction threatens one in seven of Europe's 228 species of mammals.[42]

Birdlife International have stated that out of the 524 bird species found in Europe, 68 (13%) are threatened with extinction, with 2% (10 species) marked as already Critically Endangered.[43] Out of Europe's 83 species of amphibians, nearly one-quarter are threatened with extinction. All of the 19 threatened species occur only in Europe, mostly on the Iberian peninsula, the Italian peninsula, the Balkan coast and on Mediterranean islands. These are the very regions where temperature increases from climate change are the greatest. A comprehensive review study on amphibians and reptiles found that 20 out of the 21 amphibian, and four out of the five reptilian, species assessed in Europe were already affected by climate change.[44]

According to a 2016 report "Climate change, impacts and vulnerability in Europe", distributions of European plant species are projected by the late 21st century to have shifted several hundred kilometres to the north, forests are likely to have contracted in the south and expanded in the north, and 60% of mountain plant species may face extinction. The rate of change will exceed the ability of many species to adapt.[45]

CONCLUSIONS

My conclusions are that the way we have behaved which has caused climate change means that we have not shown respect for other species. This respect is clearly seen in the teachings of all the spiritual traditions of the world but we have lost our connection with it. This is a serious mistake because our very existence depends on other species. Looking at any size of creature, they all play a role in maintaining functioning eco systems.

There is also an arrogance in our behaviour - as though we are important but other species are not. This is so true in the way that we have destroyed habitats to meet our own greed rather than our need. By destroying forests we exacerbate climate change because there are less trees to absorb excess CO_2. It is like a man sitting on a branch of a tree and cutting off the branch - with the result that he will fall to the ground. Planting more forests will greatly help. Otherwise, all we can do now is limit the damage to other species by completely decarbonising our economies as soon as possible.

Chapter 6: THE EFFECT ON HEALTH

Our physical health is dependent on the world around us. The first part of this chapter explains the attitude which the spiritual traditions have in regard to keeping our health.

THE IDEAL - SPIRITUAL TEACHINGS ABOUT HOW WE SHOULD TAKE CARE OF OUR HEALTH

Judaism and Christianity

According to the Bible, God created the world and created man in His own image (Genesis 1:27). Therefore, as the world is created by God, to Jews and Christians it is sacred. The Bible gives two main reasons why we should care for the environment. First, God Himself says that His creation is very good. The material world matters to God; He sustains it all the time. Without Him it would fall apart into chaos. "He is before all things, and in Him all things hold together" (Colossians 1.16–17). So if people neglect, abuse and spoil the environment, they are damaging something that is precious to God. The second, and even more important reason why Jews and Christians should care for the environment, is that God specifically commanded them to do so (Genesis 1.28 and 2.15). Followers see themselves as good stewards of the earth, not abusing it for selfish ends. By caring for the earth properly, they see this as proper worship of God. In relation to maintaining our health, if we create climate change through our behaviour and this affects our health, then we are not following the guidance of God. This is clear from this quote from the Old Testament: "If you listen carefully to the Lord your God and do what is right in his eyes, if you pay attention to his commands and keep all his decrees, I will not bring on you any of the diseases I brought on the Egyptians, for I am the Lord, who heals you." (Exodus 15:263)

Health is valued by God because the human body is a vessel for the spirit of God. "Do you not know that you are God's temple and that God's Spirit dwells in you?" (Corinthians 3:16). In the New Testament, John states how important health is to God: "Dear friend, I pray that you may enjoy good health and that all may go well with you even as your soul is getting along well." (3 John 1:2)

Islam

Muslims believe that the earth was created by God. The Qur'an states that "Allah created the heavens and the earth, and all that is between them, in six days". (Qur'an 7:54) As with the Bible, it follows logically that because God created the world we should take care of it. Humans are representatives of God on earth, as the Qur'an states, "It is He who has appointed you vicegerent on the earth..." (Quran 6:165) It is also clear what mankind's responsibilities are from the following quote from the Qur'an: "The world is beautiful and verdant, and verily God, the exalted, has made you His stewards in it, and He sees how you acquit yourselves." As with the Bible teachings, the Qur'an states mankind was created by God. Muslims believe their bodies are given to them as a trust by God, to use appropriately for the attainment of salvation. This belief that body and soul belong to God and will return to him, is what grounds Muslim recognition of the sanctity of human life and of the need to ensure both physical and spiritual well-being. The Qur'an speaks of God's revelation as healing for the illness of the human heart. Therefore any activity by man such as creating climate change which affects the health of mankind is against the teachings of Islam.

Hinduism

No other religion perhaps places as much emphasis on nature worship as Hinduism. The philosophy inculcates a very strong environmental conscience, rendering Hinduism a leading contender for being the most environment-friendly religion in the world. Hinduism contains numerous references to the worship of the divine in nature in its Vedas, Upanishads, Puranas, Sutras and other sacred texts. Millions of Hindus recite Sanskrit mantras daily to revere their rivers, mountains, trees, animals, and the earth. Hindus regard everything around them as pervaded by a subtle divine presence, be it rivers, mountains, lakes, animals, flora, the mineral world, plus the stars and planets. It is so because the Divine reality is present as *Prana/Shakti* energy, power, in every electron, particle, atom, and cell and in every manifestation of matter. For the Hindus the Earth is sacred as the very manifestation of the Divine Mother. She is Bhumi Devi, the Earth Goddess. One of the reasons that Hindus honour cows is that the cow represents the energies and qualities of the Earth, selfless caring, sharing and the providing of nourishment to all. Hindus see the world as a source of divinity. They would not view it as a source of ill health such as that which climate change will bring. In fact India is home to one of the oldest, still functioning, medical traditions in the world. Ayurveda medicine, dating back to the first millennium BCE, is practised in India today (as it is around the world), promoting the goal of longevity through good health. Yoga, which is also widely-known, also developed from Hinduism. Hindus are also conscious of their health because they are mainly vegetarians.

Buddhism

Buddhist religion is ecological religion. Buddhism teaches that human beings should live in harmony with nature and all other creatures. Buddhism begins with reverence for life and its recognition of the interdependence of all life. In Buddhism, health is understood as wholeness. It is the expression of harmony - within oneself, in one's social relationships, and in relation to the natural environment. Good health arises because of the law of Karma, which stresses the correlation between a deed and its subsequent consequences. If I carry out good deeds then there are good results, such as maintaining good health. For instance, the first rule or precept that Buddhists follow is to avoid killing and harming living beings. The practice of compassion is very important in Buddhism. So bad health comes from the bad karma of us causing climate change through polluting the world to satisfy our greed. Buddhists also see karma in relation to the principle of dependent origination (also referred to as the law of conditionality). This basically says, whether in the universe, the natural world, or human society, or within oneself, nothing exists as a separate unit but only as an interdependent part of the whole. So the arising of ill health through climate change is also caused by our lack of awareness of the interdependence of natural systems. Buddha was very clear that we manifest the world we live in by stating, "We are what we think. All that we are arises with our thoughts. With our thoughts we make the world." (Dhammapada)

Sikhism

Sikhism preaches the message of the One True God and the path leading to oneness with God through devotion, meditation and elimination of one's ego. The Sikh's way of living also includes living a righteous life through promoting equality, resisting discrimination, and avoiding superstition. Religion is central to the practice of health and wellness since health is not merely defined by physical functionality but by alignment with the ultimate goal in life, the path to the One True God. Disease therefore is understood as a state of dis-ease due to the attachment to the ego. Sikhs believe in the law of karma. Karma is the universal principle of cause and effect. Our actions, both good and bad, come back to us in the future. Sikhs will see the effects of bad health from climate change as the result of bad karma, where we have consumed too much energy to satisfy material desires as a substitute for pursuing the path of oneness with God.

Bahá'í Faith

Bahá'ís see that health is given by God for a purpose, and it is our responsibility to maintain it. "...you should not neglect your health, but consider it the means which enables you to serve." (Compilations, Lights of Guidance, p. 297) As 'Abdu'l-Bahá states: "Man may take good care of his body for the purpose of satisfying his personal wishes. Or, he may look after his health with the good intention of serving humanity and of living long enough to perform his duty toward mankind. The latter is most commendable." 'Abdu'l-Bahá (Star of the West, Volume 5, p. 231). From a Bahá'í viewpoint, true health extends beyond the physical. For an individual and a community to be healthy, their emotional, intellectual, spiritual, and physical well-being are all required. 'Abdu'l-Bahá stated,

"When the material world and the divine world are well co-related, when the hearts become heavenly and the aspirations grow pure and divine, perfect connection shall take place. Then shall this power produce a perfect manifestation. Physical and spiritual diseases will then receive absolute healing." 'Abdu'l-Bahá, (Tablets of 'Abdu'l-Bahá v2, p. 309) He also said: "Between material things and spiritual things there is a connection. The more healthful his body the greater will be the power of the spirit of man; the power of the intellect, the power of the memory, the power of reflection will then be greater." 'Abdu'l-Bahá (Star of the West - v5). This implies that climate change which produces health problems arises because mankind is not in harmony between the physical and the spiritual. We only focus on the material and the spiritual gets neglected, leading to ill health. We have failed to see that the real purpose is to serve the cause of God and not fulfil material desires for ourselves.

The use of foodstuffs to maintain health and provide healing means that a wide range of food needs to be available to all: "When highly-skilled physicians shall fully examine this matter, thoroughly and perseveringly, it will be clearly seen that the incursion of disease is due to a disturbance in the relative amounts of the body's component substances, and that treatment consisteth in adjusting these relative amounts, and that this can be apprehended and made possible by means of foods. It is certain that in this wonderful new age the development of medical science will lead to the doctors' healing their patients with foods."

(Abdu'l-Bahá (Selections from the Writings of 'Abdu'l-Bahá, p. 154)

Taoism

The focus of Taoism is the individual in nature rather than the individual in society. It holds that the goal of life for each individual is to find one's own personal adjustment to the rhythm of the natural (and supernatural) world and to follow the Way (*Tao*) of the universe. *Tao* is a Chinese word that has different meanings, but is typically translated as "way" or "path." Tao can be loosely defined as: the absolute principle underlying the universe, signifying the way, or code of behaviour, that is in harmony with the natural order which if followed, leads to a life of harmony and thereby a healthy life. The philosophy of Taoism is well known to have espoused a natural way of life. The Way of nature is defined as one of simplicity, contentment, authenticity and spontaneity. Contentment in the Taoist sense means to be satisfied with what we have and to refrain from excessive desires for fame, wealth, pleasure and other worldly possessions. As Lao Tzu states, "Be content with what you have; rejoice in the way things are. When you realise nothing is lacking, the whole world belongs to you." Lao Tzu (Tao Te Ching). Climate change has come from the pollution we have caused by having too many material desires, from a root cause of discontentment. Our harmony within ourselves and the environment is disturbed by the health effects of climate change and so we suffer. Taoism has given us many health practices such as acupuncture, tai chi, and qi gong.

THE ACTUAL - WHAT CLIMATE CHANGE IS DOING TO OUR HEALTH

Overall Picture

Climate change may seem distant to millions in the richer countries but when it affects their health they will sit up and take notice. I am writing this at a time when I have been told to stay at home because of the COVID-19 virus as part of the U.K. lock down. The global spread of the coronavirus illustrates what this chapter is about - it is an example of how health issues will encompass all of us as climate change develops. Important future trends for human health include an increase in the number of people suffering from disease, injury and death from heat waves, floods, storms, fires and droughts; changes in the range of infectious disease vectors such as mosquitoes; and an increase in the burden of diarrhoeal diseases. Between 2030 and 2050, climate change is expected to cause approximately 250,000 additional deaths per year, from malnutrition, malaria, diarrhoea and heat stress. Adverse health outcomes from climate change are likely to be greatest in low-income countries and in poor people living in urban areas, in elderly people, children, traditional societies, subsistence farmers, and coastal populations.[1]

Deaths from Heat Waves

With a warming world comes the threat of heat waves, where humans are exposed to temperatures which are a threat to their health. If the body temperature rises above 38°C, people suffer heat exhaustion and their physical and cognitive functions are impaired. However, above 40.6°C heat stroke occurs, with risks of organ damage, loss of consciousness and death.[2] Weather conditions such as extreme heat serve as stressors in individuals with pre-existing cardiovascular disease. There is also evidence that heat amplifies the adverse impacts of ozone and particulates on cardiovascular disease. Of particular concern for densely-populated cities is the urban heat island effect, where man-made surfaces absorb sunlight during the day and then radiate the stored energy at night as heat. This process will exacerbate any warming from climate change and limit the potential relief of cooler night-time temperatures in urban areas. By 2030, 60% of the global population will live in cities, greatly increasing the total human population exposed to extreme heat. Extreme heat gravely affects older people. As explained in the chapter on extreme weather events, a combination of high temperature and humidity which prevents the human body from cooling by sweating, is highly dangerous and is likely to become more frequent in the coming years.

In 2019 researchers found that on average across Europe the number of days with extreme heat and heat stress has more than tripled between 1950 and 2018.[3] The heat waves of 2003 in Europe caused up to 70,000 deaths, especially from respiratory and cardiovascular causes.[4] The heat waves of the summer of 2015 caused more than 3,000 deaths in France alone. In 2019 Europe suffered another heat wave.[5] According to the European Environment Agency it is virtually certain that the length, frequency and intensity of heat waves will increase in the future in Europe. This increase will lead to a substantial increase in mortality over the next decades, especially in vulnerable population groups.[6] One study estimated that, depending on measures to reduce emissions, heat-related mortality in Europe could increase by between 60,000 and 165,000 deaths per year by the 2080s compared with the present baseline, with the highest impacts in southern Europe.[7] The Meteorological Office has projected that UK summer temperatures could regularly reach 38.5°C by the 2040s. In 2018 a U.K. government report said that there could be 7,000 heat-related deaths every year in the UK by 2050.[8]

A warmer future is projected to lead to increases in future mortality of the order of thousands to tens of thousands of additional premature deaths per year across the United States by the end of this century. In 2016 US government research projected future heat deaths in 209 cities.

They found that there would be a total net increase of about 2,000 to 10,000 deaths per year by the end of the century compared to a 1990 baseline.[9]

According to an IPPC report in 2014 on Australia, the number of "dangerously hot" days, when core body temperatures may increase by 2°C, and outdoor activity is hazardous, is projected to rise from the current 4 to 6 days per year to 33 to 45 days per year by 2070.[10] The Bureau of Meteorology of Australia released its biennial State of the Climate Report in 2016 which highlighted the impact climate change is having on the continent. In the same year, an Australian Government report estimated that there will be more than 2000 heat-related fatalities in 2050, compared with about 500 recorded in 2011.[11]

Deaths from Skin Cancer

Stratospheric ozone absorbs much of the incoming solar ultraviolet radiation (UVR), especially the biologically more damaging, shorter-wavelength UVR. As the climate becomes warmer with each and every year, the ozone layer gets thinner. Due to the increase in temperatures, it is also likely that individuals' exposure to UV radiation will increase, and therefore the risk of developing skin cancer. Malignant melanoma is the most serious form of skin cancer: it is responsible for around 80% of skin cancer deaths.

Australia has some of the world's highest melanoma-related fatalities - double the mortality rates of south and central Europe. Australia already has the highest rate of skin cancer in the world - astonishingly, 2/3 of all Australians will have been diagnosed with some form of skin cancer by the time they are 70 - and the incidence is expected to continually rise in correlation with rising temperatures. In 2016, the Australian government estimated there were 13,280 new cases of melanoma and 1,770 people would be dying from this disease. As we saw from the Australian wildfires in 2019, temperatures are increasing and with them the increased risk of skin cancer.[12]

Skin cancer is the most common form of cancer in the United States.1 in 5 Americans will develop skin cancer by the age of 70.[13] According to the Skin Care Foundation, in the decade up to 2020, the number of new invasive melanoma cases diagnosed increased each year by 47%. We know from previous heat waves in the South West and Mid-West of the USA that temperatures are increasing and therefore the risk of skin cancer will increase.

Deaths Caused by Insect-borne Diseases

In 2019 the World Health Organisation (WHO) estimated that there are more than 700,000 people around the world dying from vector-borne diseases each year. Vector-borne diseases are transmitted typically by the bite of an infected arthropod. The arthropod could be something rather familiar like a mosquito, tick, or black fly. These arthropods that carry and transmit diseases are known as vectors. Current knowledge suggests that the range of mosquito-borne diseases could expand dramatically in response to climate change. Rising global temperatures can lengthen the season and increase the geographic range of disease-carrying insects. As temperatures warm, mosquitoes and other warm-weather vectors can move into higher altitudes and new regions farther from the equator.

Malaria

Malaria is caused by a parasite transmitted by *Anopheles* mosquitoes. When an *Anopheles* mosquito bites a person already infected with the malaria parasite, the mosquito becomes a carrier of the disease. When that mosquito then bites another person, that person becomes infected with the parasite too. The WHO, in 2019, stated that every year there are about 219 million cases of the disease, and more than 400,000 deaths. Children under 5 years of age account for 67% of all malaria deaths. Over 90% of malaria deaths occur in sub-Saharan Africa.[14]

Now millions of people living at higher altitudes in the tropics will be at risk of malaria as a result of rising temperatures and climate change. The WHO predicts that globally, temperature increases of 2 - 3°C would increase the number of people who, in climatic terms, are at risk of malaria by around 3 - 5%.[15] Studies by the London School of Tropical Medicine and the *Malaria Research and Treatment* journal found that by the year 2080 climate change would lead to a significant increase in the length of the malaria transmission season in parts of both eastern and southern Africa. There are also predictions for increases in malarial transmission in the highlands of Central America, southern Brazil, and parts of India and Nepal.[16]

Dengue Fever

Aedes mosquitoes are "sip feeders", preferring to take small blood meals from lots of people. This makes them prolific at spreading disease; they are the main carrier of viruses that cause dengue, Zika, yellow fever and chikungunya. Dengue Fever virus is transmitted by the *Aedes aegypti* mosquito, which usually lives in tropical regions. Dengue fever affects children and adults alike with flu-like symptoms and can lead to haemorrhagic fever where there is severe bleeding through haemorrhages. One study estimated that in 2019 there were 10,000 deaths and 100 million symptomatic infections per year in over 125 countries. Roughly half of the global population currently lives in areas that are environmentally suitable for dengue transmission. Currently there is no cure. Dengue is the most rapidly spreading mosquito-borne viral disease. Climate change, bringing significant temperature increases, will directly affect disease transmission by shifting the vector's geographic range and increasing reproductive and biting rates, and by shortening the pathogen incubation period. The study also predicted that the disease would expand to higher altitudes in central Mexico, to northern Argentina, to inland Australia, to large coastal cities in eastern China and Japan, to southern Africa and to the West African Sahel.[17] Even rich developed countries are at risk. In the south-eastern United States, the dengue vector is widely established and exists on the current fringe of dengue transmission. A study, published in 2017 in *Environmental Health Perspectives*, suggests that, as the climate changes, several areas in the south eastern U.S., particularly in southern Florida and Texas, may see elevated risk of dengue virus transmission over time.[18]

West Nile Virus

The higher temperatures and lower precipitation brought on by climate change will generally lead to more cases of West Nile Virus as it will extend its range. West Nile Virus, also, is carried by mosquitoes, and infected insects transmit the virus to human beings with a bite. The very serious symptoms include encephalitis (inflammation of the brain) or meningitis (inflammation of the lining of the brain and spinal cord) and mostly affect the elderly and individuals with a compromised immune response. The greatest risks for death in the elderly have been attributed to renal, infectious, digestive, and circulatory causes. This vector-borne disease has hit the developed world hard, particularly the USA. Following the initial outbreak in New York in 1999, it spread along the eastern seaboard, reaching Florida by 2001, and west to the Rocky Mountains and Pacific Northwest (Washington State) by 2002. Finally, in 2003, it was detected in Southern California, marking its successful establishment across the continental US. Now the virus has become endemic to the United States, where an estimated 7 million human infections have occurred, making it the leading mosquito-borne virus infection and the most common cause of viral encephalitis in the country.[19] A study of an outbreak in Texas found that 557 (13.4%) deaths occurred among the 4,142 patients reported as having the disease.[20]

The first human West Nile virus case in Canada was reported in Ontario in 2002, and it has now become endemic in several southern Canadian provinces. In 2004 it showed up in Central America and the Caribbean. Since then, evidence of the disease has been found across South America, including Colombia, Venezuela, Brazil, and Argentina.[21]

Zika Virus

You will probably have heard of the Zika virus in the press coverage of the 2015 Olympics in Brazil. Zika virus is a tropical disease spread by *Aedes* mosquitoes, *Aedes aegypti* and *Aedes albopictus,* which also carry West Nile Virus, as well as yellow and dengue fever. Since its discovery in 1947, in the Zika forest of Uganda, Zika virus has spread to many other parts of the world, where it is becoming a serious global pandemic. The virus, which can be transmitted from mother to foetus during pregnancy, has been linked to an increase in miscarriages, deaths in newborns, and birth defects - especially a condition known as microcephaly, in which the brain does not fully develop and babies are born with abnormally small heads.

A 2019 study found that the number of people exposed to one or more months of a suitable climate for transmission could rise to half a billion by 2050. This could jump to nearly a billion more people by 2080.[22] Another study in 2019 also stated that there would be significantly greater expansion between 2050 and 2080, if emissions are not reduced. The report said that by 2050, 49% of the world's population could live in places exposed to possible Zika virus infection.[23]

Again, richer nations like the USA are also vulnerable to its spread, due to climate change. For instance, a March 2016 study showed that meteorological conditions are already suitable for *Aedes* mosquitoes in the southern half of the U.S. during peak summer months, and in southern Florida and Texas during winter months. In 2016, Zika swept through southern Florida, threatening pregnant women who could contract the disease and present no symptoms but have children with significant birth defects.[24]

A new report in 2019 stated that Canada and parts of northern Europe could be newly exposed to the threat of diseases such as yellow fever, Zika, dengue and chikungunya, as well as other emerging diseases.[25] In October 2019, the first mosquito-transmitted, locally acquired cases of Zika virus were reported in Europe, according to the *Lancet*.[26]

Lyme Disease

Lyme disease was first identified in the town of Lyme, Connecticut, in 1975. The disease is caused by a bite from a deer tick, leading to a bacterial infection. Lyme symptoms include fever, headache, fatigue, and muscle and joint aches. But when it is left untreated, this bacterial infection can spread into the joints, heart, and nervous system - causing more severe and dangerous symptoms like arthritis, heart palpitations, brain inflammation and nerve pain. One of the most important determinants of where ticks can live is temperature. Lyme disease has a wide distribution in temperate countries of North America, Europe, and Asia. According to the Lyme Disease Association, it has now been reported in more than 80 countries, is the most common tick-borne disease in the northern hemisphere and the most common vector-borne disease in the United States. Climate change, with the increase of temperature, will cause an acceleration of the tick's developmental cycle, increased egg production, increased population density, and an expansion of the areas where it is a health risk.[27]

In the US, the incidence of Lyme disease has doubled since 1991. In 2015, 95% of Lyme disease cases were reported from 14 states: Connecticut, Delaware, Maine, Maryland, Massachusetts, Minnesota, New Hampshire, New Jersey, New York, Pennsylvania, Rhode Island, Vermont, Virginia, and Wisconsin. The Centre for Disease Control estimates about 300,000 cases overall, many of them untreated.[28] A study in 2018 came to the conclusion that assuming the temperature will increase by 2°C by mid-century - the forecast of the U.S. National Climate Assessment - the United States will see 8.6 more cases of Lyme disease per 100,000 people annually.[29]

Deaths Caused by the Effects of Flooding

Floods caused by climate change can increase human exposure to pathogens, as contaminants are spread by floodwaters. Floods can be one giant environmental blender, mixing industrial waste, drinking water and sewage, leaving pools of stagnant contaminated water near humans. Drought caused by climate change is also a danger as poorer people access more unsafe water supplies. Extreme weather such as hurricanes and typhoons can spread water-borne diseases by disrupting existing water systems, resulting in drinking and waste waters becoming mixed. One gram of faeces can contain 10 million viruses, a million bacteria, a thousand parasite cysts or a hundred worm eggs. According to WHO and UNICEF, more than 2 million deaths are caused by water-borne diseases annually, making it the leading cause of death around the world.[30] Here we look at 4 types of organism as an example.

Diarrhoea is the most widely-known problem linked to contaminated food and water. As rising ambient temperatures from climate change increase, bacterial survival time and proliferation, and thus the incidence of diarrhoeal diseases, might further increase. Some 829,000 people are estimated to die each year from diarrhoea as a result of unsafe drinking-water, poor sanitation and hand hygiene. The WHO predicts that by 2030 there will be 10% more diarrhoeal disease than there would have been with no climate change and that it will primarily affect the health of young children.[31]

We can look at the nasty effects of some of these infectious organisms. Cholera is an acute infection caused by ingestion of food or water contaminated with the bacterium *Vibrio cholera,* and can kill within hours if left untreated. WHO researchers have estimated that each year there are 1.3 million to 4 million cases of cholera, and 21,000 to 143,000 deaths worldwide due to cholera. It is now more widespread throughout the world - in 2017 it was found in 34 countries. A combination of poor sanitation, undeveloped health services and frequent flooding caused by rising sea levels and extreme precipitation will guarantee the future spread of this disease to the poorer countries of the world.[32]

Typhoid is a serious and life-threatening enteric fever, spread through contaminated food and water. It disproportionately impacts children and marginalised populations in Southeast Asia, sub-Saharan Africa, Latin America, and the Middle East, resulting in nearly 12 million cases globally per year. During dry spells brought on by climate change, people seek water from shallow sources that are more likely to be contaminated with microbes such as typhoid. During flooding periods caused by climate change, water sources are more likely to be tainted with faecal matter leaking from poor sewage systems and unimproved sanitation facilities.[33]

Even developed countries are at risk from climate change spreading water-borne diseases, particularly when intense downpours occur. These can overwhelm sewage systems, water treatment and distribution systems. Many older cities in the North-eastern USA and around the Great Lakes region use combined sewer systems (with storm water and sewage sharing the same pipes), which are prone to discharging raw sewage directly into surface waters after moderate to heavy rainfall. The Milwaukee *Cryptosporidium* outbreak in 1993 was preceded by the heaviest rainfall event in 50 years in the surrounding area. This led to the largest documented water-borne disease outbreak in U.S. history, causing an estimated 403,000 illnesses and more than 50 deaths.[34]

In Canada, in the year 2000, there were 7 deaths, 65 hospitalisations and more than 2,300 cases of gastro-intestinal illness in the town of Walkerton. In this case, drinking water, supplied by shallow groundwater wells, turned out to be contaminated by cattle manure from a local farm, following a period of intense spring rainfall, an event that is considered to happen once every 60 years.[35]

Research in 2018 demonstrated how hurricanes can gravely affect established sewage and water treatment facilities. Hurricane Harvey was an unprecedented rain event that delivered five consistent days of flooding and storms to Texas in August 2017. A University of Texas study found that high levels of faecal contamination were introduced into waterways. 800 wastewater treatment plants reported spills from flooding and a weight of more than two million pounds of contaminants were released into the environment. The Houston water department found some water that contained 58 times the maximum level of *E.coli* deemed appropriate.[36] Another example was the aftermath of Hurricane Maria which struck Puerto Rico. Afterwards more than 2.3 million Puerto Rican residents were served by water systems which drew at least one sample testing positive for faecal bacteria. The problem was compounded by years of under investment in the sewage system and budget cuts for staff under the Trump administration.[37]

CONCLUSION

From what we can read from the spiritual traditions, it is clear that in terms of health we have lost our way. If we followed the teachings we would inhabit healthy bodies in a healthy world. We need to heed the warnings, listen to the teachings and tackle climate change or the situation could become gravely worse for millions of us and our fellow global citizens.

Part 2

What we can do about the

Climate Emergency

Chapter 7: CHOICES IN DAILY LIFE

The cry often heard is that "I am only an individual and cannot do anything about climate change - surely that is in the hands of governments and corporations?" In this chapter I counteract that argument by showing what an individual can do to lower their carbon emissions, especially those of us in the developed countries which was where the problem was caused in the first place. If we all make even small changes it all adds up to make a difference. If you decide you wish to make a change, you can make a note of it on the personal pledge page at the end of the book.[1]

Our choices are explained under the following headings:

Changing what we eat
Changing how we travel
Saving domestic energy
Buying less, using less

CHANGING WHAT WE EAT

Eating Less Meat

Over 80% of the human diet is provided by plants but meat, aquaculture, eggs, and dairy use over 80% of the world's farmland, despite providing only 18% of our calories. As an increasing number of studies show, eating a plant-based diet is one of the most impactful behaviour changes that individuals can make to reduce their individual carbon footprint. People who eat meat are responsible for almost twice as many dietary greenhouse gas emissions per day as vegetarians and about two-and-a-half times as many emissions as vegans. If everyone in the USA did not eat meat or cheese for just one day of the week, it would be equivalent to taking 7.6

million cars off the road.[2] Going vegan can reduce emissions from food by up to 90%.[3]

I was a vegetarian for over 30 years, and in the last few years, after taking nutritional advice, added wild fish to my diet. One of my original reasons for becoming vegetarian was to protect my health. A recent report by Oxford University's Programme on the Future of Food stated, "Climate taxes on meat and milk would lead to huge and vital cuts in carbon emissions as well as saving half a million lives a year via healthier diets."[4]

There is also a moral argument for eating less meat, or no meat at all. The International Food Policy Research Institute estimates that reducing the amount of meat which is consumed in high-income countries by half could result in 3.6 million fewer malnourished children in developing countries. An area the size of the European Union is growing feed crops for industrially reared animals. This land could feed 4 billion people.[5] World hunger is on the rise for the third consecutive year, after decades of decline. Even today 1 billion people go hungry each day and 20 million die a year from malnutrition. The number of chronically malnourished people stood at 820 million in 2019, corresponding to about one in every nine people in the world, according to the most recent UN Food and Agriculture Organization data. A broader look at the extent of food insecurity beyond severe levels and hunger reveals that an additional 17.2% of the world population, or 1.3 billion people, have experienced food insecurity at moderate levels, meaning they did not have regular access to nutritious and sufficient food.[6]

Livestock production accounts for 70% of all agricultural land use, occupies 30% of the planet's land surface and is responsible for 18% of greenhouse gases, such as methane and nitrous oxide. The largest source of greenhouse gas emissions from animals (39%) is from enteric fermentation – the gaseous releases of cows and sheep. The world cattle population of 1.5 billion animals contributes 70 million tonnes of methane a year to the atmosphere and is responsible for 16% of all methane emissions. The rate of increase of methane is currently four times higher than that of carbon dioxide. In 50 years' time methane could overtake CO_2 to become the principal greenhouse gas because of its powerful warming effect. Feeding cattle is wasteful in another sense as cattle manure contributes 65% of nitrous oxide to the atmosphere.[7]

Growing animals for food is also inefficient. 70% of food fed to animals gets lost in the conversion to meat. In fact it takes ten times more land to produce one kilo of protein from meat than it does from soya.[8]

Another factor is the growing of soy to feed cattle. China now imports more than 100 million tons of soybeans per year, a figure corresponding to more than 60% of the global trade. In countries like Brazil, Argentina, and Paraguay, this has led to the clearing away of vast swathes of forests to make way for huge soybean monocultures. This is further driving up greenhouse gas emissions, since forests typically store carbon in living biomasses, soil, dead wood, and litter, while living plants take up vast quantities of carbon dioxide from the atmosphere during photosynthesis.

There is an alternative diet to eating large amounts of meat and dairy products, and research suggests that a worldwide adoption of a healthy diet would provide more than a quarter of the emission reductions needed by 2050. What do we mean by a healthy diet? Research suggests the reduction in the consumption of meat and dairy products. This is often called the "flexitarian" diet. Research by Marco Springmann at the University of Oxford has concluded that to significantly reduce carbon emissions from food production in western countries, beef consumption needs to fall by 90% and be replaced by five times more beans and other pulses. This could reduce greenhouse gas emissions by more than half, cut fertiliser application, the use of cropland and fresh water by between a tenth and a quarter.[9] A recent report by the IPCC emphasised the need for people to consume about 30% less animal products.

Eating Local Food and In Season

In the developed world we are used to having a vast choice of foods from all over the world in the supermarkets. All of this has to be transported, and the concept of "food miles" is a way of attempting to measure how far food has travelled before it reaches the consumer. The concept of food miles also includes waste, which must be transported from your home to a landfill site. In the USA, Wal-Mart publicised a press release that stated food travelled 1500 miles before it reaches customers. According to the Shop Ethical website in Australia, a typical Melbourne shopping basket has travelled a staggering 70,000 kilometres - equivalent to almost two trips around the world. So buying locally-produced food can cut your carbon footprint. The effects of food miles can be measured in the pollution that is caused - particularly producing the greenhouse gases of carbon dioxide, methane and nitrous oxide. Food travels further nowadays mainly for three reasons: we buy food, which should be seasonal, all the year round; we buy more processed food; and we like to pay as little for it as possible.[10]

Another thing to consider is making your meals from original ingredients rather than buying them pre-made as convenience foods. Using pre-made food means you have no control over the ingredients that go into the food and also no idea what additives and preservatives are added. The quality of nutrients in convenience foods is often less than in homemade food. Also all the packaging and refrigeration of the food adds to its carbon footprint. My wife and I usually cook from fresh organic ingredients, using whole foods and my health is still good even into my 70s.

Avoid Wasting Food

According to the United Nations Food and Agriculture Organisation (FAO), roughly one third of the food produced in the world for human consumption every year - approximately 1.3 billion tonnes - gets lost or wasted. Food waste emits 8% of planet-warming greenhouse gases. The UN set a global goal to cut food loss and waste in half by 2030.[11] In developed countries you can easily see why this happens in supermarkets as we have all been tempted to buy more at a reduced price and ended up throwing it away. Also perfectly good food is thrown away because of its sell-by date. I stayed with someone couch-surfing in New York, during my book promotion trip to North America, and she helped herself and me to the bin bags full of bagels which were perfectly edible, but had to be binned because of strict local environmental laws. So we in the developed world can visit the supermarket just before the sell-by date comes up on food and get a bargain or encourage out of date food to be given to the homeless, which the Salvation Army does in the U.K. We can drastically reduce the amount of food wasted by careful meal planning, buying only what we will need (which may mean shopping more frequently) and using up leftovers. In developing countries food is often wasted because of lack of infrastructure such as transport or refrigeration.

So we in developed nations can encourage governments to help the U.N. support improvements in infrastructure in the developing world.

Buying Organic

Buying locally-produced organic food can reduce your carbon emissions. Conventional farming uses synthetic pesticides and fertilisers which are often made from fossil fuels. Manufacturing and transporting them uses energy and produces greenhouse gases. Studies show that chemical farming uses more energy per unit of production than organic farming. Synthetic nitrogen fertilisers in soils produce nitrous oxide, a greenhouse gas about 300 times more powerful than carbon dioxide at trapping heat in the atmosphere. Organic farms rely on natural manure and compost for fertiliser. Organic farming not only emits lower emissions, it helps retain the carbon found in soils. For example, in-depth research in Germany found that organic management on a farm resulted in lower greenhouse gas emissions than conventional management at the same site. This was largely due to carbon sequestration in soils (which were being depleted under conventional management) and due to lower N_2O emissions due to the absence of artificial fertiliser.[12] Recent meta-analyses that have reviewed studies from all over the world show that such findings are common. One meta-analysis found that organic farms have 3.5 metric tonnes more carbon in their soils than conventional farms.[13]

Community-supported agriculture (CSA) is a food production and distribution system that directly connects farmers and growers with consumers. It is now a worldwide movement. In short: people buy "shares" of a farm's harvest in advance and then receive a portion of the crops as they're harvested. In this way farmers and growers receive a more stable and secure income and closer connection with their community, and consumers benefit by eating fresh healthy local food, feeling more connected to the land where their food is grown and learning new skills.

I am a founder member and shareholder of Canalside Community Food near Leamington Spa, which is part of the CSA network. It produces organic fruit and vegetables throughout the year, of a better quality and cheaper than from supermarkets. The community-owned organic farm is a hub of the local community, celebrating the seasons through socials and involving schools in learning where food comes from.[14]

Perhaps the most carbon-friendly way of getting your food is to grow some of it yourself. Having been involved with Eco Clubs for years, with children growing food, I can say it is a delight to grow and eat your own. You know exactly how your food is grown, especially if you do it in an organic way, and at the same time it will have given your mind and body a chance to relax in the fresh air. If you are not sure where to start, you can find out how to grow food from the websites listed at the end of the chapter.[15]

If you haven't already done so, why not make your personal pledges about food on the sheet at the end of the book?

CHANGING HOW WE TRAVEL

How we travel has a direct effect on emissions. Transportation is responsible for 24% of direct CO_2 emissions from fuel combustion. Emissions from aviation and shipping continue to rise, indicating that these hard-to-abate subsectors need more international action. More alarmingly, transportation is the fastest-growing consumer of fossil fuels and the fastest-growing source of CO_2 emissions. One reason is car buyers continuing to purchase larger, heavier vehicles, not only in the United States but increasingly in Europe and Asia. Another reason is the increased affluence and the proliferation of online commerce.[16] Road transport contributes about one-fifth of the European Union's total emissions of carbon dioxide (CO_2), the main greenhouse gas. Transport is the only major sector in the EU where greenhouse gas emissions are still rising.[17] In the U.S. 28.9% of 2017 greenhouse gas emissions were from transport, making it the largest contributor of U.S. greenhouse gas emissions.[18]

From the start, the most low-carbon way to travel is to walk or cycle, producing zero emissions, and at the same time getting health benefits from exercise.[19] Whenever I can I always ride a bike and even when I worked further away I used an electric bike. I am now over 70 but hope to be still riding a bike and walking at 80. You can always investigate other low-carbon ways to travel other than by car, such as by public transport, bus, train or ship. When I went on my Green Spirituality book tour of North America I travelled there and back on a container ship.[20]

Using a Car

For the individual the holy cow of consumerism is to own a car, yet the car has turned out to be a "pollutermobile." *Ward's Auto* estimated that in 2016 there were around 1.32 billion cars, trucks and buses in the world.[21] Yet about 40% of car trips are less than 3 miles long and, most of the time, our cars aren't being used.

I am not saying, "Do not have a car", but there are steps to use it less and therefore limit your carbon footprint. You don't have to own a car in the first place if you join a car share scheme where you pay only for the car when you are using it. When my children were young one of the most irritating things was that when I was collecting them from school on foot, so many parents used their cars to transport their kids to school that there was danger crossing the road, and pollution permeating the air. So you can encourage your kids to cycle or walk to school. In Leamington Spa, I am a member of Extinction Rebellion and we have been working with the local Cycling campaign group called Cycleways (I am a member), to develop more cycle paths so that pupils can cycle to school in safety.

You can cut down on business trips by using your phone or by video-conferencing. This latter has become very common during the coronavirus pandemic which should make it easier to continue. Let's not forget that the most environmentally-friendly car is the one you don't use, so thinking about how you can bicycle, walk, or take more public transport will help decrease your carbon footprint.

The following driving tips will help reduce the environmental impact of your car:

- Drive moderately - smooth and slow acceleration and braking, as well as keeping to the speed limit, can reduce your car's emissions by 20%!
- Get your car serviced regularly: this should keep everything working as efficiently as it should.

- When driving a car, switch off the engine if you think you will be stationary for more than two minutes. Idling for this length of time burns more fuel than it takes to restart the engine.
- Harsh acceleration and braking can use up to 30% more fuel and can lead to increased wear and tear on the vehicle. Plus, pulling away too fast uses up to 60% more fuel.
- Keep your car tyres properly inflated. It's estimated that up to 80% of car tyres are under-inflated, which can increase fuel consumption, and therefore emissions, by up to 5%.
- Avoid short car journeys. A cold engine uses almost twice as much fuel as a warmer one.
- As a car gets older, harmful deposits can build up in the vehicle's engine, reducing efficiency and increasing emissions. Adding a cleaning agent into the fuel system will help remove the deposits and lower the emissions. It's worth considering using a premium fuel that already contains these additives.
- The engine oil is the lifeblood of your vehicle: the fluid that lubricates, cleans, cools and prevents wear. It must be changed at regular intervals to keep your car running at optimum efficiency.
- When parking, always try to reverse into a parking space so that you can drive forwards out of it, as manoeuvring whilst the engine is cold uses a lot of fuel.
- If your car comes with a consumption computer, use it to get instant feedback on fuel use. Drivers who learn to adjust their habits can save up to 10% in this way. If your vehicle doesn't have one, they are easy to install. I drive a Prius and am constantly looking at the fuel consumption display.[22]

Buying an electric car is expensive - I could not afford one on my pension - but they are getting cheaper, and Elon Musk is on a mission to make this a reality. Electric vehicle sales took off in 2018, with a record two million units sold around the world, according to a new Deloitte analysis.[23] They have distinct advantages both in terms of finance and climate change. Replacing a fossil fuel-powered car with an electric model can halve greenhouse gas emissions over the course of the vehicle's lifetime, according to new research. Even when the electricity comes from the dirtiest coal-dominated grid, electric vehicles *still* produce less global warming pollution than their conventional counterparts, and with fewer tailpipe emissions (or none at all). An EU study based on expected performance in 2020 found that an electric car using electricity generated solely by an oil-fired power station would use only two-thirds of the energy of a petrol-engined car travelling the same distance. Electric vehicles charged entirely from renewable sources like wind and solar power produce virtually no global warming emissions. If you have a solar or wind facility at home you can charge them from electricity you have produced. Electric vehicles (EVs) can also save you on maintenance costs. Battery EVs have no gasoline engine, they do not need oil changes, spark plugs, or timing belts, and unlike gasoline motors, electric motors require no routine maintenance. A core component of EV batteries is lithium, but contrary to what you might hear, studies have shown lithium is relatively abundant and there are decades' worth of deposits in existing mines.[24]

Air Travel

Even air travel can be circumvented - you can travel overland by train or go by ship over the sea. A special characteristic of aircraft emissions is that most of them are produced at cruising altitudes high in the atmosphere. Scientific studies have shown that these high-altitude emissions have a more harmful climate impact because they trigger a series of chemical reactions and atmospheric effects that have a net warming. The IPCC has estimated that aviation is responsible for around 3.5% of anthropogenic climate change, a figure which includes both CO_2 and non-CO_2-induced effects. Burning jet fuel also releases water vapour, nitrous oxides, sulphate and soot. Indeed aviation generates nearly as much CO_2 annually as that from all human activities in Africa. Aircraft greenhouse emissions are projected to continue to rise and could contribute up to 15% of global warming from all human activities within 50 years.[25] In the chapter on the path of protest I describe my involvement with the Climate Camp at Heathrow airport in 2007, and recently in 2019 I was at a protest organised by Extinction Rebellion at Gatwick airport, all to stop the expansion of air travel as a source of accelerating climate change.

Deciding never to fly is a way of avoiding adding to climate change in one go. I have decided that I will not fly and in 2012 travelled to North America and back on a container ship, saving almost 2 tonnes of carbon dioxide emissions in the process. My wife and I even travelled from

London by train and bus on two holidays to southern Portugal and central Switzerland.

If you haven't already done so, why not make your personal pledges about travel on the sheet at the end of the book?

SAVING DOMESTIC ENERGY

Research indicates that the demand for energy in the world is expected to triple by the year 2050. There are many practical measures you can take to save even more carbon and to conserve the energy that goes into your home. Let's start with the building itself. If you have heat going into it then it is good to insulate everywhere you can to prevent heat escaping. Draught-proofing doors and windows and insulating lofts create a big drop in energy consumption. A quarter of lost heat is wasted through the lack of loft insulation, which should be at a depth of 270mm. Don't forget the walls: as much as a third of heat lost from homes escapes through the walls. You can have cavity wall insulation, which is what we had done to our house. Double glazing halves the heat loss which occurs with normal windows and saves 740 kg a year in CO_2. Put another way - if everyone in the UK who needed to install double glazing did so, then the total CO_2 emissions for the equivalent of 800,000 homes would be eradicated from the UK's overall carbon footprint.[26]

Even if you get your electricity from conventional energy sources, attention to efficiency savings in the home will save you money and reduce your personal emissions budget. The Energy Information Administration says that the U.S. residential sector accounts for 21% of all energy consumption and is responsible for 20% of the country's carbon emissions. To reduce the carbon footprint from your home energy use, the first thing to do is to carry out an energy audit. An audit will evaluate energy bills, insulation, heating and cooling systems, electrical systems and appliances, to determine how much energy your home consumes, and where energy is wasted. Efficient energy use is achieved primarily by means of a more efficient technology or process.[27]

In 2010, for the first time, consumer electronics (a catch-all phrase covering computers, home entertainment systems and general gadgetry) became the single biggest user of domestic electricity - overtaking lighting and major appliances. By 2020, it is estimated that these information, communication and entertainment (ICE) products will account for around 45% of home electricity use. The key to saving energy and money as far as ICE products are concerned is simple – switch them off when you are not using them, and do not leave them on standby. Consider buying a "smart" power strip, which automatically cuts off power when you turn off an appliance.[28]

Lights

Let's look at energy efficient lighting for the home. The best solution is when a building is designed from the beginning to allow more natural light through. However, this is not normally the case, so we have to do the best we can. Fit LED lights (light emitting diodes) as today's highest-performing lights consume 85% less energy than incandescent bulbs. Light fittings can be individually controlled to turn off or to dim the output as required. Switch lights off in rooms which aren't in use or install motion detector lights indoors. There is no point leaving lights on if no-one is there to benefit from them. Motion detector lights outdoors are also a good deterrent against unwanted visitors.[29]

Heating

Now let's look at heating. The first thing to consider is how high to set your thermostat. According to the Energy Saving Trust of the U.K., turning down the thermostat by just one degree centigrade can save the typical home around £90 a year. How far down should you turn it? As a general rule going below 18°C isn't comfortable, and below 16°C is unhealthy. Better still - install a "smart" thermostat which you can control from outside your home. This will allow you to turn the heating on and off from wherever you are in the world. If electricity is used to heat water you should insulate your hot water cylinder. If there are rooms that you rarely use, ensure that thermostatic valves are installed on the radiators, since these can be set to zero if the room is not in use, and the space will not be heated unnecessarily. Use radiator reflectors behind the radiators to reflect heat back into the room: this helps the radiators warm the room more effectively.[30]

As a source of heating, install a new energy-saving condensing boiler. This will recycle the heat in the waste exhaust gases, making it run far more efficiently.[31] You also might want to consider an air source heat pump which extracts heat from the outside air in the same way that a fridge extracts heat from its inside. It can get heat from the air even when the temperature is as low as -15°C. In a well-insulated property, air-source heat pumps can provide all your heating needs by themselves. They can provide lower home carbon emissions, particularly if you are replacing the heating of a house currently heated by electricity or coal.[32] Ground source heat pumps (GSHPs) use pipes that are buried in the garden to extract heat from the ground. This heat can then be used to heat radiators, under-floor or warm air heating systems and to heat water in your home. They are more efficient than air source heat pumps and therefore cut carbon emissions even more. However, they are more costly to install.[33]

Electricity

To produce some or all of your electricity yourself, you could install solar panels. Photovoltaic power is widely used in offices and homes. It uses silicon semi-conductor cells to convert sunlight directly into electricity. Photovoltaic cells (PV's) are most commonly used. Solar panels can either operate as a stand-alone or they can feed energy to a grid. Elon Musk is developing a solar panel which looks like a regular roofing tile. They work best when in direct sunlight, but they continue to produce electricity even on cloudy days. One of the problems with solar energy is that it is not easy to store the energy in batteries until it is needed. However, advances in battery technology like the Tesla Powerwall are making battery-backed solar systems more of a reality. With systems like these, solar energy will be accessible even at night.[34] There is also solar thermal heating. This efficient and reliable system is based on the ancient principle that water in a dark container will warm up when the sun shines on it. Solar thermal heating provides energy for domestic hot water without CO_2 emissions.[35] The International Energy Agency (IEA) predicts that solar power could generate 22% of the world's electricity by 2050.

Appliances

Take a look at the appliances in your home and see if they are energy efficient. In the USA, Energy Star is a voluntary programme launched by the U.S. Environmental Protection Agency (EPA) and now managed by the EPA and the U.S. Department of Energy (DOE). It helps businesses and individuals save money and protect the environment through superior energy efficiency. They test appliances for their energy efficiency and place labels on the products. This label means that a product meets strict energy efficiency guidelines set by the U.S. Environmental Protection Agency and the U.S. Department of Energy. Efficient appliances incorporate advanced technologies and use 10 to 50% less energy and water than older generation models. Since 1992, Energy Star and its partners helped save American families and businesses nearly 4 trillion kilowatt-hours of electricity and achieve over 3 billion metric tons of greenhouse gas reductions, equivalent to the annual emissions of over 600 million cars.[36]

In Europe, energy labels show how an appliance ranks on a scale from A to G according to its energy consumption. Class A (green) is the most energy efficient and Class G (red) the least. Currently - once most appliances of a given type reach Class A - up to 3 further classes can be added to the scale; A+, A++ and A+++. Similar labelling systems are found in China, South Korea and Japan.[37]

In the kitchen: when cooking food try and match the size of the burner to the right pot or pan – putting a small pan on a huge burner or electric hob will just waste power. Put lids on pots and pans to reduce cooking times. Don't open the oven to look at the food inside – peep through the window to help prevent the expensive hot air inside escaping. Lastly, leave food out to thaw before trying to cook it – this means less energy is required to cook it.[38]

If you have a dishwasher, make sure you use it – dishwashers tend to use far less water than washing by hand – but be sure to put them on ECO mode to help minimise the energy used in the process (they use less water and heat it up to a slightly lower temperature). Always use your washing machine on the lowest temperature settings – bio washing powder contains enzymes that are specifically chosen because they work at this temperature. Avoid buying a tumble dryer as they generate a lot of emissions. Instead, hang clothes outside when you can or even inside, on drying racks, as putting them on radiators makes the radiators work less efficiently. If you have a freezer make sure you fill it up. It then uses less energy since the frozen food won't warm up when the door is opened. If the freezer is partly empty, then all the empty space will fill up with warm air when the door is opened, which the freezer needs to work hard to cool down when the door is shut again. If you can access the back of the refrigerator, try and vacuum the coils once a year to ensure the fridge runs at maximum efficiency, and regularly check door seals.

These are some but not all the energy savings you can make. If you haven't already done so, why not make your personal pledges about saving energy on the sheet at the end of the book?

BUYING LESS, USING LESS

Reduce, Re-Use and Recycle

Let's make it clear from the start that I am as guilty as anyone else of being materialistic. As a child in the 1950's my material life was basic. We did not have a television for a long time and I got my first watch and transistor radio at 11 because my Dad worked in Aden and could buy them tax-free. I was brought up in a culture where to consume was the norm and so I did conform to the norm by buying a car, buying LPs and CDs, books etc. I became an addict because I succumbed to the voices emanating from my lower nature that produced the mantra "more material things will bring you happiness." Now I have changed - I no longer accumulate books which I will never read, nor music I will never hear. I now clear out something I do not use. If I have bought too many instruments I give them or sell them to people who can play them. If I accumulate too many CD's, LP's and books I give them to the OXFAM bookshop. I now focus my life more on getting satisfaction from simple pursuits around people and nature, such as writing and performing eco music with my band the Eco Messengers; going for walks in nature; listening to music; eco activism; meditating and spending time with family and friends. To me, experiences involving humans and nature are the source of happiness, not consuming more and more stuff.

The first thing we need to do is to "Reduce", i.e. to buy less, as each manufactured product increases the release of more greenhouse gases into the atmosphere. The second option is to "Reuse" if at all possible. Lastly, if this is not possible then "Recycle". It is estimated that there were about 3.2 billion people in the middle class at the end of 2016. This group are able to purchase non-essential goods. 88% of the next billion to join this group will live in Asia. This comprises 380 million Indians, 350 million

Chinese, and 210 million other Asians.[39] Heavy industry and the constant demand for consumer goods are key contributors to climate change. In fact, according to the *Independent* newspaper, 30% of global greenhouse gas emissions are produced through the process of converting metal ores and fossil fuels into the cars, washing machines and electronic devices that help prop up the economy and make life a little more comfortable.[40] The USA and Europe tend to buy goods from China. According to the Carbon Brief website, around 22% of global CO_2 emissions stem from the production of goods that are, ultimately, consumed in a different country.[41] As of 2019 the average American, it has been estimated, produces over 20 tons of CO_2 a year, which is an astonishing amount. This is 20 times more than a person who lives in India. If these CO_2 emissions were made into a solid mass of carbon they would need 40 trucks to carry them, 1540 tons in all.[42] In the next few sections I am going to explain the carbon footprints associated with commonly bought items as examples.

Cars

The carbon footprint of making a car is immensely complex. Ores have to be dug out of the ground and the metals extracted. These have to be turned into parts. Other components have to be brought together: rubber tyres, plastic dashboards, paint, and so on. All of this involves transporting things around the world. The whole lot then has to be assembled, and every stage in the process requires energy. The companies that make cars have offices and other infrastructure with their own carbon footprints, which we need to somehow allocate proportionately to the cars that are made. Research also suggests that making a new car creates as much carbon pollution as driving it, so it's often better to keep your old banger on the road than to upgrade to a greener model. I drive a used hybrid car but would love to buy an electric car. Hybrids and electric cars certainly give less or zero emissions when running but they still carry a carbon footprint from when they were manufactured.

Mobile Phones

The mobile phone is the must-have object, yet more CO_2 emissions are generated by the manufacture of smart phones than most consumers create after buying them. In France, for example, it has been calculated that the production of a smart phone generates 400 times more emissions than its utilisation. In 2019, according to the Shift Project, the share of digital technologies in greenhouse gas emissions has increased by half since 2013, to 3.7% of global emissions. There are projections that the entire communication technology industry could account for up to 14% of carbon emissions by 2040.[43] The amount of energy used by data centres which process the signals of mobile phones has doubled every four years, and is expected to triple in the next 10 years. Data Centres consume about 3% of the global electricity supply and account for about 2% of total greenhouse gas emissions. That gives them the same carbon footprint as the airline industry.[44] The sad fact is that they contribute a lot to carbon emissions because the vast majority of electricity used in the world's data centres comes from non-renewable sources, and as their numbers rapidly increase, there are no guarantees that this will change. What accentuates the problem are the phone plans which encourage users to get a new smart phone every two years. So the embedded carbon emissions in each phone are wasted.

I use my smart phone as little as possible and I have kept it as long as possible. It is best to buy a modular phone. These are smart phones built from sustainable materials and are modular in their construction. That means, rather than having to buy a new phone every time something goes wrong, the phone can be easily disassembled so the faulty part can be replaced. Or as an alternative rather than buying a brand new phone, buying a phone that has been refurbished after being returned by the previous customer is a simple but effective way to reduce your carbon footprint and cut down on electronic waste.

I text as much as I can as texting is a much lower-carbon option than calling. If you do need to make a call, using a landline is more carbon-efficient because it takes about one-third less power to transmit the call.

Fashion

The production of cloth to make clothing has a heavy impact on the environment so clothes need to be valued and well-used. The rise of what is called "fast fashion", where items are produced quickly and cheaply, then only worn a very small number of times before being thrown away, is a particular problem. According to Greenpeace, in the last 15 years production of clothing has doubled - and at the same time, between 2000 and 2015, the number of times a garment was worn before it was thrown out decreased by 36%. Apart from the vast amount of water used in the clothing industry, it emits the equivalent of 1.2 million tons of CO_2 a year.[45] We all need to think seriously about how many clothes we actually need, and, when we do buy them, wear them as much as possible and/or pass them on to someone else via a charity shop, swapping party, or whatever, rather than sending them to landfill. According to the Elle MacArthur Foundation, in 2017 less than 1% of material used to produce clothing is currently recycled into new textiles and fibres.[46] You can of course buy clothes in charity shops like I do. I furnished myself with smart shirts for years in my professional life in education. My lovely niece, who studied at the London School of Fashion, makes her fashion statement by buying clothes from charity shops.

Simple Ways to "Reduce"

There is another aspect to "Reduce", which covers simple things such as using our own shopping bags, using real plates and cups and bottles instead of disposable or single-use ones, opting for less packaging or using our own containers when shopping, where that is possible. Even things like wipes, cotton buds and floss picks have more environmentally-friendly alternatives. Every little change reduces the amount of items which need to be manufactured and therefore reduces our carbon footprint.

Repairing and Recycling

The second rule is to "Re-use". If this is not possible then we come to "Recycle". In my life I try and buy used objects, especially musical instruments, clothes and furniture. I usually give away to charity any material possessions I am not using. There are many charity shops which welcome donations of goods. There is a great centre in Leamington Spa called the Reuse Centre, run by an environmental charity called Action 21.[47] I donate things that I do not need and buy things which I do need. If I need a particular tool I advertise on our LETS scheme (Local Economic Trading Scheme) to borrow it.[48] There are other online systems like Freecycle, where items are passed from one person to another for free.[49] If things are really beyond repair or re-use, then they need to be recycled in whatever way is possible.

There needs to be, generally, a "make do and mend" approach. A relatively new phenomenon is the appearance of "repair cafés" where volunteers undertake to do their best to mend all kinds of things - bikes, electrical items, clothing, household items, in return for a donation towards costs. We have one in Leamington but if there isn't one near you, you might be able to get enough people together to start one.[50]

If you haven't already done so, why not make your personal pledges about using less on the sheet at the end of the book?

CONCLUSION

We all need to think about the things we eat, the things we use every day, and the things we plan to buy, and see if we can make any changes which will reduce the strain we place on the world's resources which has led to climate change. At the end of this book there is a page which you can use, if you wish, to plan the changes you would like to make. Not everything needs to be done at once; it can be taken step by step! But we urgently need to make a start now. We all have a part to play. It's our planet.

USEFUL WEBSITES TO HELP YOU MAKE THE CHANGE

Buying Food

U.K
www.vegsoc.org www.vegweb.com www.vegansociety.com
www.fairtrade.net https://communitysupportedagriculture.org.uk
http://www.information-
britain.co.uk/othertypes.cfm?type=Farmers%20Market
www.bigbarn.co.uk https://www.findlocalproduce.co.uk/
https://www.soilassociation.org/organic-living/why-organic
https://www.soilassociation.org/.../the-food-for-life-supplier-
scheme/find-a-supplier https://www.suma.coop
https://www.sustainweb.org/foodlegacy/local_and_sustainable_food_dir
ectories/ www.msc.org. https://www.mcsuk.org/goodfishguide/search

USA
https://americanvegan.org https://navs-online.org
https://www.localharvest.org/csa/
https://www.ams.usda.gov/local-food-directories/farmersmarkets
https://www.thedailymeal.com/cook/101-best-farmers-markets-america-
2017 https://www.localharvest.org/farmers-markets/
www.farmersmarkets.net
https://foodtank.com/news/2015/09/nineteen-organic-food-
organizations-and-businesses-working-to-protect-cons/
https://find.organic/ https://rodaleinstitute.org/
https://www.usda.gov/topics/organic www.wholefoodsmarket.com
https://greenplanetethics.com/sustainable-seafood-list-ethically-safe-fish-
to-eat-how-to-be-an-ethical-fish-consumer/
https://www.thespruceeats.com/sustainable-seafood-choices-1665724
https://www.nrdc.org/stories/smart-seafood-buying-guide

Growing your Own Food

U.K.
www.gardenorganic.org.uk
https://www.rhs.org.uk/advice/profile?PID=822

https://charlesdowding.co.uk https://www.biodynamic.org.uk
www.permaculture.org.uk

USA
https://blog.feedspot.com/organic_blogs/ https://www.mnn.com/your-home/organic-farming-gardening/stories/infographic-home.
https://www.goodhousekeeping.com/home/gardening/advice/g2104/organic-gardening-tips-460309/ verdant.net/food.htm
https://www.almanac.com/vegetable-gardening-for-beginners
https://dengarden.com/gardening/Tips-on-How-to-Grow-a-Vegetable-Garden

Transport

U.K.
http://walkit.com   : www.sustrans.org.uk / www.whycycle.co.uk
https://www.walkscore.com/cities-and-neighborhoods
https://www.usacycling.org/
https://www.bicycling.com/culture/a23676188/best-bike-cities-2018/ https://wecycleusa.org   www.liftshare.com
https://www.blablacar.co.uk/   www.nationalcarshare.co.uk
https://www.drivelpg.co.uk LPG.JustAnswer.co.uk
https://www.mylpg.eu/stations/united-kingdom
https://www.mylpg.eu/installers/united-kingdom/list
https://www.ehow.co.uk/list_7207869_government-grant-lpg-conversions.html https://www.speedyfuels.co.uk/products/biodiesel
www.vegetableoildiesel.co.uk/mybbforum/showthread.php?tid=10028
www.findafuelsupplier.co.uk/biodiesel-suppliers www.biofuel.org.uk
www.electriccars.com   www.evworld.com
https://www.carmagazine.co.uk/electric/best-electric-cars-and-evs
www.hybridcars.com   www.green-car-guide.com
https://www.whatcar.com/best/best-hybrid-cars-2020/n17013

USA
https://www.carpoolworld.com/carpool_USA_by_state.html
http://lyft.com https://www.mylpg.eu/stations/united-states-of-america
https://www.mylpg.eu/installers/united-states-of-america
https://www.prinsautogas.com/en/north_american/united_states.html
www.biodieselamerica.org/about https://www.alibaba.com/biodiesel-

united-states-suppliers.html
www.autosectorresearch.com/reports/hybrid-electric-cars-in-the-united-states https://cars.usnews.com/cars-trucks/best-hybrid-vehicles https://www.cnet.com/roadshow/news/every-electric-car-ev-range-audi-chevy-tesla https://www.msn.com/en-us/autos/news/these-are-all-of-the-electric-vehicles-on-sale-in...

Domestic Energy Efficiency

U.K.
www.energysavingtrust.org.uk/ https://www.energyagency.org.uk www.greenbuildingstore.co.uk https://energysavingadvice.co.uk https://www.gov.uk/improve-energy-efficiency https://www.gov.uk/guidance/vat-on-energy-saving-materials-and-heating-equipment...
www.lowcarbonbuildings.org.ukhttps://www.thegreenage.co.uk/100-ways-to-save-energy-in-your-home

USA
https://www.americanefficient.com
https://www.nrdc.org/stories/energy-efficiency-clean-facts
https://www.directenergy.com/learning-center/energy-efficiency/25-energy-efficiency-tips https://www.thegreenage.co.uk/100-ways-to-save-energy-in-your-home

Domestic Energy Production

U.K.
https://energysavingtrust.org.uk/renewable-energy/electricity/wind-turbines https://www.renewableenergyhub.co.uk/main/wind-turbines/wind-turbine-installers
https://www.energy.gov/energysaver/installing-and-maintaining-small-wind-electric-system www.urbanwindenergy.org
www.microgeneration.com
www.windustry.org/how_much_do_wind_turbines_cost
www.solarenergy.com https://energysavingtrust.org.uk/renewable-energy/electricity/solar-panels https://www.greenmatch.co.uk/solar-energy/solar-panels https://www.photonenergy.co.uk/solar-map-of-the-uk https://www.tesla.com/en_GB/powerwall?redirect=no

USA
https://news.energysage.com/solar-power-companies-us
www.solarenergy.com   https://www.tesla.com/powerwall
https://www.solarreviews.com/solar-companies/best-residential-solar-power-installers

Green Energy Suppliers

U.K.
https://energysavingtrust.org.uk/.../switching-utilities/buying-green-electricity https://www.uswitch.com/gas-electricity/green-energy
www.ecotricity.com   www.good-energy.co.uk
www.greenenergyuk.com   https://bulb.co.uk/energy
https://octopus.energy

USA
https://www.treehugger.com/renewable-energy/top-10-green-energy-utilities-in-usa.html   https://energyacuity.com/blog/top-10-renewable-energy-companies

Consumer Goods

U.K.
www.ethicalconsumer.org https://www.ethicalsuperstore.com
www.ethicalproducts.org.uk www.naturalcollection.com
www.simpleliving.org   www.newdream.org
https://www.frugal.org.uk https://www.frugalfamily.co.uk
https://simplelivingdaily.com

USA
https://ecocult.com/the-18-most-affordable-places-to-buy-ethical-fashion www.fairtradeamerica.org
https://www.forbes.com/.../2013/03/06/the-worlds-most-ethical-companies-in-2013
www.ecolabelindex.com/ecolabels/?st=country,us
https://www.insidermonkey.com/blog/10-most-ethical-companies-in-the-us-533013

https://www.becomingminimalist.com/simpler/
https://botw.org/top/Society/Lifestyle_Choices/Simplicity/Organizatio
ns
https://www.idealist.org/en/nonprofit/6761eefcae8e477f81cf2613554c9
749-simple-living... www.greenlivingideas.com

Recycle and Reuse

U.K.

www.recyclenow.com www.recycle-more.co.uk www.recycling-
guided.com www.salvoweb.com www.recycling-
guide.org.uk/materials/computers.html https://www.freecycle.org
https://reuse-network.org.uk/ http://www.free-
stuff.me.uk/free/recycling/ https://www.ilovefreegle.org

USA

https://www.epa.gov/americarecycles/us-recycling-system
www.reusereducerecycle.net www.zerowasteamerica.org
https://www.fundsforngos.org/donations/world-computer-exchange-
donating-computers.. www.sustainablog.org
thereusepeople.org https://buildreuse.org/promoting-wood-reuse-in-
north-america https://www.facebook.com/pages/ReUse-
America/266500450128126

Ethical Investment

U.K.

http://www.yourethicalmoney.org/ https://www.ethicalinvestors.co.uk
https://www.ethicalconsumer.org/money-finance/shopping-
guide/ethical-investment-funds https://www.theethicalinvestor.co.uk
https://www.ethicalmoney.org https://www.triodos.co.uk/ethical-
investments

USA

https://www.kiplinger.com/.../T041-C000-S002-the-7-top-funds-for-
ethical-investing.html https://www.usbank.com/newsroom/news/us-
bank-named-one-of-the-2019-worlds-most-ethical-companies.html

Chapter 8: THE PATH OF PROTEST

I take the path of protest because of the deep spiritual values that I hold. I am very aware of the suffering that climate change will bring and act from a feeling of compassion to relieve as much of it as I can. The path of protest to bring about change is one means of doing this. This chapter describes some of the history of climate protest and the effects these protests have had.

Climate Protests – the Early Years

My involvement in climate marches and climate camps began in 2001. In that year the Campaign against Climate Change (CCC) organised their first march in response to President Bush's rejection of the Kyoto Protocol.[1] They have happened every year since that time. I and an estimated 10,000 other people attended a march and rally in London on December 3, 2005. The protests on this date were not confined to the UK, but formed part of the first Global Day of Action on Climate Change, which CCC played a key role in co-ordinating. The demonstrations, in more than 30 countries around the world, were timed to coincide with the crucial Montreal Climate talks in Canada, at which preliminary agreements were made for a post-Kyoto treaty to take effect after 2012. Outside Montreal itself, a crowd of between 25,000 - 40,000 gathered in a protest organised by the American-based Climate Crisis Coalition.[2]

In 2006 the Campaign against Climate Change organized a march from the US Embassy to the iCount event in Trafalgar Square. At least 25,000 people (myself included) gathered in Trafalgar Square that day making it easily the biggest demonstration on climate change in the UK up till that time. The protests in December of that year again had an international flavour, with the London, UK protest attracting 10,000 participants.[3]

In 2006 I participated in the first ever climate camp in the world at the Drax coal-fired power station which was the largest single emitter of carbon dioxide in the UK. The camp was attended by green activists and the idea was to educate each other on climate change and focus on occupying the site of the power station to close it down. There were a wide range of topics on offer including low-tech sanitation, nuclear power, climate change and global justice, decentralised energy, aviation and climate change, introduction to permaculture, and movement-building. To this end I contributed to the learning of participants by giving a talk on green spirituality. I supported the camp by providing children's entertainment in the kids' area, putting on clowning and magic shows.

It was truly amazing to me that a small group of people just commandeered some land and were able to set up a whole community. The focus was to display a different way of creating and using energy and conserving natural resources, so there were compost toilets, comprehensive recycling, grey water systems and pedal-powered laundries. Power for lighting, radios, mobile phones, sound equipment and laptop computers was supplied by solar panels and a wind turbine. Biodiesel from recycled cooking oil was available for vehicles. All food was vegan, mostly organic and locally sourced to minimise food miles, and cooked by communal neighbourhood kitchens. The community also operated on a democratic consensus model. The site of the camp was divided into loosely bounded 'neighbourhoods', most corresponding to geographic region (one exception being the queer neighbourhood of the 2006 camp). Daily consensus-based meetings were held in each neighbourhood, with spokespeople sent to a central meeting. Anybody could block an action until the matter was resolved. On 31 August 2006, up to 600 people attended a protest called Reclaim Power, converging on Drax and attempting to shut it down. There was a lot of coverage in the media to highlight the relationship between burning fossil fuels and climate change. The Guardian newspaper reported that the Camp marked a turning point in grass-roots campaigning against the causes of climate change. There was good press coverage and it highlighted the role of fossil fuels in creating the climate crisis.[4]

This was followed by another Climate Camp in 2007, a protest against the expansion of Heathrow Airport. About 1,500 green activists attended. This camp followed the same model as DRAX, with sustainable energy and food and daily consensus-based meetings in neighbourhoods, with spokespeople sent to a central meeting. Again there were workshops which focussed on issues ranging from climate change and fossil fuels to campaigning skills and how to take direct action. I supported the camp by organising the kids' entertainment for the duration as Kristoff the clown and his magic show. Each day, after the magic show, I took a parade of children outside the tent and we sang a song about climate change to the police. This not only got media coverage that the protest was peaceful but also reminded the police that there were children in the camp and their exposure to physical violence should be avoided. I played some music at the camp and our band, the Eco Worriers, performed songs about climate change. This camp was very successful as it got international press coverage and it brought more public awareness of the role of aviation as a growing source of greenhouse gas emissions.[5]

In December 2007 I joined the National Climate March and Global Day of Action organised by the Campaign against Climate Change in London. I did an interview with Turkish television about Climate Change issues. I also met Guy Makerson from the Network of Engaged Buddhists. There were great speeches by the well-known environmentalists Michael Meacher, Caroline Lucas, George Monbiot and Zac Goldsmith. Although there were up to 20,000 on the march there was very little media coverage from a U.K. press which is dominated by billionaires with a vested interest in maintaining the status quo.[6]

The year 2008 was a momentous year for Climate Change campaigning, as Bill McKibben co-founded 350.org with students at Middlebury College in Vermont, where he was a scholar in residence. Their explicit goal was to build a grassroots movement to fight climate change. Having met the man and having him endorse this book I can say with great certainty that he has had a tremendous effect on moving the debate on climate change forward on an international level.[7]

I attended my third climate camp at Kingsnorth, in August of that same year, which aimed to highlight E.ON's plans to build another coal-fired power station, which would be the first to be built in thirty years in the UK. Again, the camp was set up in the same way, with sustainable energy and food, with daily consensus-based meetings in neighbourhoods, and spokespeople sent to a central meeting. Over 200 workshops and debates were held during the camp, including ones with George Monbiot, Caroline Lucas, and John McDonnell MP. I contributed two workshops on Green Spirituality and met Hugh Fraser who became the editor of my first book "Green Spirituality". As before I supported the camp by organising the kids' entertainment for the duration as Kristoff the clown and his magic show. The Eco Worriers also performed to entertain the participants with eco songs. On Saturday 9th August the protesters attempted to shut down the power station. The day was organised to highlight the impact on climate change of coal fired power stations with activists marching to Kingsnorth power station. I marched with the kids group and wrote a song called "Kingsnorth the Dragon" and was filmed by Channel Four news singing the song. Unfortunately, violent scenes were a feature of the over the top policing by Kent Police.[8]

In December 2008, I joined another Climate March in London organised by Campaign against Climate Change to demand a "green new deal" with more investment by the government in green energy. There was a demand to stop expansion in aviation, particularly the proposed third runway at Heathrow. Other demands were the ending of coal fired power stations and to stop deriving energy from bio fuels at the expense of food production and loss of forests. There was also the introduction of speakers from spiritual traditions. Mark Dowd from Operation Noah spoke of how peace was the one thing missing from the discussion. He compared the £33 billion military budget spent by the Ministry of Defence with the tiny amount spent on renewable energy technologies. Muzammal Hussein, from the London Islamic Network for the Environment, whom I had met previously, spoke about climate change from the Islamic perspective of achieving wholeness.[9]

By 2009 Bill McKibben had become the leader of a fast-growing movement that he dubbed the "Fossil Fuel Resistance." He saw a need for proven tactics such as civil disobedience and demonstrations. In October 2009, prior to the international climate negotiations in Copenhagen, 350.org orchestrated simultaneous rallies in 181 countries—possibly the largest coordinated protest in history.[10]

In 2009 there was another Climate Camp at Blackheath in London which unfortunately I could not attend. The camp at Blackheath was set up on 26 August on Blackheath Common, which was the site of the 1381 Peasants' Revolt, and was due to run until 2 September. It was not possible to be so sustainable in a city situation but the main emphasis was on delivering workshops and talks around Climate Change for the general public to attend. The focus was on economics and exploring different alternatives to Carbon Trading, and alternatives to Money. The link between the economic system and the climate crisis was focussed on. The spiritual dimension of climate change was expressed by Quakers and Muslims.[11]

2009 was also the year of the Copenhagen U.N. conference on climate change so all protests were focussed on trying to get a good agreement. On December 5th there was a protest organised by Stop Climate Chaos, representing 11 million members across 100 UK organisations, ranging from Greenpeace and Unison to Islamic Relief and the Women's Institute. There were similar protests in Glasgow, Dublin and Belfast. An estimated 40,000 people marched on Parliament and made a gigantic wave to remind them of the need for a climate agreement.[12] The Campaign against Climate Change also held a climate emergency rally with the focus demanding that the government create 1 million Green jobs by 2010.[13] On December 11th I joined the 'Euro-Train' of Green Activists from all over Europe travelling to Copenhagen. On the train there was a carnival atmosphere as we picked up more and more green activists en route to Copenhagen. I remember playing some of my Eco Songs on the train to entertain the activists. On Saturday 12th I joined 100,000 other protestors in Copenhagen for a Global Day of Action on Climate.[14]

In 2010, in Edinburgh there was the first climate camp established to hit a financial institution - the Royal Bank of Scotland (RBS) headquarters. The U.K. government was a majority shareholder so protestors highlighted RBS's investments in the oil, coal and gas industries which fuel climate change. Camp for Climate Action arrived in Edinburgh on 19th August to begin training and protesting against the actions of RBS. With compost loos, grey water systems and renewable energy the camp was a model of sustainable living. By taking direct action protestors managed to stop the bank opening for 2 days and thereby achieved worldwide news coverage of the issue of investing in fossil fuels. This movement has since gained momentum throughout the world.[15]

In December 2010 I joined a National Climate March organised by Campaign against Climate Change as part of a Global Day of Action, with actions and demonstrations on climate all around the world on the Saturday - midway through the UN Climate Talks in Cancún, Mexico. Next, everyone took the message to Parliament with many placards and banners twinning the 'zero carbon by 2030' message with one calling for 'a million climate jobs'. Marching off via Park Lane, Piccadilly, Lower

Regent Street, Trafalgar Square and Whitehall to finally hear the sound of 'Seize the Day' playing at the end of Abingdon Street, right in the shadow of the southern tower of the Houses of Parliament.[16]

The Occupy Movement as an Example of Protest

The Great Recession was a period of general economic decline observed in world markets during the late 2000s and early 2010s. This was caused by the greed of bankers who borrowed more than they could pay back if things went wrong. They went wrong for Lehman brothers when their bank collapsed in 2008, leading to a series of bail-outs of banks by governments around the world. By 2011 it was clear that the bankers and those who owned wealth were still doing well whereas the general populace was struggling with high unemployment and a credit squeeze. In protest an Occupy movement started in 2011 to represent the 99% versus the 1% who owned all the wealth with their slogan "We are the 99%." Although not to do with climate change the movement was organised on similar lines to the climate camps and became global very quickly. A global survey of 23 countries published by Ipsos on 20 January 2012 found that around 40% of the world's citizens were familiar with the movement. It is another model of protest to look at.

The Occupy movement was an international progressive, socio-political movement against social and economic inequality and the lack of "real democracy" around the world. It aimed primarily to advance social and economic justice and new forms of democracy.[17] Occupy Wall Street (OWS) was a progressive protest movement that began on September 17, 2011, in Zuccotti Park, located in New York City's Wall Street financial district, receiving global attention and spawning a surge in the movement against economic inequality worldwide. By 9 October, Occupy protests had taken place or were ongoing in over 951 cities across 82 countries, and in over 600 communities right across the United States.[18][19]

The movement quickly spread to Europe.[20] In October, protesters established two encampments in central London. In November a third site was opened in a disused office complex owned by the UBS bank. This site was named by protesters as the Bank of Ideas. I was part of the Occupy movement in London and observed the way the camp was run.

All decisions were consensus-based and like the climate camps people were given areas of responsibility such as food, education and security. I had the privilege to give a talk at the "Tent University" at the St. Pauls camp about eco villages. I gave a talk on Green Spirituality at the Bank of Ideas, following on from the talk on Eco villages I delivered at the Tent university in St. Pauls. I also gave a short speech to 1,000 people from the steps of St. Pauls outlining the idea that Eco Villages provided a model to follow to solve the financial crisis.[21]

There were also protests in other countries throughout Europe and in various countries of South America and throughout Oceania.[22] [23] In Asia there was a mixed picture as they had not been hit so much by the recession. There were protests in South Korea and smaller protests in China, India, Indonesia, Japan and many other countries.[24] In Africa there were quite small protests in South Africa, Tunisia, Nigeria and Egypt. All of them were connected to the idea of addressing the inequality of wealth.

What is significant about the Occupy movement is that an idea about inequality of wealth expressed in one country would quickly spread. I have described the wide geographic range to emphasise how millions of people agreed with a central message of the need for economic justice and democratic processes. Global capitalism had made a few rich and many poor, particularly those who were not insulated against the cut-backs resulting from the recession. The basic model was non-violent protest to gain the attention of the media and thereby effect change. Another common factor is that the camps when they arose were run on democratic lines, allowing full participation by the members without hierarchical structures or autocratic leaders. When climate change really starts to affect all countries - in maybe 20 years' time - the Occupy movement offers a model of how to act to effect change particularly in the drive to decarbonise economies. Looking back at my experience at the St. Pauls camp in London all these features were evident. Now I am heavily involved in Extinction Rebellion on a local and national level I know that this is also a self-organising, non-hierarchical, democratic and non-violent organisation (see later in this chapter).

Fossil Fuel Protests

Fracking is a process whereby shale rock is fractured to release shale gas. By 2011, despite opposition, the USA had long since developed a successful fracking industry. All eyes turned to Europe to develop the industry there. Opposition to the process from environmentalists was on the grounds that this was an extreme form of energy which exacerbated climate change. Professor Bob Howarth of Cornell University, a fracking critic, had said that a spike in methane measurements from 2007 measured by Nasa satellite data corresponds with the beginning of the US shale boom. Local people also felt threatened that their local water would be polluted by the fracking process which uses 2000 chemicals and an awful lot of water.[25]

In 2011 I was involved in the first ever anti-fracking protest in the U.K. I attended "Camp Frack" at Hesketh Bank, organised by the Campaign against Climate Change. There was an experimental drilling rig set up and local people were incensed that their local water would be polluted by the fracking process. The camp, as usual, was organised as sustainably as possible and run on consensus. I wrote a song against fracking and turned up in my Kristoff the clown gear to emphasise the peaceful aspect of non-violent protest. It highlighted the issue of extreme energy causing further climate change in the national media, with a sympathetic article appearing in the Guardian. From 2011 to 2019 there were many more protests and camps in the U.K., most famously at Blackpool.

The protests all over Europe had significant effects with moratoriums or bans on fracking being imposed by Bulgaria, France, Germany, Ireland and Romania. This is another example where protest yields results. Evidence that protest works is that in 2019 the U.K. government declared a moratorium on fracking declaring that the science had not proved it was safe.[26]

On Nov. 16, 2012, an estimated 2,200 New Yorkers gathered at the Hammerstein Ballroom in Manhattan to hear of a plan to prevent catastrophic climate change. It was the 10th stop of a tour, called "Do The Math", that travelled to 21 cities and featured 350.org founder Bill McKibben, author Naomi Klein and video testimonies from Kumi Naidoo, executive director of Greenpeace International, and Archbishop

Desmond Tutu. The main thrust? To stop the fossil fuel industry from extracting and burning most of earth's below-ground reserves. 350.org went on to become a global movement which is described later on in the chapter on NGO's.[27]

In 2012 the IPCC stated that to avoid dangerous climate change, only 33% of extractable fossil fuel of known reserves can be used; this carbon budget would also be depleted by an increase in other carbon emission sources such as deforestation and cement production. It was claimed that, if other carbon emissions increase significantly, then only 10% of the fossil fuel reserves could be used to stay within projected safe limits. In 2012, 350.org. started the Fossil Fuel Divestment campaign. Fossil fuel divestment and investment in climate solutions is the removal of investment assets including stocks, bonds, and investment funds from companies involved in extracting fossil fuels, in an attempt to reduce climate change by tackling its ultimate causes. Their model includes all known sources of carbon emissions. Since its inception in 2012, 350 institutions and local governments, alongside thousands of individuals - representing over $1.5 trillion in assets - have pledged to divest from fossil fuels. High-profile pledges to divest include Norway's Sovereign Wealth Fund, the Episcopal Church, the Church of England, Rockefeller Brothers Fund, the World Council of Churches, the California Academy of Sciences and the British Medical Association.[28]

2013 saw the protests increase about fossil fuel extraction contributing to climate change. America's largest climate rally occurred, where over 35,000 people from 30 states marched to President Barack Obama's doorstep. The rally was organised by 350.org to push the President for firmer action to reject the Keystone XL tar sands pipeline being built on American soil. Obama rejected the project on the grounds it would increase climate change. This is another example, like fracking, showing that protest can change government policy on climate change. When President Trump came into office, he gave the go ahead for the pipeline but it was never started, largely because there was direct action to oppose it - as in the case of the Wounded Knee protests by Native Americans - and there have been numerous legal challenges. When President Biden was elected in 2021, one of the first things he did was to cancel the pipeline. A triumph for environmental protest.[29]

The weekend of 16th and 17th November 2013 saw tens of thousands of people in Canada and Australia out on the streets in over 260 protests against the climate policies of these countries. The Saturday protests in Canada occurred from coast to coast. At Repulse Bay, in Nunavut on the Arctic Circle, more than 10,000 people gathered in over 180 events co-ordinated by Defend our Climate. Many protests focussed on stopping further expansion of the Alberta tar sands and pipelines to move the bituminous oil south to Texas, east through Ontario and Quebec, and west through British Columbia.[30] On the Sunday, more than 60,000 people attended climate protests across Australia against the government inaction on climate change. Australia is heavily dependent on its own coal reserves for its energy. There were 30,000 protestors in Melbourne, 10,000 in Sydney, 5,000 in Perth, 5,000 in Brisbane and 3,000 in Canberra.[31]

More Climate Change Protests

The People's Climate March was a large-scale activist event to advocate global action against climate change, and took place on Sunday, September 21, 2014, in New York City. This was alongside a series of companion actions worldwide, many of which also took the name People's Climate March. With an estimated 311,000 participants, the New York event was the largest climate change march in history. It was just before the Climate Summit of world leaders on September 23rd. Worldwide, nearly 600,000 people in 175 countries were estimated to have marched on September 21. Melbourne and London led the way, with 60,000 people and 50,000 people respectively, joining marches. Organisers said more than 25,000 marched in Paris, 15,000 in Berlin, and 5,000 in Rio de Janeiro. Smaller protests - attracting numbers in the hundreds or low thousands - were also seen in cities such as Bogota, Barcelona, Jakarta and Delhi.[32]

In 2015 Campaign Against Climate Change started the protest season with a "Time to Act" demonstration on March 7th in London, with 20,000 supporting the event. Then in November there was a series of Global Climate marches ahead of the U.N. talks in Paris. The event extended all over Europe, Oceania, North America, South America, Africa and Asia. There were 2,000 events around the globe, in 175 different countries. An estimated figure of 785,000 people took part in the marches. The turnout in London was the largest with 50,000 people. Cities including Edinburgh, Bristol and Belfast hosted other UK marches. 20,000 people marched in

Madrid and a similar number in Rome. On November 29th organisers said 45,000 people attended the rally in Sydney and 5,000 people took part in a rally in Canberra. 130,000 people attended rallies across Australia. The terrorist attacks in Paris put paid to a large demonstration ahead of the crucial U.N. Climate Change talks but I went to Paris with Friends of the Earth as a gesture of support. There was a small climate march which I joined and sang my climate change songs with my guitar, despite the ban put in place by the Police. I remember how moving it was to join hands with other activists from around the world near the Eiffel Tower as a symbol of solidarity, and to hear rousing speeches and positive messages from green groups from around the world at a special rally. We also did a Big Message Action in our allocated area of Paris with the banner "Climate Justice Peace".[33]

On April 29, 2017, on the 100th day of the Trump presidency, the 2017 Peoples Climate March mobilised more than 200,000 people to march in Washington, D.C. to demonstrate the public support for bold action to address climate change rooted in economic and racial justice. There were sister marches in around 300 locations throughout the United States, including Denver, Boston, New York, Seattle, and Chicago. There were also marches in Amsterdam and London.[34]

On Sept 8th 2018 over 250,000 people joined 900 events, in 95 countries, demanding real action on climate, towards a fossil fuel-free future. This was part of an international mobilisation organised by 350.org called "Rise for Climate" to show popular support for urgent measures to combat climate change in advance of a San Francisco summit on Global Action on Climate Change. On September 8th the largest ever climate march on the US west coast took place in San Francisco with 30,000 people taking part. In 2018, in Paris, up to 50,000 people showed their solidarity. The summit was held by the Governor of California, Jerry Brown, and involved political and business leaders from the USA and around the world to discuss what actions they could take to combat climate change in the light of the USA withdrawal from the Paris Climate agreement during the Trump years.[35]

The Extinction Rebellion Movement

There is no doubt that a few people with a good idea can change history. Extinction Rebellion (XR) began in Stroud in the U.K. with 15 people who had studied and researched the way to achieve radical social change. This would be achieved by embarking on a long campaign of civil disobedience to force governments all over the world to act on climate change on behalf of their citizens. On 31st October 2018, in Parliament Square in the U.K., Extinction Rebellion declared that they were in rebellion against the government because they were failing to take action to protect their citizens against present and future threats from climate change.[36] They made three demands from the outset which are :

1. TELL THE TRUTH - Government must tell the truth by declaring a climate and ecological emergency, working with other institutions to communicate the urgency for change.
2. ACT NOW - Government must act now to halt biodiversity loss and reduce greenhouse gas emissions to net zero by 2025.
3. BEYOND POLITICS - Government must create and be led by the decisions of a Citizens' Assembly on climate and ecological justice.

It is important to understand what a Citizens' Assembly is. Citizens' Assemblies are innovative processes that can empower people, communities and entire countries to make important decisions in a way that is fair and deeply democratic.

The Citizens' Assembly on Climate and Ecological Justice will bring together ordinary people to investigate, discuss and make recommendations on how to respond to the climate emergency. Similar to jury service, members will be randomly selected from across the country. The process will be designed to ensure that the Assembly reflects the whole country in terms of characteristics such as gender, age, ethnicity, education level and geography. Assembly members will hear balanced information from experts and those most affected by the emergency. Members will speak openly and honestly in small groups with the aid of professional facilitators. Together they will work through their differences and draft and vote on recommendations.[37]

Extinction Rebellion's first action, which I was involved in, took place on 18th November 2018. The aim was to block 5 London bridges across the Thames to disrupt business as usual and draw media attention to the Climate Emergency. I was blockading Blackfriars Bridge and blessed to hear George Monbiot's speech about the rebellion. This yielded international press coverage and moved climate change up the political agenda.[38]

In April 2019 they began the first phase of International Rebellion with actions occurring in the U.K., Pakistan, Austria, U.S.A., the Netherlands, Chile and Ghana. In London I joined other rebels in occupying 5 iconic locations in central London: Oxford Circus, Marble Arch, Waterloo Bridge, Piccadilly Circus and Parliament Square. The aim was to cause as much economic disruption as possible. The last site was taken back after 10 days and it had cost the city tens of millions of pounds. XR were soon invited to speak to senior politicians from all parties. This protest was effective in that the government of the UK became the first country to declare a state of climate and ecological emergency.[39]

To give you some idea of how XR works I will describe how it is set up where I live. In May 2019 my wife and I, with other locals, started the local branch of XR in Warwick District. This was in preparation for the rebellion in London in October. The way XR works is that it is self-organised with no leaders. First people set up a co-ordinating group to plan for a launch of a public meeting to gain enough members. This can be focussed on the XR talk "Heading for Extinction" which explains the science behind climate change and the social science research behind the movement, or it can be just a public meeting. Thanks to a lot of work by my wife we had a turnout of 80 people. They were then invited to join working groups and at present we have working groups focussing on communications and media, talks and training, actions, politics, finance and regenerative culture. I am involved in talks and training and in communications and media. The co-ordinating group is then made up of representatives from the working groups and they focus on the strategy of the group. Important roles are the Internal Co-ordinator who communicates with working groups and the External Co-ordinator who communicates with XR regionally and nationally.

Before anyone can join XR they have to agree to the Principles and Values which are:

1. WE HAVE A SHARED VISION OF CHANGE. Creating a world that is fit for generations to come.

2. WE SET OUR MISSION ON WHAT IS NECESSARY.
   Mobilising 3.5% of the population to achieve system change –
   using ideas such as "Momentum-driven organising" to achieve
   this.
3. WE NEED A REGENERATIVE CULTURE. Creating a culture
   which is healthy, resilient and adaptable.
4. WE OPENLY CHALLENGE OURSELVES AND THIS
   TOXIC SYSTEM. Leaving our comfort zones to take action for
   change.
5. WE VALUE REFLECTING AND LEARNING. Following a
   cycle of action, reflection, learning, and planning for more action.
   Learning from other movements and contexts as well as our own
   experiences.
6. WE WELCOME EVERYONE AND EVERY PART OF
   EVERYONE. Working actively to create safer and more
   accessible spaces.
7. WE ACTIVELY MITIGATE FOR POWER. Breaking down
   hierarchies of power for more equitable participation.
8. WE AVOID BLAMING AND SHAMING. We live in a toxic
   system, but no one individual is to blame.
9. WE ARE A NON-VIOLENT NETWORK. Using non-violent
   strategy and tactics as the most effective way to bring about
   change.
10. WE ARE BASED ON AUTONOMY AND
    DECENTRALISATION. We collectively create the structures we
    need to challenge power.

Anyone who follows these core principles and values can take action in
the name of Extinction Rebellion.[40]

I joined members of XR Warwick District to go to London on 7th
October 2019. The whole protest in central London was around
Westminster and intent on causing as much disruption as possible to
"business as usual" for the government. The three demands were stated
clearly throughout the protest.[41]

There were alliances formed with other movements such as animal
rights, peace, inter-faith and global justice and 12 themed sites were set up
run by different regional groups. Our Midlands region teamed up with
East of England and we occupied a site near the Treasury called the
"Love Rebellion" which had a theme of non-violence. Over the course of

the two week rebellion over 1000 brave souls were arrested as the Police systematically cleared all the sites except Trafalgar Square.[42]

Early on there was an effective protest in stopping Smithfield meat market functioning by protestors camping outside it. This was to highlight the need to change our diets from meat-based to plant-based as the production of meat fuels climate change.[43]

From the beginning there was an inter-faith protest when faith communities tried to block Lambeth Bridge. The message sent out was clear that the government had a moral responsibility to take action to avoid mass suffering caused by climate change. There was an emphasis on Global Justice for the South with a site dedicated to this theme. Different spiritual traditions were represented at the opening and closing ceremonies. The Quakers were particularly present and effective at the site themed around Peace.[44]

Another theme of the protest was the importance of finance in tackling the climate crisis. At the Love Rebellion site we had an "alternative budget" read out in front of the Treasury which emphasised the need to switch investment out of fossil fuels into renewables. As to further make the point I joined other protestors in closing down the city's financial district on the 10th October. This got international news coverage.[45]

The most challenging protest was against the further development of air travel as a source of emissions. They tried to close down City Airport and I had the privilege to meet a partially-sighted Paralympic cyclist, James Brown, who climbed on top of a plane to stop the plane taking off, despite having a fear of heights. I joined a peaceful protest at Gatwick Airport to protest against the further development of airports. Other musicians and singers helped me perform some eco songs interspersed with "die-ins" to emphasise the deadly nature of climate change.[46]

A notable theme of the protest was highlighting that the media did not honestly tell the public about the Climate Emergency. So protestors blocked both the BBC and Google by mass demonstrations outside. I was part of a peaceful protest against News International because of their biased reporting of climate change and encouraging scepticism.[47]

Some protests highlighted the mass extinction of species with one site being dedicated to promoting conservation through "Rewilding" as the U.K. has a dismal record of loss of native species. The biggest march was the "funeral march" for the loss of bio-diversity which I joined with

30,000 others. Typical of the selective media coverage throughout the rebellion, it was barely reported in the media.[48]

Politics was an issue which permeated the whole rebellion but not in a party political way. As the police took sites and then, illegally as it turned out, banned XR from central London, XR carried on in a democratic way. I was honoured to take part as a facilitator in 3 People's Assemblies which were held to consult rebels about how the rebellion should proceed. On the last day I took part in a march to each government department with speeches demanding what the government had done since the Declaration of the Climate Emergency in April 2019.

The effectiveness of the protest bore fruit in the following general election in December. The Climate Emergency was taken up by all parties and even the new prime minister, Boris Johnson, mentioned it in his first speech from Downing Street.

One thing that makes XR unique is that it includes the poor countries in the global south who will be most affected by climate change. There was a "die-in" in the Indian city of Mumbai with about 250 activists taking part. XR Delhi held a mixed day of regeneration. They hosted an information point and ran sessions on yoga, guided meditation, eco-anxiety, and live music, before moving on to the day's main focus: holding people's assemblies in public spaces. In the Democratic Republic of Congo, rebels travelled 5 hours down the river to start their second XR group in Bambuti. Rebels in the sinking city of Jakarta, notorious for its severe traffic conditions, marched four kilometres down the biggest major toll road in Indonesia's ill-fated capital on a Sunday. They demanded action on the climate crisis that threatens to submerge 95% of the city by 2050. In Mexico they held a Mexican Climate Crisis Carnival. Rebels in Rio staged an ocean-themed action drawing attention to controversy surrounding the auction of oil 'blocks' near the Abrolhos Archipelago, a group of islands surrounded by coral reefs off the Southern coast of Brazil's Bahia state. XR Turkey protested outside the Istanbul Biennial, a major contemporary art exhibition with fossil fuel-based sponsors. Rebels poured crude oil down the front entrance. Rebels also staged a die-in at the beach to raise awareness of the devastating effects of ocean pollution and the climate emergency.

The developed world was well represented. In Sydney, protesters staged a sit-in on a main road. Australians protested in Melbourne, Brisbane, Adelaide and Tasmania. There were a handful of arrests in New

Zealand, where activists surrounded the government building in Wellington which houses the ministry which grants oil and gas drilling permits. In New York arrests were made after protesters poured fake blood over the Wall Street charging bull statue as part of a staged "die-in". They also shut down Times Square with a lime-green boat. In Paris they set up a climate camp and 1,000 activists backed by the yellow-vest anti-government movement occupied a shopping centre. In Berlin they also created a camp and activists blocked traffic. In Amsterdam they erected a tent camp on the main road outside the Rijksmuseum, the Dutch national museum. In Vienna, activists blocked a crossroads in the central Museumsquartier district. In Madrid XR protests led to the leaders meeting the environment minister. There were also protests in Dublin, Bratislava, Hong Kong, Brussels, Prague, Tel Aviv, Amsterdam and Montreal.[49]

CONCLUSION

When people say there is nothing you can do about climate change, they probably would not think of joining a protest. Those in power want to keep it that way. Often our whole conditioning is on the premise that it is better not to "rock the boat". But you can see from this chapter that there are millions of people who have joined protests and in so doing caused climate change to go up the media agenda. If those in power are not reminded of climate change they will do nothing. Protests and camps also create models of human organisation where people co-operate for the greater good of the global community. Those in power would prefer us all to be isolated consumers competing with each other for a share of the pie. I predict that as climate change affects people's health and wealth they will protest more and change will come. You can of course make your own decision as to whether this is a path of action you wish to take.

Chapter 9: NON-GOVERNMENTAL ORGANISATIONS

If, for whatever reason, political or direct action is not for you, then you may well find that supporting one or more appropriate non-governmental organisations (NGOs) is a worthwhile course to pursue. These are usually non-profit, and sometimes international, organisations. Although they may be funded by governments, they are independent of them. They are active in humanitarian, educational, health care, public policy, social, human rights, environmental, and other areas to effect changes according to their objectives. They basically bring citizens' concerns to Governments; they advocate and monitor policies; and encourage political participation through provision of information. NGOs are usually funded by donations, but some avoid formal funding altogether and are run primarily by volunteers. The number of NGOs worldwide is estimated to be about 10 million. One characteristic which these diverse organisations share is that their non-profit status means they are not hindered by short-term financial objectives. Accordingly, they are able to devote themselves to issues which occur across longer time horizons, such as climate change. Campaigning NGOs seek to "achieve large-scale change promoted indirectly through influence of the political system". I have always believed in using my money to support NGOs. When Greenpeace carries out a direct action I would like to have had the opportunity to do it myself, but circumstances do not allow it, so at least I can pay for somebody to do it on my behalf. I am also a member of Campaign against Climate Change, Friends of the Earth, Green Spirit, Extinction Rebellion, Resurgence, United Nations Association, 350.0rg, 38 degrees, Climate Reality Project, Climate Outreach, The Alternative Living Group, and Green Party Climate Campaign Activists. The aims and objectives of some NGOs are set out below.

Friends of the Earth and the First Climate Change Law

Friends of the Earth in the U.K. wanted to do something about climate change so they launched the Big Ask campaign in 2005. This saw unprecedented numbers of people calling for a strong climate law. Nearly 200,000 contacted their MPs directly – by letter, by email, by posting a video clip, or in person. First there was a Parliamentary petition opened, calling for a new law requiring "annual cuts in carbon dioxide emissions of 3%". In July 2005, Friends of the Earth helped form a new coalition - Stop Climate Chaos - calling for a new climate law with annual carbon dioxide cuts. In 2006 David Cameron, leader of the Conservative Party, added his support to the campaign and called for a Climate Change Bill to be included in the next Queen's Speech. At the same time, Friends of the Earth produced a low-carbon economy roadmap in consultation with the Tyndall Centre. Later that same year, Environment Secretary David Miliband indicated that the Government would introduce legislation to tackle climate change. By now 412 out of 646 MPs had signed the parliamentary petition. Only three other Early Day Motions (as they are known) had ever been signed by more than 400 MPs. On 15 November 2006 the Labour government announced a new climate law would be introduced. By February 2008 it was agreed that the bill would set 5 year carbon budgets outlining the maximum amount of carbon dioxide the UK can safely release. In July of that year, Labour MPs rebelled in support of a tougher bill to cut emissions by 80% by 2050 and to include aviation and shipping emissions. The cuts target was increased from 60 to 80% by David Miliband on the advice of the Committee on Climate Change. The historic day came on 28 October 2008, when MPs voted in favour of a Climate Change Law that would cut greenhouse gases by 80% by 2050 and include all UK emissions in the first climate change bill in the world![1]

The Climate Reality Project – an Educational NGO

The Climate Project, founded in 2006 and based in Nashville, Tennessee, was partly supported by Al Gore's profits from the documentary *An Inconvenient Truth*, which he produced after his term as Vice-President of the United States. The Climate Project was an educational, worldwide grassroots organisation which trained volunteers to give public talks, similar to Gore's presentation in the film. The talks focused on the harmful effects of climate change and on ways to address climate change at the grassroots level. By 2009, the project had more than 3,000 volunteers worldwide. These volunteers, trained by Gore, delivered 70,000 presentations to a total of 7.3 million people. In 2011 the Climate Project was renamed the Climate Reality Project. Climate Reality hosts a yearly event called "24 Hours of Reality". The first event was held in 2011 from September 14 to September 15, aiming to promote the newly renamed organisation. The 24-hour event was broadcast live over the internet and featured 24 presenters across 24 time zones presenting in 13 different languages. The presentations, which stressed a link between climate change and oil and coal producers, started in Mexico City and travelled west before culminating in New York City with a presentation by Gore. The webcast received 8 million views and was awarded a "Silver Lion" at the Cannes Lions *International Festival of Creativity* event in 2012. Accompanying this event, the Climate Reality Project also released several short videos covering topics related to climate change.

A second webcast called *24 Hours of Reality: The Dirty Weather Report* was broadcast beginning on November 14, 2012. The second annual "24 Hours of Reality" followed a format similar to the inaugural event and featured speeches and presentations from more than 100 activists, business leaders and scientists in 24 locations. The 2012 webcast focused on the impact which coal, oil and gas pollution have on weather patterns. The webcast attracted a viewership of more than 16 million, which set an upstream record for the most online viewers in a 24-hour period. The event also generated 135 million tweets from Twitter users, compared with 120 million tweets in 2011. In 2013, the Climate Reality Project released the Reality Drop tool, a news aggregator that collects online news stories about climate change. The tool allows users to discuss what is said about climate change in the media, including climate change deniers. The Climate Reality Project also addresses climate change through a network of approximately 10,000 grassroots Climate Reality Leaders, which the organisation calls the Climate Reality Leadership Corps. As of 2016, 33 training events had taken place to prepare Climate Reality Leaders to communicate and conduct effective advocacy events within their local communities. Climate Reality Leaders come from 135 countries. They lead educational events and encourage activity to address climate change in their local communities.[2]

Climate Outreach

Climate Outreach was set up in 2004, with a mission to help people understand climate change, and they have become Europe's leading climate communication organisation. I have met George Marshall, who founded the organisation, and found him to be a genuinely committed campaigner as regards climate change. Climate Outreach are now Europe's leading climate change communicators, bridging the gap between research and practice and helping to widen engagement across a broader spectrum of society. Their purpose is to ensure that climate change and its impacts are understood, accepted and acted upon across the breadth of society. They produce world-leading advice and practical tools for engagement by combining scientific research methods with years of hands-on experience. Their services support governments, businesses, NGOs and grassroots organisations. They specialise in how to engage hard-to-reach audiences – developing climate connection programmes with communities such as youth, the centre-right, faith and migrant groups.[3]

Greenpeace

Greenpeace is funded by members like myself and it is an organisation which takes direct action to protect the environment, particularly with issues such as climate change. A good early example of this was the occupation of Kingsnorth power station in the U.K., prior to the climate camp protest I attended in 2008. The protestors climbed the plant's 200m chimney, forcing the plant to go offline. They were not prosecuted as their defence of protecting the U.K. from climate change was accepted. The giant chimney at that time put out as much pollution as 30 *entire countries* combined. In 2013 the power station was demolished. In 2017, 26 countries including Canada, the Netherlands and even China were closing coal plants. Also in 2017, Britain had its first ever working day without coal power since the Industrial Revolution. So direct action has had a dramatic effect.[4]

Another area Greenpeace has focussed on is climate change in relation to the Arctic. The Arctic is a unique region. It spans eight countries, is home to more than 13 million people, and provides a habitat for truly incredible wildlife. The Arctic also plays a critical role in regulating global temperatures and counteracting climate change. Arctic sea ice keeps the planet cool by reflecting sunlight. As climate change takes hold and the world gets warmer, the ice is melting and the oceans are absorbing sunlight. This makes the planet even warmer, causing the ice to melt even faster. Then, as the Arctic ice melts, the oil under Arctic waters becomes an increasingly attractive target for the oil industry. The very companies responsible for exacerbating climate change want more oil, which will make climate change worse.

The "Save the Arctic" campaign was started in 2012 by Greenpeace to protect the Arctic, principally by preventing oil drilling and unsustainable industrial fishing. It also called for a sanctuary in the uninhabited high seas area around the North Pole, similar to the Protocol on Environmental Protection in the Antarctic Treaty. At the beginning of 2013, their petition registered over 2.5 million signatures. The petition was supported by famous figures such as Paul McCartney, Robert Redford and Richard Branson. In April 2013 four young explorers travelled to the Arctic, with American actor Ezra Miller, to place a flag on the seabed floor beneath the North Pole. The Save the Arctic "Flag for the Future" was lowered together with the 3 million names of those calling for an Arctic Sanctuary. In September 2013, thirty Greenpeace activists were arrested by the Russian government when they tried to board a Gazprom drilling platform (Gazprom were partners with Shell) on its way to the Arctic. Although they were eventually released, unfortunately the Russians are still drilling for oil in the Arctic.

At the start of 2014 Shell announced it would not drill for oil in the Arctic for that coming year. It cited a huge 71% drop in profits and a court decision challenging the legality of its drilling leases. In July 2014 Greenpeace launched a global campaign calling on Lego to end its co-promotion with Shell because they believed Shell was leading the race to exploit the Arctic's oil reserves under the rapidly melting sea ice. Lego had partnered with Shell to create Shell-branded Lego sets sold in Shell service stations in 26 countries, a deal worth £68 million. The campaign was high-profile, starting with an animated Lego-style video, coming in the wake of the hugely popular Lego Movie. The initial video, which featured a Lego Arctic paradise being slowly flooded with oil, notched up more than 5 million views on YouTube. After overwhelming pressure from the campaign, Lego confirmed it would end its 50 year relationship with Shell.

In August 2015 Shell got the final go-ahead from the US government to drill in the Arctic, despite the number of Save the Arctic supporters standing at 7 million. Shell then started to move an oil rig, the Polar Pioneer, towards the Arctic. In April, six brave individuals intercepted this gigantic Arctic oil drilling rig. The six Greenpeace climbers boarded the Arctic-bound rig in the middle of the Pacific Ocean, 750 miles northwest of Hawaii, and scaled a 38,000-ton platform for the action. They remained for six days, drawing attention and support from around the world. However, the rig moved on and in May, it was stationed in Seattle on its way north to join oil drilling operations in the Arctic. History was made when activists swarmed the Puget Sound in kayaks and boats to surround Shell's rig. On June 15, many of these same kayaktivists put themselves directly in between the Polar Pioneer and the Arctic in a floating blockade as the rig left Seattle. In the same month, First Nations artist and activist Audrey Siegl stood on a small boat, bravely confronting Shell's 300-foot-tall Arctic drilling platform in Canadian waters off the coast of British Columbia on its way to the Alaskan Arctic. In the next month, hundreds of people from Seattle gathered at the port terminal for "You Shell Not Pass", a huge non-violent day of action where protesters demonstrated on the shore and in the water, disrupting Shell's ongoing Arctic drilling preparations in Seattle. Shell also found they could not repair a vital ice breaker vessel as protestors prevented it from entering Portland harbour. In September Greenpeace created a giant polar bear called Aurora, which it placed outside Shell headquarters in London and refused to remove until the company left the Arctic. The polar bear was joined by 60 activists including actor Emma Thompson. On September 28, 2015 Shell shocked the world by announcing they were finally pulling out of the Alaskan Arctic. The Guardian newspaper reported that privately Shell was taken aback by the public protests against the drilling, which was threatening to seriously damage its reputation. A clear result of action by an NGO.[5]

Passive Finance Divestment: 350. Org and Fossil Free UK

Where you invest your money has a profound effect. If you use a bank, the chances are that they will use the money in unethical ways - especially supporting fossil fuels. All most banks have to do is to make money for their shareholders by investing in anything that makes money. I am not a wealthy man but I do have savings to support my retirement activities including writing, publishing and promoting this book. I understand that the whole area of ethical investment is complicated. I have for many years employed a financial consultant to invest the money for me. What we are going on to next is the financial system which supports the fossil fuel industry.

Fossil fuel divestment is the removal of investment assets such as stocks, bonds, and investment funds from companies involved in extracting fossil fuels, all in an attempt to reduce climate change by tackling its ultimate causes. This movement is based on a moral argument which is rooted in basic maths. Scientific research shows that in order to keep to international targets to limit global warming to a 2°C rise and thus prevent catastrophic levels of climate change, between two-thirds and four-fifths of known fossil fuel deposits need to remain in the ground. But fossil fuel companies are currently banking on these targets not being met so are extracting these reserves and selling them – and are actively prospecting for more. Money supporting the fossil fuel industry comes from investments by institutions and that is where the divestment movement first started its attack.

350.org is an international environmental organisation founded by Bill McKibben which addressed climate change with a target of reducing atmospheric carbon dioxide to 350ppm from the current level of over 400 ppm. It was really instrumental in the development of the divest movement. It acted as a hub for various local and national campaigns. Beginning on campuses in the United States in 2010 with students urging their administrations to turn investments in the fossil fuel industry into investments in clean energy and in communities most impacted by climate change, Bill McKibben helped transform fossil fuel divestment into an international movement. The fossil fuel divestment movement first erupted in 2012, when McKibben published the article *"Global Warming's Terrifying New Math"* in the August edition of *Rolling Stone* magazine. It went viral. In the article he said, "What all these climate numbers make painfully, usefully clear is that the planet does indeed have an enemy – one far more committed to action than governments or individuals. Given this hard math, we need to view the fossil-fuel industry in a new light. It has become a rogue industry, reckless like no other force on Earth. It is Public Enemy Number One to the survival of our planetary civilization." A few months after his terrifying maths went viral online, McKibben biodiesel-bussed his way to 21 cities in a nationwide speaking tour called "Do the Math." He began in Seattle and wound down to Los Angeles, cross-country to Chicago, Columbus, and Madison, Minneapolis, Boston, Philadelphia, Omaha, Boulder, and more. For those too far away, 350.org developed a "Do the Math" movie. Desmond Tutu made an appearance - the South African archbishop and Nobel Peace Prize recipient who blessed the 1980s divestment movement for helping to end apartheid by withdrawing investment from South Africa. Naomi Klein, McKibben's colleague and a bestselling author, also appeared. McKibben's *Rolling Stone* article mentioned the word "divest" only in the context of a historical example, the 1980s apartheid divestment. But the lecture tour was more explicit. McKibben asked crowds to start local divestment campaigns, and to push their colleges, churches, charities, and pension funds to cancel endowment holdings in the top 100 oil and top 100 coal companies, identified in a list drawn up by the Carbon Tracker Institute. 350.org estimated at the end of 2014 that 1,162 divestment campaigns have been launched since 2012. The list of institutions throughout the USA divesting from fossil fuels is impressive - including the cities of Portland, Minneapolis, Cambridge, Boulder, Berkeley, Oakland, Palo Alto, San Francisco, Seattle, Kansas City, and the Teachers Retirement System of the City of New York. Many universities have divested from fossil fuels including well-known ones such as the California Academy of Sciences, Georgetown, Humboldt State, Salem State, Seattle, Hawaii, Stanford, the University of Massachusetts and the California Institute of the Arts.[6]

Fossil Free UK

The UK campaign started in earnest in October 2013 with the launch of Fossil Free UK, focused on the £5bn held by UK universities' endowment funds. Student campaigns have popped up on campuses across the country, including those with the three largest investments, Cambridge, Oxford and Edinburgh. At the time Naomi Klein said, "This is the beginning of the kind of model that we need, and the first step is saying these profits are not acceptable and once we collectively say that and believe that and express that in our universities, in our faith institutions, at city council level, then we're one step away from where we need to be, which is 'polluter pays'." In partnership with 350.org, *The Guardian* launched its Keep it in the Ground campaign in March 2015 at the behest of outgoing editor-in-chief Alan Rusbridger. Within its first year, the digital campaign garnered support from more than a quarter of a million online petitioners and won a "Campaign of the Year" award in the Press Gazette's British Journalism Awards. Since the launch of *The Guardian*'s campaign, "Keep it in the Ground" has become a dominant theme used by fossil fuel divestment activists. That the amount of proven reserves is five times that which is allowable within the 2°C limit forms the basis for calls to divest.

In 2017 the UK emerged as the campaign's world leader as nine new institutions announced commitments to divest from fossil fuels. Over a third of the universities in the UK had made fossil-free commitments, and nine new UK universities had committed to never invest in fossil fuel companies. These include major universities such as Edinburgh, which has the third largest investment funds, University of Wales Trinity Saint David, the universities of Warwick, Durham, Queens University (Belfast), the London School of Economics and the University of St. Andrews. As of 2018 a total of 61 UK universities have at least partially divested from oil, gas and coal.[7]

Divestment campaigns, rather like the Occupy protests, have become a global phenomenon. This has been achieved by direct action and education. The movement has spread throughout Europe. The call for divestment and more ethical investment was backed by Pope Francis in June 2018, when he addressed the heads of oil companies. He said it was "disturbing and a cause for real concern" that carbon emissions were still rising and added: "Even more worrying is the continued search for new fossil fuel reserves, whereas the Paris agreement clearly urged keeping most fossil fuels underground."[8]

In July 2018 The Republic of Ireland decided to be the world's first country to sell off its investments in fossil fuel companies, after a bill was passed with all-party support in the lower house of parliament. The state's €8bn national investment fund will be required to sell all investments in coal, oil, gas and peat "as soon as is practicable", which is expected to mean within five years.[9]

In September 2018 New York City Mayor Bill de Blasio and his London counterpart, Sadiq Khan, met in New York and challenged other cities to join them in divesting their public pensions and other assets from fossil fuels. They made a joint statement, saying, "We believe that ending institutional investment in companies that extract fossil fuels and contribute directly to climate change can help send a very powerful message that renewables and low-carbon options are the future." Bill De Blasio also said, "If we want to fund the scale of transformation the world needs, we must foster sustainable investment and use the power of institutional investors."[10]

In France, divestment has spread to local government with divestment from Regional Councils and from several municipal councils including Paris. In Germany there has been the first commitment by cities with the City of Freiburg, the Federal State of Berlin and the Federal State of Bremen all divesting from fossil fuel investments. In Sweden there has been divestment by the City of Stockholm and the City of Uppsala, and also by the University of Stockholm and the Swedish University of Agricultural Sciences. In Denmark there has been divestment by the City of Copenhagen and the University of Copenhagen. In Norway there was divestment by the Government Pension Fund Global and even discussion that Norway's Sovereign Wealth Fund, worth $1 trillion, would divest.[11]

It has also spread elsewhere in the world. In Australia there was divestment promised from prominent cities including Melbourne, as well as educational institutions. In New Zealand the local authorities of Dunedin and Auckland, as well as the educational institutions of Otago and the Victoria University of Wellington also promised divestment. Finally, in South Africa, the City of Cape Town promised to divest from fossil fuels.[12]

Reinvestment discussions become more of a focus at institutions committing to divest from fossil fuels. This means that renewable energy will get an added boost whereas at the same time fossil fuel companies may find it harder to find funds to continue their activities. By December 2019 a total of 1,200 institutions and over 58,000 individuals representing $12 trillion in assets worldwide have been divested from fossil fuels.[13] In December 2019, Mark Carney, the Governor of the Bank of England, in a speech prior to his departure, stated clearly that investment in fossil fuels by financial institutions is an economic risk for investors. He advised investors to move funds out of fossil fuels or face the consequence of great financial loss in the future. The movement started and sustained by ordinary people still gathers momentum. All this has been achieved by non-governmental organisations, supported by the people, campaigning for divestment from fossil fuels.[14]

Avaaz

Avaaz - meaning "Voice" in Farsi - describes itself as "a global web movement to bring people-powered politics to decision-making everywhere". Also, its mission is to empower "millions of people from all walks of life to take action on pressing global, regional and national issues, from corruption and poverty to conflict and climate change." I regularly sign petitions hosted on their site and am heartened by the constant display showing people signing from different countries. It is no doubt one of the biggest NGOs. In 2019 there were 55 million members. Activities include "signing petitions, funding media campaigns and direct actions, emailing, calling and lobbying governments, and organising 'offline' protests and events". It campaigns in 15 languages and is served by a small core team of 52 full-time staff worldwide and thousands of volunteers in all 192 UN member states, including Iran and China, where its website is illegal. Ricken Patel, who founded it in 2007, says it is an effective campaigning organisation because, "Our model of internet organising allows thousands of individual efforts, however small, to be rapidly combined into a powerful collective force." Since 2009, Avaaz has not taken donations from foundations or corporations - nor has it accepted payments of more than $5,000 - but relies on donations from members who have now raised over $20m (£12.4m). Prior to 2009, various foundations had funded Avaaz's staff and start-up costs.

They have consistently campaigned on climate change. At the 2007 U.N. Climate Change talks in Bali, Avaazers sent thousands of messages to leaders of countries trying to block a deal, asking them to change their minds. There were objections from the United States, Japan, Canada, Australia and Russia. Avaaz funded a newspaper advertisement in Japan appealing for the government to back the deal and this was credited with changing the government's position. In 2008, as talks leading to the Copenhagen UN Climate Change summit started to fail, Avaaz was spearheading, via the internet, hundreds of vigils and rallies around the world, made hundreds of thousands of calls to decision-makers, and delivered millions of petition signatures. Avaaz collected a hefty 14 million signatures toward its Copenhagen climate summit petition for governments to agree on a deal. The Copenhagen summit did not deliver but at the U.N. talks in Durban in 2010, via online support, they staged a protest in solidarity with developing nations. By 2014 members had grown from 3 million to over 30 million. Working with many partner organisations and after months of preparation, Avaaz helped to stage the biggest climate march ever on the eve of a critical UN Climate Summit - 400,000 people in New York City - and altogether over 785,000 people marched at 2,300 events in 175 countries, united in one voice calling for a 100% clean energy future. Weeks later, the US and China signed a landmark agreement at the Paris UN summit to reduce emissions. A great achievement.[15]

World Wide Fund for Nature

I have been a member of the World Wide Fund for Nature (formerly the World Wildlife Fund) for many years. It is a large, dynamic, global NGO. WWF came into existence on 29 April 1961, when a small group of passionate and committed individuals signed a declaration to conserve wildlife that came to be known as the Morges Manifesto. The decision was made to establish the World Wildlife Fund as an international fundraising organisation to work in collaboration with existing conservation groups and bring substantial financial support to the conservation movement on a worldwide scale. Today the World Wide Fund for Nature is a global-scale conservation organisation that works in 100 countries and consists of nearly 5 million members worldwide. The WWF's mission - in the simplest of terms - is to conserve nature. Its aims are threefold - to protect natural areas and wild populations, to minimise pollution, and to promote efficient, sustainable use of natural resources. The WWF directs its efforts at multiple levels, starting with wildlife, habitats and local communities and expanding up through governments and global networks.[16]

Although the WWF started just raising funds for the protection of species, over the years it has widened its agenda to include climate change. It has particularly focussed on climate change in recent years and the importance of preserving tropical rain forests to act as carbon sinks and to stabilise world climate.

There is no doubt amongst scientists that tropical rainforests such as the Amazon forest are vital for stabilising the climate and a big carbon sink for excess CO_2 in the atmosphere. So its destruction has a real effect on accelerating climate change. The rain forests contain 90-140 billion metric tons of carbon. Up to 2006, approximately 17% of the Amazon rainforest had already been destroyed - leading to rapid loss of biodiversity and negatively impacting communities who rely on the forest to survive. This deforestation also contributed to climate change, as up to 75% of Brazilian greenhouse gas emissions come from deforestation and forest fires - mainly in the Amazon. Because of this, Brazil is the fourth largest climate polluter in the world. Deforestation for mineral extraction, cattle-rearing and growing soya or palm oil may release significant amounts of this carbon, which could have catastrophic consequences around the world. Deforestation is currently responsible for 15% of all emissions. WWF estimates that 27% – more than a quarter – of the Amazon biome will be without trees by 2030 if the current rate of deforestation continues.[17]

In 1975 WWF's Tropical Rainforest Campaign was the first-ever conservation campaign based on an entire biome rather than a single species or individual area of habitat. In addition to raising money for new protected areas of rainforest in Central and West Africa, Southeast Asia and Latin America, the campaign contributed to widespread recognition of the biodiversity and ecological values of rainforests and the threats they face. WWF has since played a key role in efforts to build protected area networks in priority tropical forests and achieve sustainable management of their resources.[18]

In 1975 the first rainforest park was created, called the Corcovado National Park, located on Costa Rica's Osa Peninsula. Corcovado contained 13 major habitat types and was the best example of a Central American tropical forest.[19]

In 1986 WWF celebrated its 25th anniversary with a convocation of leaders from different faith traditions in Assisi, Italy. These religious leaders produced the Assisi Declarations, theological statements showing the spiritual relationship between their followers and nature that triggered a growth in the engagement of those religions with conservation around the world.[20]

In 1989 WWF brought about a new mechanism for financing conservation as it pioneered the debt-for-nature concept, in which a portion of a nation's debt is bought in return for the country allocating an equivalent amount in local currency to conservation.[21] In 1993 WWF helped create the Forest Stewardship Council (FSC), to find solutions which promote responsible stewardship of the world's forests. FSC has grown to a global network of more than 40 offices in the United States and around the world. In 1998, in a pledge developed through the WWF-World Bank Alliance, the president of Brazil committed to provide legal protection for 10% of the Brazilian rain forest. In 2000 this pledge was extended to include 70 million more acres.[22]

In 1999, worried about the destruction of the Congo tropical rainforest, WWF convened the Yaounde Forest Summit in Yaounde, Cameroon. At the Summit, six African heads of state jointly announced plans to create 12 million acres of new cross-border protected forest areas in the Congo Basin. In 2001 Central African nations surpassed the commitments made at the Yaounde Summit. With the help of WWF, these governments established nearly 13 million acres of protected areas in the Congo Basin.[23]

In 2002 the largest initiative to protect the Amazon rainforest occurred in establishing the Amazon Region Protected Areas (ARPA) programme. This was the initiative of the Brazilian government, spearheaded by WWF, aimed at tripling the Amazon protected areas to 12% of the Amazon basin, or 60 million ha, within a decade. In fact, in 2002 the Brazilian government created Tumucumaque National Park in the Brazilian Amazon with WWF committing $1 million for its management. This 9.4 million-acre park is now the largest tropical park in the world.[24] Since ARPA was established in 2002, a total of 33 million acres of new strict nature protection and 18.5 million acres of new sustainable-use areas have been created.

In 2016 WWF produced the *Living Amazon* report, outlining the current status of the Amazon, summarising some key pressures and agents of change and outlined a conservation strategy for the next decade. Today WWF are working with the Brazilian government to help it meet its pledge to restore a massive 12 million hectares of forest by 2030 – that's an area almost the size of England.[25]

In July 2018 WWF helped create the world's largest protected rainforest and a new World Heritage Site by doubling the size of the Serranía del Chiribiquete National Park, in Colombia. Chiribiquete is home to nearly 3,000 animal and plant species, including 366 birds and iconic species such as jaguars, manatees, dolphins, river otters, tapirs and the vulnerable brown woolly monkey.[26]

People like me and millions of others help WWF do all the work they do.

My Own Experience Working with NGOs

My experience of working with local and national NGOs illustrates clearly that in terms of conservation and education they make a difference. I worked at Campion School in Leamington for many years. In the first few years I ran a Gardening Club to teach children how to grow their own food but in 2004 this changed to an Eco Club. I had identified an area in the school grounds which was of no use for sport but could be the basis of a nature reserve. I was fortunate that Warwickshire Association of Youth Clubs provided the Eco Club with a £500 grant to hire the expertise of the British Trust for Conservation Volunteers to plan planting of native shrubs and trees on the land identified. With this plan I approached the Tree Council for a grant to plant the trees and shrubs.

The Tree Council was founded in 1973, with government backing, as the umbrella body for UK organisations involved in tree planting, care and conservation. They provide trees for planting every November. As part of the deal we needed to pay half of the cost but we had no funds. Then a miracle happened. The Vice President of the Tree Council was Norman Painting, a very famous actor on the extremely popular radio programme "The Archers" and he was born and bred in Leamington. The Tree Council wanted to present to Norman an 80th birthday present in the form of new woodland named after him. Norman agreed that the woodland would be planted at the school with no demand for part funding and named as "Painting's Plantation." The trees and shrubs were planted by the whole school with the help of Warwickshire Forestry Department in 2004. After starting with no money the Eco Club raised £20,000 over the following years towards developing the reserve. Norman's support, environmental grants, and donations from local business were critical. It now has pathways, an outdoor classroom and large fenced wildlife pond. In 2020 the trees and shrubs are flourishing and the reserve is used as an educational resource by the school and by local primary schools, especially for science. Age Concern Warwickshire have taken over the management of the reserve and they want to develop its use for people with senile dementia. It gives me great joy because I love nature and this means I can leave a legacy for future generations to be able to develop that connection with nature too.

CONCLUSION

There is no doubt, as this chapter shows, that NGOs have had an effect on educating people about climate change and inspiring them to act. I am a member of the WWF, Greenpeace, Friends of the Earth, Population Matters, the United Nations Association, Resurgence Trust and Green Spirit because they act on my behalf to highlight actions needed on climate change. But they are only as strong as the membership and they need to grow quickly if we have any chance of a future as a human race. More members mean more money and more widespread and powerful campaigns. More members mean that politicians - who make the decisions - will take more notice of their electorate. NGOs bring hope to people like me who want a future for my children and grandchildren and their descendants. By supporting NGOs we are taking concrete steps that there will be a future for all of humankind.

Chapter 10: THE PATH OF POLITICS

In 1981 I went to a small meeting of the embryonic Green Party which was held under an old parachute. At the time I had two young daughters and realised that I had to do something to ensure that they inherited a sustainable planet when I was gone. The Green Party was the only party which offered a model of a completely sustainable world so I joined them and have been a member ever since. I have also stood as a candidate for the Green Party on many occasions.

A Green party is a formally-organised political party based on the principles of green politics, such as social justice, environmentalism and nonviolence. Greens believe that these issues are inherently related to one another as a foundation for world peace. Green parties exist in nearly 100 countries around the world. Political parties campaigning on a predominantly environmental platform arose in the early 1970s in various parts of the world.

In this chapter I want to explore Green Parties around the world to see what progress they have made. I know of their existence as I attended the Global Greens Congress in Liverpool in March 2017 and met Dr. Frank Habineza, president of the Federation of African Greens, and Dr. Papa Meissa Dieng from Mali Green Party, who each took a copy of my book "Green Spirituality" back to Africa (www.greenspirituality.org). The Global Greens is the partnership of the world's Green parties and political movements, working cooperatively to implement the Global Greens Charter. This unique and inspiring document sets out the core values of ecological wisdom, social justice, participatory democracy, nonviolence, sustainability and respect for diversity to which Global Greens adhere. Greens came from all over the world to commit themselves to working together for their common goals.[1]

The Green Party in the UK

The Green Party of England and Wales has its roots in the People Party founded in Coventry in 1972/3. It then changed its name to the more descriptive Ecology Party in 1975 and to the Green Party ten years later. In the 1990s, the Scottish and Northern Ireland wings of the Green Party in the United Kingdom decided to separate amicably from the party in England and Wales, to form the Scottish Green Party and the Green Party in Northern Ireland. The Wales Green Party became an autonomous regional party and remained within the new Green Party of England and Wales. Jonathon Porritt, who gave me a lot of support in establishing the Green Spirituality working group in the Green Party, helped put together an election manifesto in 1979 called *The Real Alternative*. The Ecology Party fielded 53 candidates in the 1979 General Election, entitling them to radio and television election broadcasts. This paid off as the party received 1.5% of the vote in the constituencies in which it ran. The Party's greatest ever success came at the 1989 European elections, where the Green Party won 2,292,695 votes and received 15% of the overall vote. The election of a Labour government in 1997 created opportunities and focus for the Green Party. New democratic institutions were created that offered electoral possibilities for the Greens, such as the London Assembly, the National Assembly for Wales and – for the independent Scottish Green Party – the Scottish Parliament, all of which use some form of proportional representation, allowing smaller parties the chance of gaining representation. Labour also changed European Parliamentary elections to a form of proportional representation. In the 1999 European elections, two Greens were elected Members of the European Parliament (MEPs): Caroline Lucas (South East England) and Jean Lambert (London). They retained their seats in the 2004 European elections, despite a reduction in the number of seats available. Overall, the Party gained more than a million votes in the 2004 European election. The Green Party then fielded more than 300 candidates in the 2010 general election. Caroline Lucas became the first Green candidate to gain a seat in Westminster, after being elected MP for Brighton Pavilion. Green membership doubled between March and December 2014, reaching 30,900 by the end of the year. By 2015 the membership had more than doubled again to 63,000. In the 2019 local elections, the Green Party secured its best ever local election result, more than doubling its number of council seats from 178 to 372 councillors. This success was followed by a similarly successful European election where Greens (including the Scottish Greens and the Green Party in Northern Ireland) won over two million votes for the first time since 1989, securing 7 MEPs, up from 3. The membership also saw another climb in 2019, returning to 50,000 members in September.

The Influence of the Green Party in England and Wales

Despite the Green Party of England and Wales having only 1 Member of Parliament (due to the "first past the post" electoral system) Caroline Lucas has used her position to gain maximum media attention for the green cause. She is regularly on national radio and television stations. She is not afraid to stand up against policies such as fracking. At the Balcombe fracking protest she was arrested and so highlighted the issue of fracking being dangerous and a form of extreme energy contributing to climate change. As we know, fracking was eventually put on hold by the U.K. government.[2]

I know from my experience that green politics makes a difference at the local level. After years and years of leafletting for my local Green Party (Warwick and Leamington), there was a breakthrough in the 2019 local elections, when we went from 1 councillor to 8 councillors. In 2020 there was a remarkable happening when, largely because of the influence of the Greens, all parties in the District Council agreed on action to tackle the climate emergency they had declared. Basically they agreed to raise the council tax to create a special fund for initiatives to deal with the climate emergency. Warwick District Council is the first local authority in the U.K. to do this. This has not yet been implemented as the COVID 19 virus has delayed the carrying-out of a referendum to approve the change.

The Success of the Scottish Green Party

The Greens have had a lot of success in Scotland. The 2007 election saw the Scottish National Party (SNP) take power in Scotland with a minority government. Reduced in number but not reduced in influence, the two Green MSPs (Members of the Scottish Parliament) who had been elected discovered that they held the balance of power in the Parliament and that the minority SNP administration required Green support for the election of the First Minister and for its annual budget. The Scottish Greens negotiated an agreement with the SNP – they would back Alex Salmond as First Minister and his initial Ministerial appointments, and in return Green Party MSP Patrick Harvie would chair the Transport, Infrastructure and Climate Change Committee and the SNP would back a Climate Change Bill. Patrick Harvie then steered the Climate Change Act through the Scottish Parliament. On 4th August 2009, the Scottish Parliament passed the Climate Change (Scotland) Act which introduced world-leading legally-binding targets for reductions in emissions of 42% by 2020 and 80% by 2050. It also established a Climate Challenge Fund, to help communities to transform their local environments and reduce carbon emissions. So this was a clear example of how political means can have a positive effect in dealing with Climate Change.[3]

The Success of the Green Party in Germany

The German Green party was founded in 1980, unifying a whole array of regional movements made up of people frustrated by mainstream politics. It brought together environmental, peace and human rights activists. They viewed themselves as a peaceful, ecological, feminist, grassroots democratic movement, more than an actual political party. Many felt that those in power were ignoring environmental issues, as well as the dangers of nuclear power. Adopting a phrase coined by one of its founding leaders, Petra Kelly, the Greens described themselves as the "anti-party party". They established the four pillars of the Green Party which were social justice, ecological wisdom, grassroots democracy and non-violence. After some success at state-level elections, the party won 27 seats with 5.7% of the vote in the Bundestag, the lower house of the German parliament, in the 1983 federal election. They gained more members from those who were against the deployment of nuclear missiles by the Americans on German soil. They also gained supporters who were opposed to nuclear power in the light of the Chernobyl nuclear disaster in the U.S.S.R. in 1986. Joschka Fischer, a former left-wing activist, became Germany's first Green office-holder, when he became Environment Minister in the State of Hesse in 1985. Before the unification of Germany the Greens increased their share of the vote to 8.3% in the 1987 federal election.

In 1991 the Green Party had their first real success of "greening the economy" with the passing of the Electricity Feed-in Act. This established the feeding of electricity from renewable energy sources into the public grid. This legislation was the first green electricity feed-in tariff scheme in the world. The law obliged grid companies to connect all renewable power plants, to grant them priority dispatch, and pay them a guaranteed feed-in tariff over 20 years. With the merger of East and West Germany, the Green Party merged in 1993 with the civil rights movement *Bündnis 90* of the former German Democratic Republic (GDR). Since 1983, there has been a continuous representation of either the Greens or Alliance 90 in the German Bundestag. In the 1998 federal election they retained 47 seats and joined the federal government for the first time in a 'Red-Green' coalition government with the SPD (Social Democratic Party). Joschka Fischer of the Greens became Vice-Chancellor of Germany and foreign minister in the new government, which also had two other Green ministers. The Greens achieved a major success as a governing party through the 2000 decision to phase out the use of nuclear energy. Minister of the Environment, Nature Conservation and Nuclear Safety, Jürgen Trittin, reached an agreement with energy companies on the gradual phasing-out of the country's nineteen nuclear power plants and a cessation of civil usage of nuclear power by 2020. In the 2002 federal election, the Greens increased their total to 55 seats and 8.6% of the vote. The party also continued its coalition government with the SPD. However, relations with the SPD soured in 2005 over Chancellor Schröder's decision to call an early election. The Greens campaigned on their own and did not get enough seats to be part of the government.

In the 2009 parliamentary elections the Greens improved on their 2005 results, winning 10.7% of the national vote and increasing their seats in the Bundestag from 51 to 68. In March 2012, following elections in the German state of Baden-Wuerttemberg, the Green Party headed its first-ever state government. In October 2012, Green Party candidate Fritz Kuhn became mayor of Stuttgart, the first German state capital to elect a Green mayor. In the 2013 elections the Greens got a lower share of the vote at 8.4%, but by 2016 they had bounced back, reaching a membership of 70,000 for the first time in their history. In the 2017 elections the Greens expressed their recovery by winning 67 out of 709 seats in the Bundestag. In 2018 the Greens surged to second place in the Bavarian regional elections, almost doubling their vote. A national poll also saw them in second place across Germany, leapfrogging both the far right AfD and the centre-left SDP. In 2019 the Greens became the second largest party at a national level for the first time in German history. The Greens' massive success in Germany, nearly doubling their 2014 result to win more than 20% of the vote, was apparently in large part down to their new popularity among young voters. They also did well in the European elections with almost 21% of the vote - nearly double their 2014 total.

The effectiveness of Green politics in terms of the German Green Party has been seen in the great progress made in renewable energy resources. Germany has been called "the world's first major renewable energy economy". Renewable energy in Germany is mainly based on wind, solar and biomass. In 2016 Germany had the world's third largest photovoltaic installed capacity. It is also the world's third country by installed wind power capacity, at 50 GW, and second for offshore wind. Peak generation from combined wind and solar power reached an all-time high of 74% in April 2014. Biomass is a key provider of electricity. For instance, 40% of German wood production is also used as a biomass feedstock. Agriculture is the main source of rapeseed oil, which is used for the production of biodiesel and making substrates for the production of biogas. Hydropower meets 3.5% of the electricity demand. As of 2020, 52% of electricity was coming from renewable energy. There will be a phasing-out of nuclear power in 2022.

In food and agriculture the German Green Party has advanced the cause of sustainable organic farming so much that Germany is a leading nation in Europe for organic farming. The Green Party's Renate Künast became Minister of Consumer Protection, Food and Agriculture in 2001. The farming policy was changed to extend the share of organic farming from 3% to 20% of the agricultural land in Germany by 2010. The spread of organic farming was supported by government aid in converting, certifying, training, marketing and advertising. There was also a law requiring organic labelling of food. Also subsidies for agriculture were made more conditional on the fulfilment of ecological criteria.[4]

The Green Party in the USA

At the other extreme to the growth and success of the German Green Party is the Green Party of America, which has struggled to get a foothold. Green activists in the United States first convened in Minnesota in 1984 and approved the "10 Key Values" platform which was based on environmentalism, nonviolence, social justice, participatory grassroots democracy, gender equality, LGBT rights, anti-war and anti-racism. In 1990, Alaska became the first state to put the Green Party on the ballot paper. In 1996, state Green Party organisations banded together and formed the Association of State Green Parties. Four years later, the state parties united as affiliates under the national Green Party of the United States. The group officially obtained recognition as a national political party with the Federal Election Commission in 2001.

The Green Party has its strongest popular support on the Pacific Coast, the Upper Great Lakes, and the Northeast, as reflected in the geographical distribution of Green candidates elected. The Greens gained widespread public attention during the 2000 presidential election, when they won 2.7% of the popular vote.

As of October 2016, 143 officeholders in the United States were affiliated with the Green Party, the majority of them in California, but several in each of Illinois, Connecticut, Maine, Massachusetts, Oregon, Pennsylvania, and Wisconsin. In 2017 there were over 255,000 registered Greens across 21 states, according to their website. The Green Party supported 171 candidates for federal, state, and local office in 2017, with 51 candidates being elected. Difficulties arise because different states have different rules for which parties can stand, so ballot access for independent parties is hard in many states.[5]

The point is that the Green Party is still there and somewhere to go for people who do not think that the Democrats or Republicans can represent them, because these parties for funding purposes are allied to large corporations, which have vested interests in the current economic system which drives climate change. They have also been a place to go to be amongst like-minded people who have had to endure the Trump administration. Thank goodness in 2021 they elected a non-climate-denying president in Joe Biden. Biden now controls the Senate and is planning a massive investment in a Green Recovery to tackle climate change. He has revoked many of Trump's disastrous policies on wildlife protection and climate change. He is rejoining the 2015 Paris agreement and this augurs well for co-operation with the U.K. government to achieve ambitious reduction targets at the IPCC international climate summit in Glasgow in November 2021. The Green Party of America gives the option for people to follow the path of politics in relation to climate change. The movement will probably grow rapidly as the effects of climate change develop more quickly and directly affect individuals.

One survey found that 1 in 4 people in the 18-24 age demographic say that they will consider voting for the Green Party.[6]

Pioneering the Way in Finland

The Finnish Green Party is historically the first Green Party to make inroads into national government. It was founded on February 28, 1987, and registered as a political party the next year. In 1995 it was the first European Green party to be part of a state-level Cabinet. In that 1995 election the Green League received a total of nine seats (out of 200), joined the coalition cabinet led by the Social Democrats and Pekka Haavisto became the minister for Environment and Development Aid, thus becoming the first Green minister in Europe. By 1999 they had a total of 11 seats. The Greens continued in the next coalition cabinet, but resigned in protest in 2002, after the cabinet's decision to allow the construction of a new nuclear plant. In the 2003 election the Green League received 8% of the vote, giving a total of 14 seats. In 2007, the party gained 15 seats, and joined the centre-right-led government. At the 2011 election, the party fell to ten seats. Nevertheless, the Greens were invited to join a six-party cabinet. They made it a condition of their participation in the government that there would be no nuclear plants built. In the 2015 parliamentary election, the party returned to 15 seats but then in September 2018 the Green League left the coalition government in protest at a decision to build a nuclear power plant in the north of the country. The Green League has since changed their views on the nuclear issue. In 2019 the greens won 20 seats and were part of the coalition government holding three ministerial posts: Minister of the Interior, Minister for Foreign Affairs and Minister of the Environment and Climate Change.

At the municipal level, Greens are an important factor in the largest cities of Finland. In the municipal election of 2008 the Greens' vote share was considerably higher in Helsinki (the capital), where the Greens were the second largest party. In several other cities the Greens achieved the position of the third largest party. In the 2017 municipal elections the Green League emerged as a major victor, winning 12.4% of the national vote and consolidating its foothold as the second-largest party in the Finnish capital.

The Greens have had a definite influence on bringing forth climate change legislation and promoting renewable energy. The national Climate Change Act for Finland entered into force on 1 June 2015. The Act lays down provisions in the planning system for climate change policy and monitoring of the implementation of climate objectives. The Act describes a long-term strategy for a greenhouse gas emission reduction target of at least 80% by 2050, compared to 1990. This has now been exceeded as the government coalition aims to get Finland to net zero emissions by 2035.[7]

After Sweden, Finland has the second-highest proportion of renewable energy in Europe. In 2015, the share of renewables in electricity generation was 45%. Within it, the largest share was hydro power followed by wood and wind power. Almost 80% of electricity generation was emission-free, which will rise to 90% by 2030. By 2014 Finland had already exceeded its 2020 target for renewable energy use under the EU Renewable Energy Directive.[8]

Progress in Australia

The United Tasmania Group was the first "green" party anywhere in the world and ran candidates in the 1972 Australian election. Other state-based Green parties sprang up in the early 1980s. In 1992 Australia's state-based Green parties joined together, to form the new federal party, the Australian Greens. They could now take part in elections to the national government. In addition to environmentalism, the party cites four core values: ecological sustainability, social justice, grassroots democracy and peace and non-violence. In 2010, 1.6 million Australians voted Green. The numbers elected expanded, with four new seats in the Senate, plus Adam Bandt becoming the first Green elected to a federal seat. In 2018 the Australian Greens had 9 federal senators, 1 federal MP (Adam Bandt), 23 state MPs, and more than 100 Green councillors including Green mayors.[9]

Australia is the world's largest exporter of coal, according to the International Energy Agency, and the country is also a leading exporter of liquefied natural gas (LNG). In 2015, about 40% of Australia's export income was related to energy. Australia in 2018 did not ratify the Paris Agreement and would not be held to the targets. This is plainly because of business interests in the fossil fuel industry. So although the green political presence is not great, it is at least there as a pressure group to highlight the issue of climate change. This has been even more important given the rampant bush fires of 2019. There have been a lot of protests by farmers and others about large mining developments adding to emissions. Not only have Greens been the voice of protest about coal mining, they have been instrumental in highlighting the need to build renewable energy resources such as solar and wind.

Greens believe Australia has the capacity to become a world leader in climate action and renewable energy, phasing out coal and building a renewable energy economy. An Expanded Renewable Energy Target was passed by the Australian Parliament, with the support of the Greens, on 20 August 2009, to ensure that renewable energy would achieve a 20% share of the electricity supply in Australia by 2020. A key policy encouraging the development of renewable energy in Australia involves the mandatory renewable energy targets (MRET) set by both federal and state governments. There are also domestic feed-in tariffs which guarantee a good and stable price for electricity from wind and solar. The Australian government has no renewable energy policy beyond the year 2020, raising concerns about environmental sustainability for future generations, as the government will not be replacing the "Renewable Energy Target" (RET) after 2020. This shows the need for the Greens to continue to grow as a force in Australian politics - to bring about a dramatic change in energy policy. As of August 2017, it is estimated that Australia could generate enough renewable energy to power 70% of the country's households. In 2019, Australia met its 2020 renewable energy target of 23.5% of the total energy produced. Now many Australian states and territories want to reach a 40% target of all energy produced from renewables by 2030.[10]

New Zealand

The New Zealand Green Party traces its origins to the Values Party. The Values Party originated in 1972 at Victoria University in Wellington. While it gained a measure of public support in several elections, the then first-past-the-post electoral system meant that the party did not win any seats in parliament. In May 1990, remnants of the Values Party merged with a number of other environmentalist organisations to form the modern Green Party. This sparked a resurgence of support, with the new group winning 6.85% of the vote in the 1990 election. The following year, the Greens became co-founder members of the Alliance, a five-party grouping. The Greens contested the 1993 and 1996 elections as part of the Alliance. With the adoption of the mixed-member proportional (MMP) electoral system in 1996, the Alliance gained entry to parliament, bringing 3 Green MPs with them. In the 1999 election, the Greens gained 5.16% of the vote and 7 seats in Parliament. In the 2002 election, the Greens polled 7%, increasing their strength in parliament to 9 seats. In the 2005 election, their support dropped a little, but in the 2008 election they restored their number of seats. They became the third largest parliamentary party in New Zealand. In the 2011 election, the Green Party received nearly a quarter of a million party votes, equating to 11.06% of the total valid party votes nationwide, earning them 14 seats in the new Parliament. In the 2014 general election, the Green Party's share of the party vote fell slightly to 10.7%. Despite this, they retained all of their 14 seats and remained the third largest party in parliament. During the 2017 general election, the Green Party's party vote dropped to 6.3%, with the Party gaining 8 seats in the House of Representatives.

Having the greens in politics has made a difference to climate change as they have had success in promoting renewable energy and cutting carbon. Early on, an Energy Efficiency and Conservation Act was set up which created the Energy Efficiency & Conservation Authority (EECA), a crown entity. The Greens also got legislation for feed-in tariffs to guarantee a fair price to households producing electricity using renewables. In October 2017, the Greens entered a confidence and supply arrangement with the Labour Party which gives them three ministers outside cabinet and one under-secretary role. Green Party leader James Shaw was appointed Minister for Climate Change. As a support partner of the Labour-New Zealand First coalition government, the Greens secured several policies and concessions. The most important achievement is passing the Zero Carbon Act into law. The Act makes greenhouse gas emissions targets legally binding. A Climate Change Commission has been created to oversee implementation of the Act. The coalition has agreed an energy strategy which includes a target of 90% electricity from renewable sources by 2025. In 2017, 82% of the electricity generated in New Zealand came from renewable sources. Under the agreement with the Green Party, the Government will prepare a transition plan to achieve 100% renewable electricity generation by 2035. The Greens have helped to pass legislation which bans new offshore oil and gas exploration to make sure that fossil fuels stay in the ground. There are moves now by the Greens to bring a bill to Parliament which will outlaw further investment in fossil fuels.[11]

CONCLUSION

It is clear from the examples shown in this chapter that people who think politics is a good way to bring change can join their local Green party, and will know that locally and nationally they will make a difference to the onset of climate change. In a time when we have had the election of leaders such as Donald Trump in the USA and Jair Bolsonaro in Brazil, many people need an alternative political home. Green parties may be small at the moment but when the full effect of climate change hits ordinary citizens they will grow. I have been attending Green Party conferences in the U.K. for many years and they have, through full debate and democratic processes, produced policies which could readily be adopted by governments when the full force of climate change hits societies around the world.

Chapter 11: THE PATH OF A SPIRITUAL LIFE

What I mean by the path of a spiritual life is acting in a way which acknowledges that the physical world only tells part of the story of who we are, and that the complete story is told when we recognise there is a metaphysical dimension of life. Trying to understand the spiritual dimension becomes the focus of a lifetime's work (or perhaps many lifetimes). After all, we have limited senses that only take us so far. The spiritual traditions all express different ways of working with the greater metaphysical reality but they also all contain teachings about how we should interact with the natural world.

What this whole book is about is getting over the message that the deepest values come from the spiritual traditions and these values should act as our guide to how we treat the earth and the beings that live on it. Since the time of the emergence of language in humans, spiritual values have given guidance on how to relate to the natural environment. It started in the shamanic tradition over 40,000 years ago and continues into the more modern spiritual traditions such as the Bahá'ís, Spiritualism and Sikhism.

In this chapter I am going to focus on looking at the spiritual life of Buddhists, Muslims, Christians and Hindus. I explain briefly the basic guidelines of each religion which, if followed by adherents, would lessen their personal impact on climate change. This is followed by a brief look at the more demanding and deeper spiritual practice which can only followed by a few but is the ultimate as regards its lack of materialism and therefore its low carbon footprint.

The Buddhist life as a path to combat climate change

I am a lay Buddhist and what I say in this section is what I have found to work in my own life in trying to minimise my contribution to climate change. Trying to be a genuine Buddhist through my everyday activities, by way of thought, word, and deed, is the most important thing in my life. For millennia, Buddhism has been making people more aware, more caring, and more skilful. I apply ethical self-discipline, and avoid acting destructively. Acting destructively is acting under the influence of the disturbing emotions – anger, greed, attachment, jealousy, arrogance and so on.

My guidelines are what are called precepts, or rules to follow. These precepts were outlined in the first Buddhist texts. They constitute the basic code of ethics undertaken by lay followers of Buddhism. The three pure precepts which encapsulate the Buddha's teaching are:

- Desist from evil - by refraining from that which causes suffering.
- Do only good - doing good arises naturally when we cease from evil.
- Do good for others - to train in Zen is to devote one's life to the good of all living things.

You can apply this to climate change. I try to lead my life in a way that does not accentuate climate change, which I know causes suffering to others. I see doing good as when I serve others who might be affected by climate change, as I support many charities doing work in this area. I see doing good for others as sharing my knowledge about climate change so that they too can become aware of how they can avoid actions that can make climate change worse for everybody. This is the whole point of writing this book. There are also five further precepts I try to follow as follows:

- Do not take life **but rather cultivate and encourage life.**
- Do not steal **but rather cultivate and encourage generosity.**
- Do not indulge in abusive or inappropriate sexuality **but rather cultivate and encourage honest and caring relationships.**

- Do not lie **but rather cultivate and encourage truthful communication.**
- Do not abuse intoxicants **but rather cultivate and encourage clarity.**

The last one of these I mostly follow but sometimes I drink alcohol - although I try not to take so much that I become intoxicated.

I meditate every day for half an hour and before I do I say this: "How great and wondrous are the clothes of enlightenment, formless and embracing every treasure. I wish to unfold the Buddha's teaching so that I may help all living beings." This sets the intention for the day that I am not living just for myself and my needs but I am living to help fulfil the needs of all living things. My intention is based on the values expounded by the Buddha when he summarised his teachings by saying that we should be free from evil, do only good and do good for others. At the very heart of Buddhist teachings is that compassion should permeate all that we do. Theravada Buddhism describes this in terms of *metta* which is goodwill, loving-kindness, universal love; a feeling of friendliness and heartfelt concern for all living beings, human or non-human, in all situations. The chief mark of *metta* is a benevolent attitude: a keen desire to promote the welfare of others. So all through the day I am trying to be aware of what I say and do and the effect it has on all beings. What I eat, what I think, what I say, how I travel, what consumer products I buy, and what leisure interests I choose to pursue and so on. Mindfulness is an important element in Buddhism - after all the word "Buddha" actually means "someone who is totally awake." This brings in another fundamental teaching of Buddhism, that of karma or cause and effect. I try to be aware of the good and bad effects of my actions.[1]

I am now going to look at the Buddhist monastery, which is a more dedicated type of Buddhist practice, and which probably has a bigger effect on mitigating the effects of climate change.

The Zen monastery as a model to lessen the effects of climate change

Zen Buddhism evolved out of the Ch'an School, a Buddhist sect that was founded in China in the 8th century A.D. Ch'an is pronounced Zen in

Japanese. It means "contemplation" or "meditation". Zen Buddhism was introduced to Japan from China during the Chinese Sung Dynasty in the 10th century by a Chinese monk named Huineng. It had a relatively small following for two centuries and didn't take hold and flourish in Japan until the 12th century.

Zen Buddhist monastic life is based upon simplicity, silence, self-investigation and wholehearted effort. A core part of many Zen monasteries' daily life is daily service in the spirit of mindfulness, love, and great compassion. I have focussed on the monastic element of Buddhism because it is the most radical and perhaps has least impact on the natural world compared to the life of a lay Buddhist.[2]

I have been going to Throssel Hole monastery in Northumberland in the U.K. for some years. It is a Zen monastery which follows the Soto Zen tradition. If materialism is the cause of carbon emissions they are the antidote to it. Monks own few material objects and all wear the same type of clothing. The carbon footprint of each monk (a term used for both male and female members) is low because everything is communally shared. The food is vegetarian, avoiding the damaging effects of climate change from meat-eating. Food is prepared in one kitchen to save fuel and then eaten communally. A measure of their thought is the meticulous way they use and rewash plastic bags to store food in. Any vehicles are communally shared and they travel with the maximum number of passengers if possible.

From my experience of attending retreats at the monastery there is little time to even think of what material thing you are going to buy next. Both monks and those on retreat carry out tasks which are vital for the monastery to function as an act of service. At Throssel Hole tasks such as such preparing and cooking food, cleaning, washing, looking after the garden and woodlands are completed in the time allocated to work periods.

The focus of life for a Zen monk is to foster "awakening the enlightened mind". In the life of a Zen monk, sitting meditation (zazen) is one of the most important parts of the day. Each day, there is time designated just for sitting. This meditation is really practice for learning to be present. If the focus is on enlightenment and realisation of the truth, monks therefore do not pursue activities which accentuate climate change.[3]

The Christian way of life as a way to combat climate change

Christianity is the most widely practised religion in the world, with some 2.4 billion followers - one-third of the global population. The Catholic Church alone has 1.09 billion followers.

Christians believe that God has commanded them to take care of his creation by respecting and honouring it. The Bible gives clear instructions of how man should relate to the earth, as quoted in Genesis; "...work it and take care of it," (Gen. 2:15). So Christians from the very beginning are meant to take care of God's creation. So leading a Christian life should mean that any action that contributes to climate change should be avoided as it harms God's creation.

It is also clear from the fundamental teachings of Christ that love should be the basis of relations between humans. Jesus said that the two greatest commandments that Christians should follow are firstly to love God completely and secondly to love your neighbour as yourself (Matthew 22:36-40). The way that this love is demonstrated in the world is stated by this simple quote from the Bible: "And as you wish that others would do to you, do so to them." (Luke 6:31)

Surely if this is the case, a practising Christian would be concerned about the global suffering caused by climate change and as an act of love through their lives not make the situation worse.

Another focus of the Christian way of life is worshipping God, carrying out His will and practising the teachings of Jesus Christ. It is clear that Christianity is a mystical religion where the focus of life is to have a direct spiritual relationship with God and Christ. So spiritual rather than material concerns are paramount. According to Christian teachings a major obstacle to living in this way is the desire for money and material wealth. We know that materialism and consumption cause climate change as everything we buy requires more emissions of CO_2 to make it. These quotes from the Bible really succinctly make this point:

"No one can serve two masters, for either he will hate the one and love the other, or he will be devoted to the one and despise the other. You cannot serve God and money". (Matthew 6:24)

"Watch out! Be on your guard against all kinds of greed; a man's life does not consist in the abundance of his possessions." (Luke 12:15)

"If you want to be perfect, go, sell your possessions and give to the poor and you will have treasure in heaven. Then come, follow me." (Matthew 19:21)

So you would expect moderate consumption of material goods from a Christian and this definitely means they would not add to the problem of increasing CO_2 and the dramatic effects it has on our world.

I am now going to look at a Christian monastery, which is a more dedicated type of Christian practice. This involves minimal consumption so it is unlikely to contribute to climate change.

Monastic life in a Benedictine monastery as a model to lessen the effects of climate change

The monastery is the place where monks and nuns are called to live the Christian Gospel. It involves a return to God through attention to the classic spiritual disciplines of silence, chastity, prayer, fasting, confession, good works, obedience and vigils. To be a monk or nun is to be "dead to the world" in order to be "alive in Christ". Monks and nuns who join any monastery make their vows of poverty, chastity and obedience.

St. Benedict was one of the first Christians to establish monasteries. The *Rule of Saint Benedict* has been used by Benedictines for 15 centuries, and thus St. Benedict is sometimes regarded as the founder of Western monasticism. The Rule is comprised of 73 short chapters, containing two kinds of wisdom: spiritual and administrative. How to live through Christ and how to run a monastery wisely. Many of the chapters focus on being obedient and humble. The *Rule of Benedict* constitutes a basic guide for living the Christian life. In the *Rule*, Benedict tells his monks and nuns to live a balanced life filled with work and prayer. In Benedictine monasteries the day is ordered around communal prayer and reflection on Holy Scripture. A Benedictine community prays together six or seven times a day, consecrating the whole day to God. Manual labour is seen as a way of honouring God and serving the needs of the community.[4]

On my travels to India in 2002 as part of my research for my first book I had the privilege to visit Asirvanam Benedictine Monastery in Bangalore. I was inspired by the monks and their commitment to the spiritual life and their active involvement in the surrounding poor community. They had a farm which provided employment for the locals, a clinic for medical needs and a school. I was struck by their humbleness and purity of intention which meant that they focussed on their spiritual practice of prayer and service.[5]

The first point about a monastery is that monks and nuns share resources between them which means that there is less energy used for heating, cooking, and transport by each individual. In the life of the householder such energy needs contribute a greater amount of greenhouse gases and hence have a greater effect on climate change.

The second major point is that Benedictines and other monks and nuns follow a rule to have minimal consumption. They have only 2 sets of clothes and do not spend money on consumer goods. The focus of their life is getting closer to God and their time is very structured throughout the day in order to achieve this, mainly through prayer and work from early morning to early night. With minimal consumption each monk and nun has a small carbon footprint and does not contribute to climate change.

Benedictine Nuns of Holy Trinity Monastery, Herefordshire, U.K., offer a good example of the lifestyle. They rise at 5am and their day is full of services, prayers, study, work and contemplation, which ends about 9pm. There is also a minimum requirement that they do at least one hour of contemplative prayer every day and at least half an hour of prayerful reading. Benedictines prize learning so there is a well-stocked library.[6]

The Muslim life as a way to combat climate change

Historically, Islam is a religious tradition which originated in seventh century Arabia with the prophet Muhammad (570-632) and the divine revelation which he received from God that is recorded in the Qur'an.[7] Islam is the world's second-largest religion, with over 1.8 billion followers, or 24% of the world's population. Muslims make up a majority of the population in 50 countries. "Islam" is an Arabic word that means "peace through the submission to the Lord".

True Islam is a complete and comprehensive way of life leading to a balanced way of living. Islam doesn't view "spirituality" separately from everyday activities. In Islam everything is "spiritual" because all actions must be in accordance with God's will. Consequently there is no great tradition of monks or nuns. The central fact of the Muslim religious experience is Allah (God). Everything in this world belongs to Allah. As such, man's life and wealth, which are part of this world, also belong to Him, because He has created them and has entrusted them to every man for his use. The God of the Qur'an is one and transcendent, creator and sustainer of the universe, and the overwhelming concern of the believer. Islam generally discourages the isolation of one's self in devotion to God, and tells its adherents that you should find a balance between practising your faith and living life as a part of society. It encourages raising families and getting married, and donating from your net wealth to charitable causes.[8]

Central to the life of a Muslim is prayer, which they do five times a day. For prayer, Muslims stand facing the direction of Mecca in Saudi Arabia, where the Holy House of God, known as the Ka'ba, is situated. Muslims pray in the early morning before sunrise, in the middle of the day, in the afternoon, at sunset and at night. Muslims pray in obedience to God because they believe God created humankind for no other purpose except to worship Him. Prayers are a set of ritual movements and words said at fixed times of the day and night. Prayer at fixed times serves as a reminder of the presence of God in their lives.

- Fajr: This prayer starts off the day with the remembrance of God; it is performed before sunrise.
- Dhuhr: After the day's work has begun, one breaks shortly after noon to again remember God and seek His guidance.
- 'Asr: In the late afternoon, people take a few minutes to remember God and the greater meaning of their lives.
- Maghrib: Just after the sun goes down, Muslims remember God again as the day begins to come to a close.
- 'Isha: Before retiring for the night, Muslims again take the time to remember God's presence, guidance, mercy, and forgiveness.

Muslims are also required to attend the mosque each Friday for prayers.[9]

In Islam, Allah (God) created everything. The Qur'an states that God has granted human beings the responsibility of stewardship (*khilafah*) of the Earth as "He who appointed you viceroys of the Earth". (Qur'an 6:165) "The world is sweet and verdant green and Allah appoints you to be His regents in it and will see how you acquit yourselves…" (Sunnah of the Prophet) "It is he who has made you his agents, inheritors of the Earth: He hath raised you in ranks some above others: that he may try you in the gifts he hath given you." (Qur'an - Cattle: 165) From these words it is clear that mankind represents the interests of God on Earth. Mankind is thus entrusted with its maintenance and care and, as a trustee, therefore it follows that because climate change causes such damage to the earth, Muslims must act in ways that prevent the worst effects of climate change. This is especially so since, according to the Qur'an, God had created everything in balance and we know that climate change puts the climate out of balance. "And the firmament He has raised high and He has set up the balance; in order that ye may not transgress balance." (Qur'an 55:5-9). "Verily, all things have we created in proportion and measure." (Qur'an 54:49)

A major Islamic teaching is that for a Muslim, the primary duty is to be good and to strive for spreading goodness. This is seen as carrying out the will of God. These quotes from the Qur'an illustrate this:
"Do good to others as God has done good to you." (Qur'an 28:77)
"Will the reward for doing good be anything other than good?" (Qur'an 55:60)
"So compete with each other in doing good." (Qur'an 5:48)
"Those who believe and do good deeds - the Gracious God will create love in their hearts." (Qur'an 19:97)

If this is the case then any action by a Muslim which causes evil or suffering instead of good is contrary to the teachings of Islam. The teachings emphasise taking care of God's creation but just as importantly warn against overzealous consumption. It is sad to me that oil wealth in places like Dubai, which I have visited, seems to take pride in displaying affluence and materialism, in complete contradiction to the message of moderation found throughout Islamic teachings. The Qur'an and the Hadiths (sayings) of Muhammad are clear on this issue as seen from these quotes:
"The most enviable of my friends is a believer with little property who finds pleasure in prayer, who performs the worship of his Lord well, who obeys Him in secret, who is obscure among men, who is not pointed out by people, and who is content with his provision." (Tirmidhi)
"Watch out for greed because the people before you perished from it. Greed led them to be miserly so they became misers. Greed led them to

break the ties (of kinship) so they broke them. Greed led them to sins so they committed sins." (Abu Dawud)

"Do not forbid the good things Allah has made lawful to you and do not overstep the limits. Allah does not love those who overstep the limits." (Qur'an 5:87)

We know that consumerism is a major cause of the production of greenhouse gases as all material objects carry a carbon footprint. Moderation is a central theme of Islam so if Muslims limit their consumption they limit their contribution to climate change.

Another principle of Islam which applies to climate change is similar to the idea of karma in Buddhism in that simply all actions have consequences. According to Islam, man is answerable to God for all his actions and will be called on to render an account of them in the Hereafter on the Day of Judgement. Therefore logically Muslims should be aware that if they contribute to climate change and thereby cause suffering to others by their actions in this life, they will suffer the consequences in the next life. Two quotes from the Qur'an illustrate this:

"And truly the Lord will repay everyone according to their works for he is well aware of what they do." (Qur'an 11:113)

"Conduct yourself in this world as if you are here to stay forever and yet prepare for eternity as if you are to die tomorrow." Muhammad

The life of a Hindu as a way to combat climate change

With over a billion Hindus worldwide, Hinduism is the world's third largest religion, after Christianity and Islam. Hinduism has been described as a way of living in harmony with nature and growing inwardly over many lifetimes. Its authority rests upon a large body of sacred texts that provide Hindus with rules governing rituals, worship, pilgrimage, and daily activities, among many other things.

The summary of Hinduism is sometimes said to be "simple living and high thinking". By doing his or her social and religious duty, a devotee simultaneously progresses spiritually and obtains material necessities without undue complication and without harming the environment.

The Hindu *dharma* is a way of life. Hindu scriptures make it abundantly clear that when a person lives from an egocentric viewpoint he or she incurs sin, whereas when he or she lives for God or in the service of God they attain liberation. In other words, the life of a human being upon earth is not for his enjoyment but for service to God. Hindus believe in rebirth so when people engage in selfish actions they accumulate evil and remain bound to the cycle of births and deaths as they are in essence an eternal, indestructible, transcendental self. When they offer the fruit of their actions to God they attain liberation. In other words they espouse the law of karma, as discussed in the Buddhist section. This states that people have to bear the consequences of what they do - if not in this life, then in the next life. Good deeds result in spiritual progress, bad deeds result in spiritual regression. A human birth is seen as precious and a chance to attain liberation, but a person may be reborn in animal form and have no opportunity for liberation.

When I travelled to India in 2002 and carried out interviews with 130 spiritual leaders for my previous book, the Hindu leaders, with few exceptions, were worried about consumerism and western values decimating Hindu culture. Materialism comes from selfish desires and we know that the consumerism which accompanies it, adds to the destruction of our climate. Following the Hindu *dharma* means that a person acts from a selfless point of view and is always aware of how their actions may create negative karma for themselves. The ideal practitioner of Hinduism, as put forward by the holy scriptures of the Upanishads, is that a person reaching about the age of fifty should cast aside all material possessions and become a wandering *sannyasin*. So they become an anti-consumerist archetype with minimal contribution to greenhouse gas emissions.[10]

The world is considered by Hindus to be divine in all its aspects, being the work of Brahma, the supreme creator. The Vedas (early scriptures) state that the "Earth belongs to all" and there needs to be a deep respect for all creation. (Atharvaveda 12 1-45). These quotes from the scriptures illustrate this viewpoint:

"In this cosmos, whatever exists - living and non-living, all that is - is pervaded by one divine consciousness." (Isa Upanishad 1)

"For the world is a living whole, a vast interconnectedness of cosmic harmony, inspired and sustained by the One Supreme." (Bhagavad Gita X.20.)

If the planet is an expression of the divine, and life on earth has the purpose of union with the divine, then any action taken by a Hindu to destroy the divine world through contributing to climate change is wrong.

Ashram life as a model of combatting climate change

The ashram takes Hindu spiritual life to a different level and has a more profound effect on combatting the worst effects of climate change. Traditionally the ashram is a place of spiritual learning as they were often founded by a spiritual teacher or guru to give the opportunity for residents to pursue a spiritual life under their guidance. They can vary in size from a small hermitage, housing just a few people, to multiple building complexes which are home to hundreds, including whole families. Material needs are basic and residents are content with simple living rather in the style of a Christian monastery. Each resident is expected to serve the community by carrying out tasks such as gardening and cooking. Part of the time when not working is taken up by *Satsang* which is a Sanskrit word meaning gathering or coming together of seekers of truth. *Satsang* involves chanting, meditation and talks given by the resident guru. It is usually held morning and evening.

Amritapuri is the name of an ashram which was founded by the spiritual leader called Mata Amritanandamayi, known as Amma. Amma or "Mother" was born in a remote coastal village in Kerala, South India in 1953. Even as a small girl, she spent many hours in deep meditation. She also composed devotional songs and could often be seen singing to the divine with heartfelt emotion. She lived in poverty so in the beginning the ashram was simply Amma's family's cow shed. I met her for the first time in 1988 and she gave me a hug and I felt an amazing energy going up my spine. I met her for another hug in 2019 and the energy and compassion was still there. It is no wonder people were attracted to her spiritual qualities and now there are 3,500 members of her ashram. Amma has many ashrams following her model of spiritual life throughout the world. All the residents are asked to dedicate their lives to realising God and serving the world. The ashram way of life does not contribute to climate change because the focus of residents is on the accumulation of spiritual experience, not consumer products. Those who do not consume do not produce greenhouse gas emissions. Here is the daily schedule of life at the ashram:

05:00 a.m. – 06:00 a.m. Chanting
06:30 a.m. – 07:30 a.m. Meditation
08:30 a.m. – 09:30 a.m. Breakfast
10:00 a.m. – 12.30 p.m. Seva or service
12:30 p.m. – 02:00 p.m. Lunch
02:00 p.m. – 05:00 p.m. Seva or service
05:00 p.m. – 06:00 p.m. Meditation
06:30 p.m. – 08:00 p.m. Bhajans devotional singing
08:15 p.m. – 09:00 p.m. Dinner
09:00 p.m. – 10:00 p.m. Personal study, Meditation, Diary Keeping

Various yoga, meditation and scripture classes also take place.

The ashram is as sustainable as it can be. "Green Friends" is an organisation established by Amma for the preservation and protection of the environment. They carry out various projects at the ashram. Their recycling department collects all the non-biodegradable waste from the ashram and sorts it into many different useful categories. It is then sold to recyclers who re-use it. All proceeds directly support Amma's many charities. There is also a composting department which makes sure all food waste produced in the ashram is converted to compost for growing crops. The "Amrita Plastic Project" uses non-recyclable plastics to make saleable goods. There is an ecology department which runs a centre for environmental education, outreach and innovation. It encourages local people to produce organic and natural products. This means that greenhouse emissions of products bought are reduced.

Conservation projects at the ashram and throughout India are carried out by "Amrita Forests". 200 greenhouses have been established to produce tree saplings and 100,000 saplings are planted every year. There has also been the planting of 100,000 casuarina saplings to beautify the Kerala shoreline and also protect the beaches from erosion.

Amma also founded an organisation called "Embracing the World", which is a global network of charitable projects. It is a member organisation of the United Nations' *Billion Tree Campaign*, and has organised the planting of more than a million trees globally since 2001. There is now a new pledge to plant six million trees worldwide.

Throughout the world, "Embracing the World" has centres which are working to become local models of sustainable living. The centres run workshops in sustainable living, permaculture, beekeeping, gardening and conservation techniques. The centres practise rainwater harvesting; produce food from organic farms, gardens, and orchards; and make organic fruit and vegetables available to their local communities.[11]

CONCLUSION

It is my view that someone following a spiritual life is not usually contributing many greenhouse gases to the atmosphere through their lifestyle. Their focus is on spiritual rather than material progress. The emphasis on awareness of how our actions effect the environment through karma also means that people living a spiritual life will think carefully if they contribute to climate change. I have chosen only the four main religious traditions but my previous book on green spirituality examines the green credentials of eight other religious traditions. (see www.greenspirituality.org)

Part 3

The

Future

Consequences

of what we do

Chapter 12: GLOBAL WARMING BELOW 2°C

This is the best case scenario. The future of our planet depends on the choices we make now. What we do at this moment will affect the whole of humanity – and many other species which share the earth with us. If we make the right choices then the effects of climate change will not be so drastic – the majority of life on earth will survive. But if we choose to follow our current path then the climate will soon change beyond our ability to adapt and cope. My hope is that many people will read the second part of this book and will act upon it so that we can avoid that worst case scenario.

For one thing, when a system is as large and complex as the global climate, it just cannot be predicted with any degree of precision, and understanding the long-term impact of emissions is near impossible. The IPCC (Inter-governmental Panel on Climate Change) is the leading world body for assessing the science related to climate change, its impacts and potential future risks, and the possible responses. They have been producing assessment reports for many years.[1] In 2018 the IPCC brought out a *Special Report on Global Warming of 1.5°C* and included a *"Summary for Policymakers"*. I am basing a relatively good outcome scenario on acting on the advice of this report. If we do act on this then we will have a chance of keeping global warming to 1.5 degrees overall. However, the report stated that even limiting global warming to 1.5°C would require rapid, far-reaching and unprecedented changes in all aspects of society. It also showed that there would be clear benefits to people and to the natural ecosystems of limiting global warming to 1.5°C even compared to 2°C – and that if the temperature rise is even higher than this, it is likely to be catastrophic. Unfortunately, current pledges in the Paris Agreement will not restrict us to 1.5° - on the contrary, they will get us to about 3 degrees Celsius of warming by 2100.

The report highlights a number of climate change impacts that could be avoided by limiting global warming to 1.5°C, rather than 2°C or more. Limiting global warming would also give people and ecosystems more time to adapt. It is described as a "soft landing", as under those conditions scientists believe we will be relatively safe.[2]

To achieve this 1.5° outcome, global greenhouse emissions would need to fall by half in just 12 years and zero out by 2050. To stay below 2°C, emissions have to decline to zero by about 2075. Virtually all of the coal-fired plants and gasoline-burning vehicles on the planet would need to be quickly replaced with zero-carbon alternatives. Any remaining emissions would need to be balanced by removing CO_2 from the air. The recommendation that prompted the creation of Extinction Rebellion, mentioned in the chapter on Protest, was the need to cut CO_2 emissions by half within 12 years.[3]

Temperature increases are the drivers of climate change. World Meteorological Organization (WMO) Secretary-General Petteri Taalas stated "The 20 warmest years on record have been in the past 22 years. The degree of warming during the past four years has been exceptional, both on land and in the ocean." [3] The IPCC Report of 2018 states that global warming is likely to reach 1.5°C between 2030 and 2052 if emissions continue to increase at the current rate. Half a degree more than the current 1 degree Celsius increase might sound small, but it means a significant change. That number is an average of temperatures all over the globe, so some places will become significantly hotter. The Arctic, for example, is likely to be several degrees warmer, increasing ice melt and therefore sea level rise. That half of a degree will make drought-prone regions much more likely to experience severe drought, and areas prone to heat waves or intense hurricanes will get more of those disasters, too. These factors could trigger huge migrations of people and mass extinctions of animals. Most coral reefs will die, which could trigger rippling effects throughout the oceans. The new report says that we will see those effects in just 20 years unless major changes are implemented. Extreme weather affects our water supply, our food supply and our health. If carbon emissions continue to grow, rather than dropping, the weather is predicted to change dramatically, with most weather events becoming more extreme. Stronger hurricanes, longer droughts, more and wetter thunderstorms, and more catastrophic flooding are all among the results predicted by climate models.[4]

Soil

One source of CO_2 that people do not often think about is the soil itself. Soils play a key role in the carbon cycle by soaking up carbon from dead plant matter. Plants absorb CO_2 from the atmosphere through photosynthesis, and pass carbon to the ground when dead leaves and roots decompose. Organic carbon commonly makes up 50 to 60% of the organic matter in soils. The top metre of the world's soils contains three times as much carbon as does the entire atmosphere, making it a major carbon sink, alongside forests and oceans. Currently, soils absorb about 25% of the world's fossil fuel emissions each year.[5]

Agricultural practices that disturb the soil - such as tilling, planting mono-crops, removing crop residue, excessive use of fertilisers and pesticides, and over-grazing - expose the carbon in the soil to oxygen, allowing it to burn off into the atmosphere. A loss of this carbon from the soil, due to inappropriate land use or the use of poor soil management and cropping practices, can cause a decline in soil quality and soil structure, and increase soil erosion, all of which lead to emissions of carbon into the atmosphere. Globally, about 25% of the total land area has been degraded. Fertile soil is being lost at a rate of 24bn tonnes a year through intensive farming as the demand for food increases.[6] On the other hand, appropriate land use and soil management can lead to increased ability of the soil to retain carbon and even partially mitigate the rise of atmospheric CO_2. A United Nations study in 2017 found that with better management, global croplands have the potential to store an additional 1.85 gigatons of carbon each year - as much as the global transportation sector emits annually. There is a lot of evidence that growing organically stabilises carbon in the soil. In theory, soils could be managed in a way that would allow them to reabsorb all of the carbon that has been lost from the soil since the agricultural revolution.[7]

Extreme Weather

Let's look at extreme weather events, assuming that temperature increase is restricted to 1.5 degrees Celsius around the world. The strength of the winds associated with tropical storms is likely to increase, along with the amount of precipitation falling in them. The intensity of Atlantic hurricanes is therefore likely to increase as the ocean warms. Climate models project an increase in the number of the strongest (Category 4 and 5) hurricanes, as well as greater rainfall rates within them. Such hurricanes cause more extreme sea levels, which means the combined height of the high tide plus any storm surge. Driven by hurricanes or other large storms, these extreme sea levels flood coastal areas, threatening life and property.[8]

Global average annual precipitation up until the end of the century is expected to increase, although changes in the amount and intensity of precipitation will vary significantly by region. One thing all the climate models agree on: big rainstorms will be getting even bigger, dumping a lot more rain. The intensity of precipitation events will increase. This will be particularly pronounced in tropical and polar regions, which are also expected to experience general overall increases in precipitation. Heavy downpours that currently occur about once every 20 years are projected to occur between twice and five times as frequently by 2100, depending on the location. This can lead to widespread flooding, and research has predicted that in the 2080s around four times as many people will be exposed to flood water compared with the 1980s.[9]

More intense precipitation in the United States is most likely in the Northeast, in Alaska and in the upper Midwest. This could increase the chances of river flooding, especially along the coast where sea level is also rising. Weather records show that extreme rains are already beginning to increase in the USA.[10] The Pacific Ocean near the equator will be much wetter, as will India and areas near the North and South Poles, such as Canada, Russia, and northern China. Europe is also expected to see a considerable increase in flood risk in coming years.[11] Research by the EU Science Hub suggests that most of Central and Western Europe will experience substantial increase in flood risk at all warming levels, and the higher the warming, the higher the risk both from storm surges and heavy precipitation.[11] Even at 1.5 degrees warming, more than 100 million people worldwide may be exposed to inundation by 2100, according to

IPCC climate research. The most vulnerable communities often don't have the financial resources to cope with this flooding. [12]

Rising Sea Levels

Over the next century, as the temperature increases, it is expected that the amount of sea ice will continue to decline, glaciers will continue to shrink, snow cover will continue to decrease, and permafrost will continue to thaw. Whilst snow-covered ice reflects more than 80% of the sun's heat, the darker ocean absorbs up to 95% of solar radiation, so melting accelerates. Marine ice sheet instability in Antarctica and/or irreversible loss of the Greenland ice sheet will result in a rise in sea level which could eventually amount to several metres. In 2019 researchers were able to calculate the shrinkage of the Greenland ice sheet at the rate of a billion tonnes a day. Meanwhile research has shown that in 2017, the Antarctic ice loss was 252 billion tonnes per year. [13] These sea level rises will make flooding elsewhere more frequent. With 1.5°C of warming, according to the IPCC, average sea level rise is predicted as 24-30cm (10-12 inches) by 2065 and 40-63cm (16-25 inches) by 2100. Sea level will continue to rise well beyond 2100, although the magnitude and rate of this rise will depend on future emissions. A slower rate of sea level rise enables greater opportunities for adaptation in the human and ecological systems of small islands, low-lying coastal areas and deltas, which is a good argument for trying to restrict the warming to 1.5°.

If the sea level rises, the coastline will retreat. More than 600 million people live in low-elevation coastal areas, less than 10 metres above sea level. The consequences of economic loss even at 1.5°C are great, but not as horrendous as any temperature above that. Residential properties, factories, roads, bridges, power plants, airports, ports, public buildings, military bases and other critical infrastructure along coasts also face the risk of chronic inundation. With them go tax revenues as well as creating thousands of homeless people. [14]

In the United States, some places are more exposed than others in the near term; many more will be exposed by mid-century and beyond. Higher sea levels worsen flooding, affecting the 40% of Americans who live in coastal counties. Florida, New Jersey, New York, and California are among the states with the most homes and property value at risk. Unfortunately, slightly higher sea levels also make hurricanes even more damaging. Just a few more inches of sea level rise allow a hurricane to push more water onto the land, even if the hurricane itself doesn't make landfall. Higher sea levels also create a higher launching point for storm surge. [15]

At least 275 million city dwellers live in vulnerable areas, the majority of them in Asian coastal megacities. In China a lot of the population is in coastal cities. For instance, with a 1 metre rise in sea level more than a third of Shanghai would be under water. Other major cities at risk of flooding are Miami, Shenzhen, Bangkok, Osaka, Tokyo, Jakarta and Singapore. Singapore is an economic hub of Asia and is threatened by sea level rise as it lies only 15 metres above the mean sea level, with about 30% of the island at less than 5m above the mean sea level. [16]

Rising sea levels increase migration. Residents from coastal areas in emerging market countries will have to move elsewhere. They don't have the ability to erect barriers or install pumps. Some atoll island nations, such as the Maldives, will soon be completely underwater. By 2050, 17% of Bangladesh is likely to be flooded, displacing 18 million people. The Government of Bangladesh has acknowledged that by 2050, one in every 7 people in the country will be displaced by climate change. [17] Residents of the densely populated river valleys of Asia would be forced into already crowded interiors. Rising sea level could create millions of climate refugees in China, India, Indonesia, the Philippines and Vietnam. They may not all be content to stay within their own countries.

Heatwaves

Now let's look at the direct effect of rising temperatures on people. Global average temperature is expected to warm at least twice as much in the next 100 years as it has during the last 100 years. According to the 2018 IPCC report, another half a degree increase, bringing it to 1.5 degrees, will expose 14% of the world's population to extreme heat every 5 years. The number of hot days is projected to increase in most land regions, with the highest frequency in the tropics. The report states that with a 1.5° increase, extreme hot days (in mid-latitudes) will be 3°C warmer, while the coldest nights in high latitudes (i.e. nearer the poles) will be about 4.5°C warmer. [18]

Heat deaths have been explained in a previous chapter. According to a study by The Lancet, extremes of heat have caused a rise in deaths among older populations in every region of the world, with the Western Pacific, South-East Asia and African regions all seeing an increase of more than 10% since 1990. [19]

The London School of Hygiene & Tropical Medicine (LSHTM) published a study, the first that evaluates global temperature-related health impacts under scenarios consistent with the Paris Agreement. They found a net increase in heat deaths was still projected for warmer regions such as South America, southern Europe, and South-East Asia. Some estimates predict up to 152,000 heat deaths yearly in Europe by 2100 if global warming is not restricted to 1.5°. That number is 50 times more deaths than reported now. There is an even more serious situation for India as there is little medical infrastructure to deal with heat stress. In India, heat-waves caused 22,562 deaths between 1992 and 2015. [20]

Australia has a long history of deadly heat waves and since 1950 the annual number of record hot days across Australia has more than doubled. As even more Australians move into urban areas, they are increasingly moving into the inner city, and thus into areas where the urban heat island effect is more likely. Without adaptation, it has been estimated that heat waves could cause an additional 6,214 deaths by 2050. [21]

The USA has problems too, according to the Centers for Disease Control and Prevention. Extreme heat now causes more deaths in U.S. cities than all other weather events combined. A 2017 National Resources Defense Council study looked at how an increase in the number of dangerously hot days will increase the number of heat-related deaths in 45 U.S. cities. According to the estimate, by 2040 there would be more than 13,000 heat-related deaths annually, equating to an average of 150 every summer day. This would double by the 2090s, and the total would then be twice the number of people who are killed by gun violence annually in the U.S. today. [22] New research led by scientists at the University of Miami Rosenstiel School of Marine and Atmospheric Science and NOAA shows that the future holds more heat waves in the U.S., thanks to human-caused climate change. Heat waves will gradually develop over the whole country and it predicts that Californians and residents of Southwestern states could see them as soon as the 2020s; for the Great Lakes, 2030; for the Northern Plains, 2050; and for the Southern Plains, 2070. [23]

Disease

Diseases carried by insects are set to affect more and more people as we head towards an increase of 1.5 degrees. Insects regulate their body temperature by taking in heat from the environment. This means that increases in temperature could help some species survive and incubate in new areas, thereby spreading any disease-causing organisms they carry, such as parasites, bacteria and viruses. Increased rainfall, flooding and humidity create more viable areas for certain insects to breed in, and allows breeding to occur more quickly, as eggs hatch faster in hotter climates.

Vector-borne diseases are human illnesses caused by parasites, viruses and bacteria that are transmitted by mosquitoes, sand flies, triatomine bugs, black flies, ticks, tsetse flies, mites, snails and lice. These major vector-borne diseases together account for around 17% of all infectious diseases. Every year, according to the World Health Organization (WHO), there are between 700,000 and 1 billion deaths globally from diseases such as malaria, dengue, schistosomiasis, yellow fever, Japanese encephalitis and others. This will increase with higher temperatures. [24]

Rising global temperatures can lengthen the season and increase the geographic range of disease-carrying insects. One study reports that tropical climates are spreading both northwards and southwards (away from the equator), and the disease-carrying insects that thrive in these regions are spreading with them. In the past decade, according to the European Centre for Disease Prevention and Control, there have been cases where one of the tropical mosquito species has been implicated in outbreaks of chikungunya and dengue in southern France, Italy and Croatia. Climate assessment has suggested that one species of mosquito which spreads dengue fever, malaria and chikungunya could theoretically live in warmer parts of the UK by 2030. [25]

Droughts and Wildfires

According to the IPCC, around the world, somewhere between 75 million and 820 million hectares of land burn each year. There is also a risk of death from wild fires. It is estimated that the fire season has lengthened by 20% since 1979, due to climate change. Climate models predict that higher temperatures and longer droughts will increase wildfire frequency, particularly in semi-arid regions.[26] In southern Europe hot and dry summers like 2003 are likely to become more common in a warmer world; some scenarios project that by 2080 such conditions could arise every other year.[26]

In Australia drought has persisted for more than a decade in the southeast, setting the stage for catastrophic fires. Research has indicated that fire risk days increase even with a 2°C increase in temperature. I watched on television the bushfires raging at the beginning of 2020.[27]

The USA has problems too. Across the western United States the annual wildfire season has lengthened by 78 days in the last 15 years. The U.S. Forest Service projects that a rise of around 1.5° C in summer could double the wildfire area in 11 western states.[28] In Alaska and Canada the trends of higher temperature, drought and insect outbreaks are predicted to worsen. By the end of the century, the area burned in parts of Canada's northern forest could double, even with a 2°C increase in temperature.[29]

Food

Higher temperatures mean that drought will be more common at 1.5 degrees and this inevitably leads to food shortages, according to the IPCC report. The probability of drought and risks to water availability will be substantially increased if warming is not limited to 1.5°C. Depending on future socio-economic conditions, limiting global warming to 1.5°C, compared to even 2°C, may reduce the proportion of the world population exposed to a climate change-induced increase in water stress by up to 50%, although there is considerable variability between regions. At 1.5 degrees increase, 350 million people worldwide are estimated to be exposed to severe drought. There are projected extreme drought conditions for the Middle East under 1.5°C of global warming. The Mediterranean region will get much drier - including Spain, Portugal, Italy, Greece, Turkey, and the North African coast. In Africa the western Sahel and southern Africa - South Africa, Namibia, and Botswana - will be much drier. Drought will be more frequent in south-western Australia and parts of South America.[30]

One study in 2019 predicted that at 2°C there will be up to 20% increase in drought overall. This will result in increased duration and frequency of drought in virtually the entire African continent, Australia, the Middle East, western India, China, SE Asia, most of South America and the western half of North America.[31] The most important detrimental effect of climate change on agriculture, however, is quite simple – the *direct* influence of the temperature rise itself, manifesting as heat stress. Crops are particularly vulnerable for a specific time period in the growth cycle (the crop's 'thermal sensitive period'). The IPCC have predicted a significant reduction in the global production of wheat, maize and soybean, for each degree Celsius increase in global mean temperature. So the higher the temperature the greater the losses. [32]

Researchers led by the University of Exeter in the UK examined how climate change could affect the vulnerability of different countries to food insecurity – and the ones at the greatest vulnerability when moving from the present-day climate to 2°C global warming. These countries found most vulnerable are Oman, India, Bangladesh, Saudi Arabia and Brazil. [33] Research by The International Food Policy Research Institute shows that by 2050, relative to a world with no climate change, global average crop yields will decline by between 5 and 7%.[34]

According to the IPCC's report from 2014, every decade of warming that happens decreases the amount of food the world can produce by 2%, or 4.4 million metric tons. The IPCC's *Fourth Assessment Report* estimated that, depending on the climate change scenario and socio-economic development path, somewhere between 34 million and 600 million more people could suffer from hunger by 2080.[35] According to a study in the journal *Science*, half of the world's population could face severe food shortages by the end of this century as rising temperatures shorten the growing season in the tropics and subtropics, increase the risk of drought, and reduce the harvests of dietary staples such as rice and maize by up to 40%.[36] In 2017, an estimated 124 million people faced crisis-level food insecurity or worse, up from 108 million in 2016.

The Food and Agriculture Organisation estimates that about one billion people world-wide rely on fish as their primary source of animal protein. Their data suggests that a consistent source of fish is essential for the nutritional and financial health of a large segment of the world's population. But the rise in sea temperature is making some waters too hot for the target fish and they are migrating to cooler waters. People then lose that food supply. [37] The IPCC states that global warming of 1.5°C is projected to shift the ranges of many marine species to higher latitudes as well as to increase the amount of damage to many ecosystems. This effect will be even worse at 2°C. It is also expected to drive the loss of coastal resources and reduce the productivity of fisheries and aquaculture, especially at low latitudes.[38]

Coral reefs are also very important in the life cycle of many fish, because they act as nursery areas for growing fish. 25% of all species of fish are found in coral reefs. 500 million people depend on coral reefs for fish, coastal protection, building materials and tourism. At high sea temperatures the reefs bleach and die. Coral reefs are projected to decline by 70-90% with warming greater than 1.5°C. With an additional half degree of warming to 2°C, more than 99% losses are expected. Latest figures in 2016 show that 20% of coral reefs have already died.[39]

With the oceans absorbing more CO_2 they are becoming more acidic, and this threatens much marine life, including plankton, molluscs, shellfish and corals. As ocean acidification increases, the availability of calcium carbonate will decline. Calcium carbonate is a key building block for the shells and skeletons of many marine organisms. The current rate and magnitude of ocean acidification is at least 10 times faster than any event within the last 65 million years.[40] At temperatures up to 2°C this process will accelerate.

Ocean deoxygenation refers to the loss of oxygen from the oceans due to climate change, caused by the increase in the temperature of the oceans. As a physical rule, warmer water holds less oxygen. As the surface waters warm due to climate change, the ocean loses its ability to hold oxygen, leading to an oxygen decline. Long-term ocean monitoring shows that oxygen concentrations in the ocean have declined during the 20th century and the new IPCC *5th Assessment Report* predicts that they will decrease by 3-6% during the 21st century, in response to surface warming. Oxygen makes up about 21% of the air we breathe and half of this oxygen is produced by phytoplankton in the ocean, which need an appropriate environment to thrive. Species like fish and crustaceans require higher oxygen levels and are highly vulnerable to oxygen declines and so often migrate away from deoxygenated zones and this means there is a loss of food supply. There have been declines in Pacific tuna and cod. Currently Namibia, the Philippines, India, Chile, Peru, and the US are just some of the coastal nations that are vulnerable to the impacts of deoxygenation.[41]

If there is drought, flood, shortage of food and rising sea levels, migration is the only answer to survival. The number of people being displaced by weather-related disasters has more than quadrupled since the 1970s. Since 2008, extreme weather has displaced 22.5 million people, according to the United Nations High Commissioner for Refugees.[42] In 2018 a World Bank report predicted that climate change would displace 143 million people by 2050, mainly from Africa, South Asia and Latin America.[43]

Loss of species

For people like me, who think that all life has a right to exist on this planet, the way climate change will decimate species is shameful. The latest IPPC report states that on land, impacts on biodiversity and ecosystems, including species loss, are projected to be lower at 1.5°C of global warming compared to 2°C. In a 1.5°C scenario, 6% of insects, 8% of plants, and 4% of mammals, birds, reptiles, amphibians, and fish would lose more than half their habitat range. They predict for global warming of 2°C the situation would be far worse, with a loss of 18% of insects, 16% of plants and 8% of vertebrates.[44]

A 2018 study by the University of East Anglia, the James Cook University and the World Wide Fund for Nature (WWF), which analysed the impact of climate change on nearly 80,000 species of plants and animals inhabiting 35 "Priority Places" for conservation, came to some startling conclusions. The good news is that the report stated that limiting global warming to 1.5°C would save the vast majority of the world's plant and animal species from likely extinction caused by climate change. The study looked at the ability of species to move to more suitable locations as the planet warms. Mammals, birds and butterflies have the greatest ability to relocate, which could allow some species to expand their range by 2100. But there were dire warnings for the Amazon, one of the most bio-diverse places on Earth, which could lose about 70% of its plant and amphibian species and more than 60% of its birds, mammals and reptile species from unchecked climate change. Most plants, amphibians and reptiles, such as orchids, frogs and lizards cannot adapt quickly enough to keep up with these climatic changes.[45]

CONCLUSIONS

You can come to your own conclusions but these are mine. Although it will still have a detrimental effect, it seems that the scenario of 1.5°C increase is manageable. The sad thing is that those that suffer the most are those who did not cause the problem in the first place, the world's poor - plus all the innocent species on earth. It is clear then that we should individually and collectively do everything we can in the next 12 years to keep the temperature rise to no more than 1.5 degrees. There is a real role for science and technology here which we can use to decarbonise the economies of the world and even devise machines to extract excess CO_2 from the atmosphere. I remember Nicholas Stern in 2007 warning of the great financial cost of not tackling climate change, but we have ignored this warning and it is certain that there will be an individual and collective economic cost to bringing in the necessary changes. Perhaps we have reached the highest material standard of living today and it will decline in the future. The information in this book gives you the tools to make the necessary changes. The next chapter illustrates what will happen if the information in this book is ignored and we carry on in our mist of delusion.

Chapter 13: GLOBAL WARMING ABOVE 2°C

I was privileged to meet Bill McKibben (who has endorsed this book) and I am inspired by his work. He describes the worst case future scenario in these terms: "Huge swaths of the world will be living in places that by the end of the century will have heat waves so deep that people won't be able to deal with them, you have sea level rising dramatically, to the point that most of the world's cities are drowning, the ocean turning into a hot, sour, breathless soup as it acidifies and warms."[1] I also have deep respect for science journalist Mark Lynas, who endorsed my last book and has written a new book entitled "Our Final Warning - Six Degrees of Climate Emergency." In a business as usual model he sees us reaching 2°C increase by 2030, 3°C by 2050, 4°C by 2075 and possibly 6°C by 2100 when more tipping points come into play.[2] Jonathon Porritt (who has also endorsed this book) in his new book "Hope in Hell - a decade to confront the climate emergency" reminds us that the voluntary commitments of the Paris agreement, if delivered, will result in an increase of temperature of more than 3°C which he describes as "essentially game over for human civilisation."[3]

Right now, we are on track to be living in a world that will be, on average, 3.2°C warmer than pre-industrial levels by 2100. A 3°C degree increase in global temperature – possible as early as 2060 according to a report by the Hadley Centre – would throw the carbon cycle into reverse. Instead of absorbing carbon dioxide, vegetation and soils start to release it. So much carbon pours into the atmosphere that it pumps up atmospheric concentrations by 250 parts per million by 2100, boosting global warming by another 1.5°C. This means that after a 3°C global temperature rise, global warming may run out of control and efforts to mitigate it may be in vain. Millions of square kilometres of Amazon

216

rainforest could burn down, releasing carbon from the wood, leaves and soil and thus making the warming even worse, perhaps by another 1.5°C. A world in which warming reaches 4°C above preindustrial levels, would be one of unprecedented heat waves, severe drought, and major floods in many regions, with serious impacts on human systems, ecosystems, and associated services.[4]

Soil

What becomes clear as the temperature rises is that mechanisms which were a sink for our excess CO_2 become sources of it instead. Take soil for example. A study published in the journal *Nature* calculated that an increase of 1°C in temperature may cause soils to release two to three times the carbon emitted each year by human activity. This will happen more towards 2°C and beyond. As heat increases, soils become a source of carbon rather than a sink. This is because the microbes in the soil release more carbon dioxide with the increase in heat. As the heat is turned up the soils will be heated to a greater depth.[5]

Extreme Weather

Extreme weather will get worse with each degree increase of temperature. Tropical cyclones occur as hurricanes in the northern hemisphere and as typhoons in the southern hemisphere. One primary driver of the planet's increasingly extreme hurricanes is the warming of oceans as we reach over 2°C. Hurricanes can only become more intense. According to research by the Geophysical Fluid Dynamics Laboratory it is likely that greenhouse warming will cause hurricanes in the coming century to be more intense globally and have higher rainfall rates than present-day hurricanes. A new computer model, created at the NOAA's Geophysical Fluid Dynamics Laboratory has predicted that for the period 2016 to 2035, there will be an 11% increase in hurricanes of categories 3, 4, and 5, compared to the late 20th century. Also they predict that the lifetime maximum intensity of Atlantic hurricanes will increase by about 5% during the 21st century. This will have a massive effect on property and people near the coast through rising sea levels accompanied by powerful storm surges.[6]

As regards typhoons, research has shown that the intensification of typhoons making landfall occurs because warmer coastal seas provide more energy to growing storms, enabling their wind speeds to increase more rapidly. The destructive power of the typhoons that wreak havoc across China, Japan, Korea and the Philippines has intensified by 50% in the past 40 years due to warming seas, a new study has found.[6] The researchers warn that global warming will lead to the giant storms becoming even stronger in the future, threatening the large and growing coastal populations of those nations. Research has indicated that there will be an increase in typhoon intensity in the Pacific Basin in this century. Cyclones, including hurricanes and typhoons, are now moving across the planet at a slower pace than they did decades ago, dragging out and amplifying their devastation. This means they have time to drop more rain, leading to devastating flooding.[7]

With more severe climate change there will be changes to the hydrological cycles associated with severe risks of floods and droughts. Heavy downpours that currently occur about once every 20 years are projected to occur between twice and five times as frequently by 2100, depending on the location. The moisture in the air changes depending on temperature: heat that air by 1°C and it can hold approximately 7% more water. Research has shown that precipitation rates are increasing between 5% and 10% for every degree Celsius increase. In the tropics, there is more than a 10% increase in precipitation for each degree Celsius increase in temperature. Depending on how resilient a natural or a man-made landscape is, heavier rain could exacerbate floods that disrupt traffic and transportation, overburden storm water and runoff systems, damage property and infrastructure, and reduce crop yields due to excess water or field flooding, among other impacts.[8]

Wetter conditions are projected in particular for the northern high latitudes - that is, northern North America, northern Europe, and Siberia - and in some monsoon regions. Rain will fall even more intensely over shorter periods if warming is above 2°C, increasing the flood risk. At 4°C, according to one study, a large area of south and east Asia, equatorial Africa and South America will see floods increase and 62 million more people will be exposed to regular flooding.[9]

According to the European Environment Agency, projections show an increase in heavy daily precipitation in most parts of Europe in winter, by up to 35% during the 21st century.[11] According to one study at 3°C flooding is estimated to affect 780,000 people in Northern Europe.[12]

We can also look at the USA. Across most of the United States, the heaviest rainfall events have become heavier and more frequent. Extreme downpours - like those that flooded Louisiana, Houston and West Virginia in 2019 - will happen nearly three times as often in the United States by the end of the century, and six times more frequently in parts of the Mississippi delta, according to a new study. The number of summertime storms that produce extreme downpours could increase by more than 180% by 2100.[13] The amount of rain falling on the heaviest rain days has also increased over the past few decades. By mid-century, some places could experience two or more additional days per year on which the rainfall totals exceed the heaviest rains historically experienced in the area.[14]

Rising Sea Levels

The sea levels are rising because of thermal expansion of ocean waters due to rising temperatures, as well as due to melting of glaciers and polar ice. Flooding will be exacerbated by sea level rise. Estimated figures for sea level rise vary widely in the research, because nobody can predict accurately the rate at which sea levels will rise, although we are certain it will happen in the lifetimes of most people alive today.

Even back in 2012 a report by the World Bank in 2012 predicted that if the currently-planned actions are not fully implemented, a warming of 4°C could occur as early as the 2060s. Such a warming level would not be the end point: a further warming to levels over 6°C would be likely to occur over the following centuries. With 4°C increase, it is predicted that both poles are certain to melt causing an eventual sea rise of 50 metres. Warming of 4°C will likely lead to a sea-level rise of 0.5 to 1 metre and possibly more, by 2100. [15]

If the world sees warming above 2°C, then ice sheet collapse in Antarctica becomes far more likely. 2°C of global warming above the preindustrial level is widely suggested as the threshold beyond which climate change risks become unacceptably high. According to some research in 2016, this 2°C threshold is likely to be reached between 2040 and 2050. Warming of above 2°C will lead to an average global ocean rise of 20 cm (8 ins), but more than 90% of coastal areas will experience greater rises.[16] If warming continues above 2°C, then, by 2100, sea level will be rising faster than at any time during human civilisation. The IPCC

Fifth Assessment Report estimates that under high emissions, sea levels may rise between 0.52m and 0.98m (20 to 39 inches) by 2100.[17] A report quoted in the Scientific American magazine predicted that sea levels may rise by about 2.3 metres for each degree Celsius of global warming within the next 2000 years.[18]

The rate of rise of sea level will be dependent on melting ice at both poles. Anders Levermann, leading a study by the Potsdam Institute for Climate Impact Research in 2020, found that if the warming temperature goes beyond 2°C degrees centigrade then the Antarctic rate of melting ice doubles. The study found that at 2°C of warming, the melting and the accelerated ice flow into the ocean will, eventually, entail 2.5 metres of global sea level rise just from Antarctica alone. Further melting at 4°C will yield a 6.5 metres of sea level and at 6°C almost 12 metres. Levermann commented : "If we give up the Paris Agreement, we give up Hamburg, Tokyo and New York."[19]

At 4°C we are heading to an eventual ice-free planet. A 2-4 metre rise in sea level per century could be possible with tipping points coming into play with Greenland, West Antarctic and majority of East Antarctic gone. Over 10,000 years there could be a sea level rise of 30-40 metres.[20] Another piece of research tried to predict what would happen at 5°C. They forecast a 12-15 metre rise in sea level by 2500. They further calculated that if the entire Antarctica ice sheets melts in 10,000 years this could yield a 50 metre sea level rise.[21]

Flooding

Flooding is the inevitable result of rising sea levels. A 2020 study by Melbourne University found that in a high emissions scenario of "business as usual" where there are poor flood defences built, there will be an increase of 48% of the world's land area, 52% of the global population and 46% of global assets at risk of flooding by 2100. A total of 68% of the global coastal area flooded will be caused by tide and storm events. North West Europe, South East England, the east coast of the USA and the Bay of Bengal region of India are identified as most at risk.[22] Another report in 2018 predicted that at 5°C, 2 million sq. km. of land would be inundated and 800 million people flooded out of their homes.[23]

Whichever figure is taken, this is a serious problem for the large populations of the world who live near the coast, especially in cities.

Ashley Dawson in his book *"Extreme Cities"* has calculated that 2 billion, or 38%, of the world's population live near coasts prone to flooding. Also 500 million live in river deltas prone to flooding because there is a subsidence of 10cm a year at the same time as the sea levels are rising. Half a billion people live in mega cities near the coasts.[24]

Among all nations affected, a report by Climate Central found that China has the most to lose from a lack of action on emissions, because sea level rises resulting from 4°C of warming could risk 145 million of its citizens being inundated. The report found that 12 other nations have more than 10 million people living on land that could be inundated due to 4°C warming - India, Bangladesh, Vietnam, Indonesia, Japan, the United States, Philippines, Egypt, Brazil, Thailand, Myanmar, and the Netherlands, in descending order of total threats. For example, 17 million people would be flooded in Bangladesh.

Global megacities in developing nations with the top ten populations under threat of flooding include Shanghai, Hong Kong, Calcutta, Mumbai, Dhaka, Jakarta, and Hanoi. 4°C warming could lead to submergence of land inhabited by more than half the population of Shanghai, Mumbai and Hanoi. The numbers of people affected in developing countries are staggering. 17.5 million people living in Shanghai could be displaced by rising waters if global temperatures increase by 3°C. Jakarta is the second largest metropolitan area and is sinking at 7.5cm (3ins) a year. It will be affected badly by a 4°C rise and threaten flooding to 30 million people. Also Alexandria and the Nile Delta region could be flooded by even a 3°C rise in temperature, displacing 8 million people.[25] By 2060, there could be about 1.4 billion climate refugees because of rising sea levels, estimates Charles Geisler, Professor Emeritus of Development Sociology at Cornell University. By 2100, the number might be as high as 2 billion - about a fifth of the world's anticipated population.[26]

The developed world will not escape the devastation and human displacement. We can consider some specific examples of nations and cities affected. The Trump climate-denying administration in the USA may have left a legacy of suffering and hardship for millions of American citizens. According to Jeff Goodell in his book *"The Water Will Come"*, already New York sea level rise is 50% faster than the global average. Eventually 400,000 people in the New York area will be susceptible to flooding and this will probably bring to an end its role as a global financial centre. Even at 3°C warming, Miami, home to 2.7 million people, would simply cease to exist. At above 2°C, forecasts show almost the entire southern third of Florida - currently home to more than 7 million people - will be submerged. In New Orleans an estimated 500,000 people could have to leave the area in the next century to stay above sea level.[27]

In my own country of the UK we have experienced significant flooding. At temperature increases of 3°C and above, the Lancashire/Humber corridor is expected to be among the worst affected regions for flooding, as would be the Thames Valley, eastern Devon and towns around the already flood-prone Severn estuary, like Monmouth and Bristol. The entire English coast from the Isle of Wight to Middlesbrough would be at risk from flooding as would be the whole of Cardigan Bay in Wales.[28]

Heatwaves

Four billion people live in hot areas worldwide. We have talked about heat deaths earlier. As the temperature climbs, fatalities will increase. A heatwave is often defined as a hot outdoor temperature or hot weather that lasts for several days, and is outside the normal range of ambient temperatures. Extreme heat is dangerous because it stresses the human body, potentially leading to heat exhaustion or heat stroke and sometimes death. This is especially so in cities - where the majority of humanity live - as they will be hotter than the surrounding countryside. If we do not get our emissions under control according to one study they found that at 4°C world global exposure to extreme heat increases 30 fold with 75% of the entire world population being exposed to deadly heat at least 20 days a year.[29]

Heatwave-related excess mortality is expected to increase most in tropical and subtropical countries/regions (close to the equator), while European countries and the United States less so. According to research by the WHO carried out in 2014, in which they compared projected heat deaths in 2030 and 2050, there are startling statistical increases if emissions are not curtailed and therefore temperatures rise. They found that the global estimate for increases in heat-related deaths (each year) was 92,207 for 2030 and 255,486 additional deaths for 2050. The relative increase in excess deaths from 2030 to 2050 is large in sub-Saharan African regions, Latin America, and south/south-east Asia.[30]

According to the Fifth IPCC report of 2014, over the mid-term (2046–2065), an increase of 2 to 4°C is projected for Asia, with the warmest temperatures concentrated in Iraq, Saudi Arabia, Iran, Russia, China, Mongolia, Nepal and Bhutan. Over the long-term (2081–2100), an increase of 4 to 6°C is projected over similar areas.

As temperatures climb over 2°C in South East Asia, unusual heat extremes in summer will cover a majority of the land surface for longer periods. As the planet warms, a crescent-shaped area encompassing parts of India, Pakistan, Bangladesh, and the North China Plain, where about 1.5 billion people (a fifth of humanity) live, is at high risk of experiencing much higher temperatures in the next half century.[31]

This will greatly affect people who work outside in agriculture or in factories, slowing down their rate of productivity. One study projected that if higher temperatures are reached, heat stress threatened to cut labour productivity in SE Asia by up to 25% within 30 years. It further predicted the biggest losses in productivity in Singapore and Malaysia, with about 25% decreases from current levels. The number of extreme heat days will increase, making working difficult or impossible. The study projected that under a high emissions scenario, by 2045 the number of heat stress days in both Singapore and Malaysia would rise to 364, and to 355 days for Indonesia and 337 days for the Philippines.[32]

So-called "wet bulb" temperatures take humidity into account, providing a better measure of potential health impacts. To measure the wet bulb temperature a damp cloth is put around the bulb of the thermometer to introduce the aspect of humidity. Experts estimate that a healthy adult may not survive outdoors at "wet bulb" temperature of 35°C for more than six hours. This is because if the wet bulb temperature exceeds the human body's skin temperature of 35°C, perspiration no longer works as a cooling mechanism and therefore the body will quickly overheat, resulting in death. An example is that at 55% relative humidity, it would take a searing air temperature of 44.4°C to reach the 35°C wet bulb threshold. This is just the sort of temperature that would be reached at 2°C extra warming and above.

One study looked at the wet bulb predictions for South Asia. Under the business-as-usual scenario of future greenhouse gas emissions they projected that extremes of wet-bulb temperature in South Asia were likely to approach and in a few locations exceed, the critical 35°C threshold by the late 21st century. The most intense hazard from extreme future heat waves is concentrated around densely populated agricultural regions of the Ganges and Indus river basins. In an agrarian economy, like India, this would have a devastating effect on producing food and providing an income from agriculture as people would be severely restricted as to how many hours they could work on the land.[33]

China is the largest developing country, and has a faster increase in surface air temperature than the global average. The elderly population is increasing and will continue to increase further in the 21st century. According to an IPCC study, in a worst case scenario mainland China will see a 308% increase in heat deaths.[34]

Heat waves in the North China Plain - China's breadbasket - are predicted to become so severe, they would limit habitability in the most populous region of 400 million people. One study predicted that these heat waves would emerge between 2070 and 2100. They predicted that they would see a 3 to 4°C increase in wet bulb temperature by 2100 under a business-as-usual emissions scenario. This is very serious as China is basically an agrarian economy and if people cannot work outside they cannot produce food. This would result in the double whammy of food shortages and unemployment. The third factor is that if the 400 million cannot survive in the area, where will they move to?[35]

Over the last 30 years, on average, exposure to extreme heat was the top cause of weather-related deaths in the United States. In the United States, the number of individuals of 65 years of age and older (who are more susceptible to heat effects) is expected to increase from 12.4% in 2000 to 20% in 2060. The Union of Concerned Scientists produced a report in 2019 looking at the predictions for the heat index temperatures over the whole country. The heat index is a measure of how hot it really feels when relative humidity is factored in with the actual air temperature. They found that in the worst case scenarios, where there is more than 2°C of warming, the number of days per year above 40.5°C heat index would quadruple, whereas the average number of days per year with a heat index above 37°C will more than double. Assuming no changes in population, the number of people experiencing 30 or more days with a heat index above 40°C in an average year will increase from just under 900,000 to more than 90 million - nearly one-third of the US. This would include 60% of the urban areas.[36]

In the USA, above 2°C there will be further warming in the south west and Midwest. One recent study predicted that if 4°C is reached then

224

virtually all of Texas, Oklahoma, Kansas, Missouri and Arkansas will experience peak temperatures exceeding Death Valley conditions every year.[37] The Midwest is home to more than 61 million people who largely reside in cities, including Chicago, Indianapolis, Detroit, Milwaukee, Kansas City, Cincinnati, Cleveland, Minneapolis and St. Paul. A report in 2009 by the Union of Concerned Scientists predicted that on a high emissions scenario, by mid-century Cincinnati would experience a heat wave comparable to the 1995 Chicago heat wave nearly every year and Cleveland would experience one every three years. Projections for Indianapolis and Chicago show that these cities are very likely to suffer a heat wave comparable to the 2003 European heat wave in the next several decades. Under the higher-emissions scenario a heat wave of this magnitude would occur at least every five years by mid-century, and every other year toward the end of the century.[38]

The Southwest is the hottest and driest region in the USA, extending from the Pacific Ocean east to the Rocky Mountains and south to the Mexican border. This region is home to about 56 million people, about 90% of whom live in cities, including Albuquerque, Phoenix, Las Vegas, Salt Lake City, Denver, San Diego, Los Angeles, Sacramento and San Francisco. The population of the Southwest is expected to increase by nearly 70% by mid-century. Heat deaths in urban areas are bound to increase if temperatures rise above 2°C, especially because some have high elderly populations. One study in 2012 found that major urban centres in California could have a greater than tenfold increase in heat-related mortality in the over 65 age group by the 2090s.[39]

Because urban areas absorb and retain heat they are centres for future heat deaths. One study of 12 US cities found that nearly 200,000 heat-related deaths are projected to occur in these cities by the end of the century due to climate warming under a high emissions pathway and therefore a higher than 2°C increase in temperature. Twelve northern US cities with populations over 250,000 were selected for evaluation because of their potential for vulnerability to future heat-related fatality risks under a changing climate. These were Washington DC, Chicago, Detroit, Minneapolis/St. Paul, Cincinnati, Cleveland, Columbus, Toledo, Portland, Philadelphia, and Pittsburgh. Already by the 2020s, most cities will show increases in the 20% to 30% range. By the 2050s, deaths could increase by as much as 50% to 70% for some cities. Even higher impacts could be seen by the 2080s.[40] In a more recent study they found that if the global average temperature rises 3°C above pre-industrial levels, future heat waves could claim 6,000 lives in New York City, 2,500 in Los Angeles and 2,300 in Miami every year.[41]

Let's look at the future situation in Europe. In the last two decades Europe has experienced a series of high-impact heat extremes. According to the European Environment Agency, if emissions are not curtailed, and by implication the temperature increases above 2°C, they estimate that heat-related mortality in Europe will increase by between 60,000 and 165,000 deaths per year by the 2080s compared with the present baseline, with the highest impacts in southern Europe.[42] In a study in *The Lancet Planetary Health* in 2017, their findings suggested that if emissions are not cut - and therefore the likelihood is of temperature increases over 2°C - heat waves would be the most lethal weather-related disaster and could cause 99% of all future weather-related deaths in Europe - rising from 2,700 deaths a year between 1981 and 2010 to 151,500 deaths a year in 2071 to 2100.[43]

In the U.K., research done by the Committee on Climate Change in 2017 predicted between 700 and 1,000 more heat-related deaths per year in south-east England. It also stated that heatwave events such as that in 2003 are projected to become the norm in the UK by the 2040s if there are not sufficient emissions reductions.[44] In 2018 there was a report given to Parliament by the Committee on Climate Change stating that the average number of heat-related deaths in Britain will more than triple to 7,000 a year by the 2050s if emissions are not tackled.[45]

Disease

Vector-borne diseases are caused by pathogens transmitted among hosts by intermediate species, primarily arthropods such as mosquitoes or ticks. Mosquitoes are some of the deadliest creatures in the world because of the many diseases they can transmit. Mosquito-borne diseases include the Zika virus, dengue, malaria, West Nile virus, chikungunya, yellow fever, and more. We discussed earlier the health risks from the spread of vector-borne diseases up to 2°C increase in temperature. Generally as the temperature rises above that limit the range where vector-borne diseases are found increases.

Some research has found that current emissions scenarios, producing over 2°C of warming, will sometime in the next 50 years result in 1 billion more people being exposed not just to dengue and yellow fever, but to emerging diseases such as chikungunya, Zika, West Nile and Japanese encephalitis, all carried by just two species of mosquito. Also predicted is that within 80 years the health of twice as many people as today could face a serious mosquito risk, not only in the tropics.[46]

Dengue fever and dengue haemorrhagic fever are important arthropod-borne viral diseases. Rising temperatures attributed to climate change have increased concerns that dengue will intensify in already endemic areas through faster reproduction and biting rates, ultimately leading to longer transmission seasons and a greater number of human infections, more of which are expected to be severe. Increasing temperatures over 2°C may further exacerbate this situation by enabling greater spread and transmission in low-risk or currently dengue-free parts of Asia, Europe, North America and Australia. A study in 2019 predicted that there may be a billion more people at risk of dengue in 2080 compared to 2015, bringing the total population at risk to over 6.1 billion, or 60% of the world's population. The areas most affected by the increase in dengue would be southern Mexico, the Caribbean, Ecuador, Colombia, Venezuela and the coastal regions of Brazil.[47]

Malaria has been declining thanks to efforts by Bill and Melinda Gates and other donors. One study suggests that with progressive global warming, malaria will creep up the mountains and spread to highlands in East Africa and South America. The problem is that people who live in these areas have no protective immunity because they are not used to being exposed to malaria. They will therefore be particularly vulnerable to more severe and fatal cases of infection. This will of course be more profound with temperatures over 2°C.[48]

Droughts and Wildfires

Boreal forests and Arctic tundra cover 33% of the global land area and together store an estimated 50% of the total soil carbon. According to the IPCC, as the climate warms, there is a general expectation that fire activity will increase in many flammable landscapes, with associated increases in severity and a lengthening of the fire season. Many studies indicate that fire frequency, extent, and severity will increase significantly in many regions, including North and South America, central Asia, southern Europe, southern Africa and Australia. As temperatures climb above 2°C, the danger of death from wild fires becomes more likely. Not only do wildfires threaten lives directly, but wildfire smoke can linger in the atmosphere long after the fire has been controlled, and can contain carbon monoxide, lung-damaging particulates, and toxic, volatile organic compounds.

Projections indicate that the wildfire frequency and burned area in North America will continue to increase over the 21st century due to climate change. According to the United States Forestry Service their research has shown a predicted increase in wildfires in the Southwest, the Rocky Mountains, northern Great Plains, the Southeast, and Pacific coast. The effects of these fires will be most pronounced in summer and autumn, mainly caused by future warming trends. Fire seasons will become longer in many areas. These effects will be profound, as the IPCC projects that by 2050, summer temperatures in the U.S. West will increase between 2°C and 5°C.[49]

Alaskan tundra and forest wildfires would increase under warmer and drier conditions. One study made the prediction that the total area burned would increase between 25% and 53% by 2100.[50] Another study of the whole of the northern boreal forests and tundra found that in 43% of the region the probability of burning is projected to more than double by mid-century, if emissions rise.[51]

In Australia fire frequency and intensity of wildfires is expected to increase substantially in coming decades, because of long-term drought coupled with higher temperatures and low humidity. This will be especially in those regions currently most affected by bushfires, such as southern and eastern Australia, where a substantial proportion of the human population live. The country's summers are now typically a month longer than they were in the 1950s. By 2070, warming is projected to be 2.2 to 5.0°C for a high emissions scenario.[52] According to World Weather Attribution, future predictions by some climate models say that a Fire Weather Index at the 2019/20 level would be at least four times more likely with a 2°C temperature rise, compared with 1900, commenting that this is likely an underestimate.[53]

Food

Drought results from below-normal precipitation, often combined with warm temperatures, over a period of months to years. It often causes extensive damage to crops and natural ecosystems, creates water shortages, and increases risks of heat waves, wildfires and of course land turning into deserts. According to one 2018 study, at 4°C half of the worlds surface area will be classified as arid.[54] Another study in 2019 predicted that in a 4°C world an additional 3 billion people will suffer from water stress.[55] Drought is one of the four horsemen of the Apocalypse. According to the American Meteorological Society, the frequency of moderate to severe agricultural drought could increase by 50%-100% by the 2090s over most of the Americas, Europe, and southern Africa and parts of East and West Asia and Australia.[56]

Water scarcity already affects more than 40% of the world's population, according to the U.N.'s 2019 *World Water Development Report*. The United Nations estimates that by 2025, half of the countries worldwide will face water stress or outright shortages. That number is expected to rise due to global warming, with one in four people projected to face chronic or recurring shortages by 2050, it added. By 2050 there is a predicted increase of 20 to 30% above the current level of water use, mainly due to rising demand in the industrial and domestic sectors.[57] According to the World Bank, within the next three decades demand for water from agriculture could increase by 50%, and for urban uses by between 50% and 70%. Meanwhile, by 2035, the energy sector is projected to consume 85% more water.[58] According to a recent IPCC report, risks from droughts and precipitation deficits are projected to be higher at 2°C compared to 1.5°C of global warming in some regions.[59]

The Middle East and North Africa is the most water-scarce region in the world. According to a report by the World Resources Institute in 2019, 12 out of the 17 most water-stressed countries in the world are in the Middle East or North Africa.[60] Over 60% of the region's population lives in areas with high or very high surface water stress, compared with a global average of about 35%. And with temperatures set to increase across the region above 2°C this will get worse. Across the Middle East and North Africa, the lack of surface flows and reliance on non-renewable groundwater reserves for irrigation makes agriculture especially vulnerable to predicted warming across the region. The countries of Iraq, Qatar, Kuwait, Saudi Arabia and the UAE, Yemen, Lebanon, Jordan, Israel, Syria, Bahrain, Oman, Eritrea and Morocco will all experience significant increases in surface water stress driven by climate change. Projections from climate models based on temperatures exceeding 2°C almost uniformly point toward drying in the Middle East and North Africa, and suggest that the region will experience more severe and intense droughts.[61]

Sub-Saharan Africa is particularly susceptible to drought since more than 90% of the economy depends on a climate-sensitive natural resource base such as rain-fed, subsistence agriculture. At 3.5°C, southern Africa and most of West Africa is expected to experience reductions of up to 50% in water available for agriculture. East Africa, Angola, the Democratic Republic of Congo, South Africa and most of West Africa, are expected to become water scarce. The main impacts of the drought in this region are death of livestock and poor crop yields leading to widespread hunger. Research has shown that yield potential, particularly along the margins of arid and semi-arid areas, is expected to decrease as rising temperatures makes land likely to turn to desert.[62] A Massachusetts Institute of Technology report found, in a paper published online in the journal *Earth's Future*, that by 2080 Africa generally is expected to experience marked reductions in yield, decreases in production, and increases in the risk of hunger as a result of climate change. Generally, crop yields in Africa may fall by 10–20% by 2050 because of increases of temperature but there are places where yield losses may be much more severe. For instance, maize is a very important subsistence crop and the researchers reported that, if the world's average temperatures rise by 4°C by the year 2100, much of southern Africa and the Sahel region (just south of the Sahara desert) - regions that contribute a significant portion of Africa's maize production - will experience increased aridity, which in turn is predicted to decrease maize crop yields in some nations by over 20%. In fact future warming increases the probability of globally synchronized maize production shocks. The most pessimistic simulations predict a 30% reduction in maize production in southern Africa by 2090.[63]

China is also very vulnerable to drought if temperatures rise above 2°C. According to research by the International Food Policy Research Institute, seasonal drought driven by climate change could lead to substantial losses of nearly 8% in China by 2030 in yields of three main crops - rice, wheat and maize. Typically, a 1°C increase in temperature in the full growth cycle can reduce the growth period of rice by nearly 4 days, wheat by 10 days, and maize by 7 days. This could reduce yields of wheat by 4%, yields of maize by 3% and yields of rice by 2%. If emissions are not held to 2°C or under by the latter third of the 21st century, when global temperatures are predicted to be more than 3°C higher than now,

China's agricultural production could crash, causing widespread hunger and migration of climate refugees.[64]

Drought is projected to increase over north-western India, Pakistan, and Afghanistan. India is one of the most water-challenged countries in the world, including its deepest aquifers and its largest rivers. According to the World Resource Institute, groundwater levels are falling as India's farmers, city residents and industries drain wells and aquifers. What water is available is often severely polluted. A future of increasing temperatures above 2°C will result in more droughts of greater frequency and increased length. The dire fact is that the national supply of water is predicted to fall 50% below demand by 2030. This will have an effect on future food supply as north-west India (its breadbasket) suffers increasing water stress. The states of Punjab and Haryana alone produce 50% of the rice and 85% of the wheat. Both crops are highly water intensive.[65] A report by the World Economic Forum stated that by 2030, it is predicted that 40% of the Indian population will have no access to drinking water - and 21 cities, including Chennai and New Delhi, will run out of groundwater, impacting 100 million people.[66]

Hungry people move and so the refugee crisis is set to get worse above 2°C warming. It is estimated by UNCCD that 135 million people are at risk of being displaced by desertification. UNCCD predict that by 2025, 2.4 billion people will live in water-stressed areas and this might displace 700 million people by 2030.[67] A World Bank report of 2018 focused on three regions - Sub-Saharan Africa, South Asia, and Latin America - as regions of internal migration. It projected that by 2050, without a significant emissions reduction, just over 143 million people of these three regions could be forced to move within their own countries to escape the slow-onset impacts of climate change. Drought could be a major factor.[68]

Loss of Species

The predicted extinction of many species will not go away but if temperatures climb above 2°C it will be accelerated with devastating consequences for all species. According to Richard Pearson of the Natural History Museum in London, after each previous mass extinction event it took 10 million years to rebuild the former levels of diversity.[69] According to Elizabeth Kolbert, extinction is a part of evolution, but biologists calculate that it is now happening at least a thousand times faster than the average rate for the past 500 million years.[70] We humans destroy wildlife habitats at an alarming rate through agriculture and urbanisation, so much so that in 2018 it was estimated that only 23% of the habitable land surface area remains as undisturbed wilderness. When we add climate change into the mix the picture gets worse.

The geographic ranges of most plant and animal species are limited by climatic factors, including temperature, precipitation, wind strength, soil moisture and humidity. Any shift in the magnitude or variability of these factors in a given location will impact the organisms living there. Species sensitive to temperature may respond to a warmer climate by moving to cooler locations at higher latitudes or elevations. If species cannot disperse fast enough they will die out. This is more likely with a temperature increase above 2°C. Also with natural events in spring and summer occurring earlier, plants and different animal species are becoming out of sync, leading to concerns that food will not be available when creatures need it. This lack of food supply could make species extinct.

As the temperature rise goes above 2°C ecosystems are gravely affected and species die out at an alarming rate. In 2020 a study gave a depressing prediction that in just 50 years' time, a third of all plant and animal species on our planet could be wiped out due to man-made climate change, if emissions rise unabated.[71] A 2015 study found that if temperatures rise to 4.3 °C then up to one in six species would become extinct. This would be highest in South America at 23% and 14% for Australia and New Zealand.[72]

In 2020 another new study by researchers from the University of Arizona presented detailed estimates of global extinction from climate change by 2070. They studied 538 species at 581 sites around the globe. The study identified maximum annual temperatures – the hottest daily highs in summer – as the key variable that best explains whether a population will become extinct. The new research indicates most species will not be able to disperse or adapt to the change in climate quickly enough to avoid extinction. About 95% of the species had local extinctions if maximum temperatures increased by more than 2.9°C. Professor Wiens who led the study said, "If humans cause larger temperature increases, we could lose more than a third or even half of all animal and plant species, based on our results." In the study the projections of species loss are similar for plants and animals - but

232

extinctions are projected to be two to four times more common in the tropics where the majority of plant and animal species live - than in temperate regions.[73]

Another study in 2018 looked at 35 "Priority Places" around the globe, which have been scientifically identified as being home to irreplaceable and threatened biodiversity. They analysed the ability of species to adapt to climate changes by dispersal. They studied 80,000 species of plants, mammals, birds, reptiles and amphibians. Most plants, amphibians and reptiles, such as orchids, frogs and lizards, cannot adapt quickly enough keep up with climatic changes. They found that in the worst case scenario, which would mean temperatures rising to 4.5°C, up to half of plant and animal species in these naturally-rich areas, such as the Amazon and the Galapagos, could face local extinction by the turn of the century.[74]

Recent research suggests that large-scale loss of biodiversity is likely to occur with a temperature increase of 4°C. At 6°C warming and above, we can look to what happens by looking at the end of the Permian period, 251 million years ago. This was not caused by humans of course, but 95% of species were wiped out, almost certainly by climate change. The immediate cause of this was probably a huge series of volcanic eruptions. This episode was the worst ever endured by life on Earth, the closest the planet has come so far to ending up as a dead and desolate rock in space.

Insects are a crucial part of any ecosystem on land. The insects comprise two-thirds of all the species of life on Earth – they pollinate flowering plants, decompose waste, control pests and serve as prey for many other species. According to research in 2019 by Sánchez Bayo of Sydney and Queensland University, more than 40% of the world's insects could go extinct in the next few decades. He gave a terrifying prediction that, "In 10 years you will have a quarter less, in 50 years only half left and in 100 years you will have none." This would be a devastating blow to everything that relies on them.[75]

The oceans are where life came from. One of the most serious consequences of rising carbon dioxide concentration in the atmosphere occurs when it dissolves in the ocean and results in acidification. Water which is more acidic can corrode minerals that many marine creatures rely on to build their protective shells and skeletons, so they die out. Zooplankton are very small creatures and almost all larger life eats zooplankton or other animals that eat zooplankton. Evidence suggests that increasing acidity kills off zooplankton and hence the food supply for larger species. In higher emission scenarios, by the end of this century the average ocean would be about 1.5 times more acidic than the waters were before industrialisation.[76] Another problem is that bleaching kills off coral reefs. This can occur when corals are subject to sea surface temperatures only 1 to 2°C above long-term average maximum temperatures, so temperatures above 2°C will be catastrophic. The research group Coral Watch at Queensland University says all reefs will disappear by 2050 if temperatures continue to rise.[77]

CONCLUSIONS

This is a grim picture but it can be avoided if we start to act individually and collectively to change the system: as the motto says, "System Change not Climate Change." What people need is information about what is happening around climate change so that they can make an informed choice of how to respond. At the moment the message is not being understood or getting through. What we need is the political will to make great changes to our economic system so that instead of the exploitative model we replace it with the sustainability model. A sick patient does not get better by being given ineffective medicine. If we do not match the disease with the cure then the patient dies and in this case that means we humans, plus most of the other species we share this planet with. We do not want our legacy as a species to be that we allowed cockroaches to inherit the earth.

As individuals we need to act now. It is up to us to make the necessary changes to our lifestyle and to put pressure on governments and businesses (in whatever way) to make the drastic changes which are necessary as soon as possible. The time is now.

Part 4

The Final Word
of
Hope

Chapter 14: SPIRITUAL GUIDANCE ON HOW TO LEAD A CLIMATE-FRIENDLY LIFE

If you have read the last two chapters outlining possible future scenarios you may have begun to feel despair. However, this chapter shows that we can really make a difference and that we can build a better future for all of us. The secret is found in the collections of these spiritual words emphasising that we need to live by spiritual values – if we do not, then the likely outcome is that materialistic consumerist values will lead us to extinction.

These spiritual words are grouped under the following headings:

- **How to be Satisfied**

- **Creating Good Karma**

- **Achieving Balance and Harmony**

- **Connecting with Nature**

- **The Importance of Doing Good**

- **Finding Deeper Happiness**

- **Practising Love and Compassion**

Some of the extracts in the first four sections are also found in the first chapter of this book. They serve as a reminder of the spiritual advice in that opening chapter, which explained the underlying spiritual causes of climate change.

HOW TO BE SATISFIED

If we address any greed which arises within ourselves and live in moderation, then our behaviour will not contribute to climate change.

Christianity

"What good will it do for a man if he gains the whole world, yet forfeits his soul." (Matthew 16:26)

"If you want to be perfect, go, sell your possessions and give to the poor and you will have treasure in heaven. Then come, follow me." (Matthew 19:21)

"The love of money is the root of all evils and there are some who, pursuing it, have wandered away from the faith and so given their souls any number of fatal wounds." St. Paul (Timothy 6:10)

"No one can be a slave to two masters: he will hate one and love the other; he will be loyal to one and despise the other. You cannot serve both God and money." Jesus (Matthew 6:24)

"Watch out! Be on your guard against all kinds of greed; a man's life does not consist in the abundance of his possessions." (Luke 12:15)

"Do not save riches here on Earth, where moths and rust destroy and robbers break in and steal. Instead save riches in heaven, where moths and rust cannot destroy and robbers cannot break in and steal." Jesus (Matthew 6:19-20)

"Give and it will be given to you. A good measure, pressed down, shaken together and running over, will be poured into your lap. For with the measure you use, it will be measured to you." (Luke 6:37-38)

"The suffering of some can be blamed on the greed of others." Mother Teresa

Judaism

"You shall not set your heart on your neighbour's house. You shall not set your heart on your neighbour's spouse, or servant, man or woman, or ox, or donkey, or any of your neighbour's possessions." Ten Commandments (Exodus 20:17)

"You shall have no other Gods to rival me." Ten Commandments (Exodus 20:3)

"Wealth may be like waters gathered in a house, which, finding no outlet, drown the owner." The Talmud

"Although the pursuit of money, love and power provide temporary satisfaction, nothing is as satisfying as pursuing a relationship with the Infinite." Rabbi Noach Weinberg

"Just as Death and Destruction are never satisfied, so human desire is never satisfied." (Proverbs 27:20)

"For what is the hope of the hypocrite, though he hath gained, when God taketh away his soul?" (Job 27:8)

"Be moderate in all things." The Talmud

Islam

"Refrain from greed for those who were before you perished as a result of greed. Greed commanded them to be stingy and they obeyed: it ordered them into alienation and they obeyed; and it commanded them to sin and they sinned." (Nahj Al-Fasahah)

"Oh you who have believed let not your wealth and your children divert you from remembrance of Allah." (Qur'an 63:9)

"The richest of the rich is one who is not a prisoner of greed." Imam Ali

"He is not a believer who eats his fill while his neighbour remains hungry by his side." (Hadith Baihaqi)

"Allah created the earth and all that is in it – it is people's heritage." (Qur'an, 6:165; 2:256-7)

"And what is the worldly life except the enjoyment of delusion." (Qur'an 57:20)

"Anyone who has property that exceeds his needs, let him support someone whose property does not (meet his or her needs), and anyone whose food exceeds his needs, let him share it with someone who does not have food." (Fiqh-us-Sunnah, Volume 3, Number 93C.)

"Greed is permanent slavery" Hazrat Aliibn Abi Talibas

"..But people are prone to selfish greed. If you do good and have faith, Allah is aware of what you do." (Qur'an an Nisa.128)

"You are obsessed by greed for more and more until you visit your graves." (Qur'an 102. 1-2)

"In his love for the world, the greedy is like the silkworm: the more it wraps in its cocoon, the less it has escaping from it, until it dies of grief." Muhammad al-Baqir "The desire to know your own soul will end all other desires." Rumi

"If you want money more than anything, you'll be bought and sold your whole life." Rumi

"Anything which is more than our necessity is poison. It may be power, wealth, hunger, ego, greed, laziness, love, ambition, hate or anything." Rumi

Hinduism

"When a man dwells on the objects of sense, he creates an attraction for them; attraction develops into desire, and desire breeds anger." (The Bhagavad Gita)

"Pleasure from the senses seems like nectar at first, but it is bitter as poison in the end." (The Bhagavad Gita)

"In this world three gates lead to hell - the gates of passion, anger and greed. Released from these three qualities one can succeed in attaining salvation and reaching the highest goal." (The Bhagavad Gita)

"Everything in the universe belongs to the Lord. Therefore take only what you need, that is set aside for you. Do not take anything else, for you know to whom it belongs. (Isa Upanishad)

"If one is a slave to his passions and desires, one cannot feel the joy of real freedom." Swami Vivekananda

"Earth provides enough to satisfy every man's need but not every man's greed." Mahatma Gandhi

"Do not get attached to worldly things and pursuits. Be in the world, but do not let the world be in you." Sathya Sai Baba

"Desire is storm, greed is whirlpool, pride is precipice, attachment is avalanche, ego is volcano. Discard desire and you are liberated." Sathya Sai Baba

"Detachment is the beginning of mastery." Sri Aurobindo

"Desire nothing, give up all desires and be happy." Swami Sivananda
"Live simply so others may simply live." Mahatma Gandhi

Buddhism

"The root of suffering is attachment." Buddha (Pali canon)
"Live with no sense of 'mine', not forming an attachment to experiences." Buddha (Sutta Nipata)
"Follow the middle path. Neither extreme will make you happy." – Buddha (Dhammacakkappavattana Sutta)
"Contentment is the best form of wealth in that it gives us the highest satisfaction." 17th Gyalwang Karmapa, Ogyen Trinley Dorje
"As the Buddha said, chasing our desires is like drinking salty water. The more we drink, the thirstier we become. Therefore, I believe that where we find meaning in life as individuals and as society will need to change in the 21st-century. We need to pause, slow down and simplify." 17th Gyalwang Karmapa, Ogyen Trinley Dorje
"We must attempt the impossible. I am convinced that if we continue to follow a social model that is entirely conditioned by money and power, and that takes so little account of true values such as love and altruism, future generations may have to face far worse problems and endure even more terrible forms of suffering." Dalai Lama (The Dalai Lama's Little Book of Inner Peace: The Essential Life and Teachings)
"We should be contented in material areas, for those are bound by limitation, but not with regard to the spiritual, which can be extended limitlessly." Dalai Lama (How to Practice: The Way to a Meaningful Life)
"The entire teaching of Buddhism can be summed up in this way: Nothing is worth holding on to." Jack Kornfield (Living Dharma: Teachings of Twelve Buddhist Masters)
"Only when the mind sees for itself, can it uproot and relinquish attachment."
Ajahn Chah (A Tree in a Forest. A Collection of Ajahn Chah's Similes)

Jainism

"Persons should refrain from accumulation of unlimited property due to unquenchable thirst as it becomes a pathway to hell and results in numerous faults." (Saman Suttam, 23/315 & 316)

"The more you get, the more you want. The greed increases with the gain." Mahavira (Uttaradhyayana, 8/17)

"Know that birth is accompanied by death; youth is succeeded by old age, wealth is perishable. Thus should one reflect that everything is transient." (Saman Suttam, 30/507)

"To abandon attachment is the art of living as it is also the art of dying." Acharya Shri Mahaprajna, Head of the Jain Terapanth Sect

"The first rule of ecology is limitation." Acharya Shri Mahaprajna

Sikhism

"Riches cannot be gathered without sin." Guru Nanak (Guru Granth Sahib)

"The fire of desire is quenched by the water of virtue." Guru Nanak (Guru Granth Sahib)

"Lust and wealth are poisons - heavy and hard." (Guru Granth Sahib p.1187)

"True wealth does not burn; it cannot be stolen by a thief." (Guru Granth Sahib)

"Greed is a dog; falsehood is a filthy street-sweeper." (Guru Granth Sahib)

"I have seen the world being destroyed by greed and egotism. Only by serving the Guru, God is realised and the true gate of salvation is found." (Guru Granth Sahib p. 228).

Taoism

"Without desire there is stillness, and the world settles by itself." Lao Tzu (Tao Te Ching Chapter 37)

"Those who know when they have enough are rich." Lao Tzu (Tao Te Ching Chapter 33)

"To have enough of enough is always enough." Lao Tzu (Tao Te Ching Chapter 46)

"There is no greater misfortune than greed." Lao Tzu (Tao Te Ching Chapter 46)

"If you want to be given everything: give everything up." Lao Tzu (Tao Te Ching)

"The Master has no possessions. The more he does for others, the happier he is. The more he gives to others, the wealthier he is." Lao Tzu (Tao Te Ching Chapter 81)

"It is he who can live in simplicity and purity whom we call the true man." Chuang Tzu

"The perfect man uses his mind as a mirror. It grasps nothing. It regrets nothing. It receives but does not keep." Chuang Tzu

"Although gold dust is precious, when it gets in your eyes, it obstructs your vision." Hsi-Tang

Paganism

"In a culture where profit has become the true God, self-sacrifice can seem incomprehensible rather than noble." Starhawk (Webs of Power: Notes from the Global Uprising)

"The role of religion and spirituality (in environmental activism) is to hold up the values that go beyond the value of profit and the value of somebody winning and somebody losing, to say... there are things that are more important than money or gain. The value of generosity, the value of putting good of community and the good of the whole before your own personal gain those of the things that every religion at its core has always stood for." Starhawk

Bahá'í Faith

"If carried to excess, civilisation will prove a prolific source of evil as it had been of goodness when kept within the restraints of moderation." Bahá'u'lláh (Gleanings, CLXIV)

"Take from this world only to the measure of your needs, and forego that which exceedeth them." Bahá'u'lláh (The Summons of the Lord of Hosts, p. 194)

"Put away all covetousness and seek contentment; for the covetous hath ever been deprived, and the contented hath ever been loved and praised." Bahá'u'lláh (The Persian Hidden Words, no 50)

242

CREATING GOOD KARMA

If we are aware of the effects of our actions then our behaviour will not contribute to climate change.

Christianity

"Do not be deceived: God cannot be mocked. A man reaps what he sows." St. Paul (Galatians 6:7)

"Man has lost the capacity to foresee and to forestall. He will end by destroying the earth." Albert Schweitzer

Islam

"And truly the Lord will repay everyone according to their works for he is well aware of what they do." (Qur'an 11:113)

"Corruption doth appear on land and sea because of (the evil) which men's hands have done, that He may make them taste a part of that which they have done, in order that they may return." (Qur'an 30:41)

"Believe in Allah and His messenger, and spend of that whereof He hath made you trustees; and such of you as believe and spend (aright), theirs will be a great reward." (Qur'an 57:7)

"And do good as Allah has been good to you. And do not seek to cause corruption in the earth. Allah does not love the corrupters." (Qur'an 28:77)

Judaism

"Who is the wise person? The one who foresees the consequences." (Talmud, Tamid, 32a)

"For they have sown the wind, and they shall reap the whirlwind." (Hosea 8:7)

"As ye sow, so shall ye reap." (Jeremiah 1–19)

"There is no dark place, no deep shadow, where evil doers can hide." (Job 34:22)

Buddhism

In Buddhism the need to be fully aware of karma or cause and effect is paramount. Doing good and practising compassion and accumulating wisdom are the focus of Buddhism, not the accumulation of material wealth.

"If you should speak or act with mind defiled, suffering will follow just as a wheel follows the hoof of a drawing ox." The Buddha (Dhammapada)

"Avoid doing wicked actions, practise most perfect virtue, and thoroughly subdue your mind." The Buddha (Dhammapada)

"The universe we inhabit and our shared perception of it are the results of a common karma. Likewise, the places that we will experience in future rebirths will be the outcome of the karma that we share with other beings living there. The actions of each of us, human or non-human, have contributed to the world in which we live. We all have a common responsibility for our world and are connected with everything in it." Dalai Lama.

Hinduism

"There is nothing mightier in the world than karma: karma tramples down all powers as an elephant tramples down lotuses." (Hindu Scriptures)

"The world is like a river and our acts are like its ripples." (Hindu Scriptures)

"They say that this world is unreal, with no foundation, no God in control. Following such conclusions, the demoniac, who are lost to themselves and who have no intelligence, engage in unbeneficial, horrible acts meant to destroy the world. They believe to gratify the senses is the primary necessity of human civilisation." (Bhagavad Gita 16.4, 7-16.)

"No one who does good work will ever come to a bad end, either here or in the world to come." (Bhagavad Gita)

"As the young calf is able to recognise its mother from among a thousand cows, so does karma find the person destined to experience it. As the flowers and fruits of a tree, unurged by visible influences, never miss their proper season, so does karma done previously bring about its fruits in proper time." (Mahabharath)

"By harming Nature, he is paving the way for his own destruction." Sri Sri Amritanandamayi Devi

Sikhism

"According to one's own actions and deeds, they will get near to God or they will get far away from him." (Jaap Ji Sahib-Salok, Guru Granth Sahib.)

"As are one's deeds, so will one become." (Dhansari Mahalla I p.662.)

"The soul knows, that as one sows, so will one reap." (Guru Granth Sahib p1243)

Jainism

"A person of right world-view reflects on karma and its results." (Bhasyam Sutra 53)

"All unenlightened persons produce sufferings. Having become deluded, they produce and reproduce sufferings, in this endless world." Mahavira (Uttaradhyayana, 6/1)

"Attachment and aversion are the root cause of karma, and karma originates from infatuation. Karma is the root cause of birth and death, and these are said to be the source of misery. None can escape the effect of their own past karma." Mahavira

Taoism

"Never take over the world to tamper with it. Those who want to tamper with it are not fit to take over the world." (Tao Te Ching Chapter 48)

"Natural laws of the universe are inviolable... what you say and do determines what happens in your life... You are the master of your life and death. What you do is what you are." Lao Tzu (Tao Te Ching)

Shamanism

"In our every deliberation, we must consider the impact of our decisions on the next seven generations." (Iroquois saying)

Paganism

"Because everything is interdependent, there are no simple, single causes and effects. Every action creates not just an equal and opposite reaction, but a web of reverberating consequences." Starhawk (The Earth Path: Grounding Your Spirit in the Rhythms of Nature)

"An it harm none, do what ye will." Doreen Valiente (Witchcraft for Tomorrow, p.36)

Bahá'í Faith

"If a man eats too much, he ruins his digestion; if he takes poison he becomes ill or dies. If a person gambles he will lose his money; if he drinks too much he will lose his equilibrium. All these sufferings are caused by the man himself, it is quite clear therefore that certain sorrows are the result of our own deeds." 'Abdu'l-Bahá (Paris Talks, p. 51)

ACHIEVING BALANCE AND HARMONY

If we deeply understand the need for balance and harmony for the planet and in ourselves then our behaviour will not contribute to climate change.

Islam

"And the firmament He has raised high and He has set up the balance; in order that ye may not transgress balance." (Qur'an 55:5-9)

"Verily, all things have we created in proportion and measure." (Qur'an 54:49)

"He is raised high and set up the measure, that ye may not exceed the measure." (Qur'an 55: 8-10)

"Do no mischief on the earth, after it has been set in order, but call on Him with fear and longing (in your hearts): for the Mercy of God is (always) near to those who do good." (Qur'an 7:56).

"This world is a universal guest house given to us by God. We have to live here like a guest and not disturb the house." Mr Maulana Wahiduddin Khan, Delhi, India - Mullah and published scholar on Islam.

Buddhism

"When we bring our concern for ourselves into harmony with our concern for others, our life comes in balance. When our life feels imbalanced and pointless, usually we notice that our relationships have

246

also become unhealthy. By thinking carefully about how we orient ourselves toward others and toward ourselves, we can build and enjoy healthy relationships. We can learn to cultivate relationships that are warm and truly meaningful." 17th Gyalwang Karmapa, Ogyen Trinley Dorje

"Because we all share this planet earth, we have to learn to live in harmony and peace with each other and with nature. This is not just a dream, but a necessity." Dalai Lama

Hinduism

"Happiness is when what you think, what you say, and what you do are in harmony." Mahatma Gandhi

"The highest education is that which does not merely give us information but makes our life in harmony with all existence." Rabindranath Tagore

"God has made the balance of Nature perfect." (Hindu scriptures)

"The world is a living whole, an interconnectedness of cosmic harmony." (Hindu scriptures)

"A large number of man's activities are polluting the physical environment around him and creating an imbalance in the ecological situation, which is difficult to restore or cannot be restored at all." Swami Smarananda, General Secretary of the Ramakrishna Mission, Kolkata, India

"If the balance in Nature is lost, harmony of human life will also be lost and vice versa." Sri Sri Amritanandamayi Devi

"To live in harmony with the whole of existence - this is what we call environmental religion." Swami Shatrananda

Sikhism

"In intuitive balance, love is balanced and detached. In the state of intuitive balance, peace and tranquillity are produced. Without intuitive balance, life is useless. (Guru Granth Sahib)

Taoism

"When you know Nature is part of yourself, you will act in harmony." Lao Tzu

"Fill your bowl to the brim and it will spill. Keep sharpening your knife and it will blunt." Lao Tzu

247

"When you stand with your two feet on the ground, you will always keep your balance." Lao Tzu (Tao Te Ching)

Bahá'í Faith

"For every part of the universe is connected with every other part by ties that are very powerful and admit to no imbalance." 'Abdu'l-Bahá (Selections from the Writings of 'Abdu'l-Bahá, p. 157)

"This nature is subject to a sound organisation, to inviolable laws, to a perfect order, and to a consummate design, from which it never departs." 'Abdu'l-Bahá (Some Answered Questions, Ch. 1, p. 3)

"The purpose of man's creation is, therefore, unity and harmony, not discord and separateness. If the atoms which compose the kingdom of the minerals were without affinity for each other, the earth would never have been formed, the universe could not have been created. Because they have affinity for each other, the power of life is able to manifest itself, and the organisms of the phenomenal world become possible." 'Abdu'l-Bahá (The Promulgation of Universal Peace)

Judaism

"Look at my creations. See how beautiful and perfect they are. Do not desecrate or corrupt my world. For if you corrupt it, there will be no one to set it right for you." (Talmud)

"It's not how much or how little you have that makes you great or small, but how much or how little you accomplish with what you have." Rabbi Samson Raphael Hirsch

"One should see the world, and see himself as a scale with an equal balance of good and evil. When he does one good deed the scale is tipped to the good - he and the world is saved. When he does one evil deed the scale is tipped to the bad - he and the world is destroyed." Maimonides

Christianity

"Man always travels along precipices. His truest obligation is to keep his balance." Pope John Paul II

"The disastrous feature of our civilisation is that it is far more developed materially than spiritually. Its balance is disturbed." Albert Schweitzer

248

Shamanism

"Touching the earth equates to having harmony with nature." (Native American Lakota proverb)

CONNECTING WITH NATURE

If we were really connected to nature we would not do it any harm, and our behaviour would not then contribute to climate change.

Hinduism

"For the world is a living whole, a vast interconnectedness of cosmic harmony, inspired and sustained by the One Supreme." (Bhagavad Gita 10.20)
"He on whom the sky, the earth and the atmosphere are woven and the wind, together with all life-breaths, Him alone knows the one Soul." (Mundaka Upanishad 2.2.5)
"Hinduism teaches us to understand the laws of Nature and respect them." Swami Dharammanda, Rishikesh, India.
"We are not different from nature; we are an interdependent part of it. Our lives depend on the well-being of the whole. Therefore, it is one of our foremost duties to lovingly care for all living things." Sri Sri Amritanandamayi Devi
"Steeped in selfishness, people have forgotten that it was from Mother Nature that we received everything – and without her, we will lose everything." Sri Sri Amritanandamayi Devi

Buddhism

"I don't need to have books made up of paper and ink. Everything I see around me teaches me the Dharma." Milarepa
"Interdependence is a fundamental law of nature." Dalai Lama
"The earth is not just our environment. The earth is our mother." Dalai Lama
"All parties are changed by being in relationship. Just being connected to someone or something means we are each forming part of the other. This is true in all forms of interdependence, from those that form planetary

systems to our most intimate and personal relationships." Ogyen Trinley Dorje, 17th Kalmarpa

"Recognising our intimate dependence on the natural environment allows us to see its true value and treasure it." Ogyen Trinley Dorje, 17th Karmarpa

"Living close to nature is a very healing experience - to have few activities, few distractions." Ven. Asabho

"Everything depends on everything else. The One contains the many, and the many contains the One" Thich Nhat Hanh, (Old Path White Clouds: Walking in the Footsteps of the Buddha)

"We can learn from Nature enough to be enlightened because everything flows the way of truth. It does not diverge from truth." Ajahn Chah

"Once you understand our innate power to purify ourselves and our surroundings you will act properly." Shunryu Suzuki (Zen Mind Beginners Mind)

Jainism

"One who neglects or disregards the existence of earth, air, fire, water and vegetation disregards his own existence which is entwined with them." Mahavira

Paganism

"The Earth's biosphere may be understood as a single ecosystem and that all life on Earth is interconnected." (A Pagan Community Statement)

"Perceiving the world as a web of connectedness helps us to overcome the feelings of separation that hold us back and cloud our vision. This connection with all life increases our sense of responsibility for every move, every attitude, allowing us to see clearly that each soul does indeed make a difference to the whole." Emma Restall Orr

"A real relationship with nature is vital for our magical and spiritual development, and our psychic and spiritual health. It is also a vital base for any work we do to heal the earth and transform the social and political systems that are assaulting her daily." Starhawk (The Earth Path: Grounding Your Spirit in the Rhythms of Nature)

"Becoming a Druid involves taking responsibility to bring your own life in harmony with nature." Michael Greer

250

"Our belonging to the Earth community is the most fundamental in which we exist and know ourselves." Jason Kirkey (The Salmon in the Spring: The Ecology of Celtic Spirituality)

"We are part of the whole and that whole changes when we are no longer consciously a part of it." Pam Montgomery (Partner Earth: A Spiritual Ecology)

Bahá'í Faith

Bahá'u'lláh stated, "Nature is God's Will and is its expression in and through the contingent world." Bahá'u'lláh (Tablets of Bahá'u'lláh, p. 142)

"By nature is meant those inherent properties and necessary relations derived from the realities of things. And these realities of things, though in the utmost diversity, are yet intimately connected one with the other." 'Abdu'l-Bahá, (Tablet to Dr. Forel, in The Bahá'í Revelation, p. 223)

"We cannot segregate the human heart from the environment outside us and say that once one of these is reformed everything will be improved. Man is organic with the world. His inner life moulds the environment and is itself also deeply affected by it. The one acts upon the other and every abiding change in the life of man is the result of these mutual reactions." Shoghi Effendi (Compilation on Social and Economic Development, p. 4)

Islam

"Bread feeds the body, indeed, but flowers feed also the soul." (Qur'an)

"Devote thyself single-mindedly to the Faith, and thus follow the nature designed by Allah, the nature according to which He has fashioned mankind. There is no altering the creation of Allah." (Qur'an 30:30)

Shamanism

"With all beings and all things we shall be relatives." Black Elk

"We are all flowers in the Great Spirit's Garden; we share a common root, and the root is Mother Earth." Grandfather David Monogye

"The whole universe is enhanced with the same breath, rocks, trees, grass, earth, all animals and men." Intiwa, Hopi

"The earth does not belong to us. We belong to the earth." Chief Seattle

251

"Humankind has not woven the web of life. We are but one thread within it. Whatever we do to the web, we do to ourselves. All things are bound together. All things connect." Chief Seattle

"Nature is not our enemy, to be raped and conquered. Nature is ourselves, to be cherished and explored." Terence McKenna

"We are not separate, rather we are connected to one source and to a web of life." Sandra Ingerman

"Man's heart away from nature becomes hard." Standing Bear

"The Great Spirit is in all things, he is in the air we breathe. The Great Spirit is our Father, but the Earth is our Mother. She nourishes us, that which we put into the ground she returns to us...." Big Thunder

"All men were made brothers. The earth is the mother of all people, and all people should have equal rights upon it." Chief Joseph

"Regard Heaven as your Father, Earth as your Mother, and All That Lives as your Brother and Sister." (Native Wisdom)

"Holy Mother Earth, the trees and all nature, are witnesses of your thoughts and deeds." (Winnebago saying)

Sikhism

"By divine prompting, look upon all existence as one and undifferentiated." (Guru Granth Sahib p 599)

"I perceive Thy form in all life and light; I perceive Thy power in all spheres and sight." (Guru Granth Sahib p 464)

Christianity

"Whether you like it or not, whether you know it or not, secretly all Nature seeks God and works toward him." Meister Eckhart

"You will find something more in woods than in books. Trees and stones will teach you that which you can never learn from masters." St. Bernard

"As stewards of God's creation, we are called to make the earth a beautiful garden for the human family. When we destroy our forests, ravage our soil and pollute our seas, we betray that noble calling." Pope Francis

"A truly human intimacy with the earth and with the entire natural world is needed." Thomas Berry

"Logic does not lead us from the fact that we are an integral part of the web of life to certain norms of how we should live. However if we have deep ecological awareness, or experience, of being part of the web of life, then we will (as opposed to should) be inclined to care for all living nature. Indeed, we can scarcely refrain from responding in this way." Wendell Berry

"Nature compels us to recognize the fact of mutual dependence, each life necessarily helping the other lives who are linked to it. In the very fibres of our being, we bear within ourselves the fact of the solidarity of life." Albert Schweitzer

Taoism

"He who regards all things as one is a companion of Nature." Chuang Tzu

"Life comes from the earth and life returns to the earth." Chuang Tzu

THE IMPORTANCE OF DOING GOOD

If we focus our lives on doing good for others then our behaviour will not contribute to climate change.

Christianity

"In everything, do to others as you would have them do to you; for this is the law and the prophets." (Matthew 7:12)

"And let us not grow weary of doing good, for in due season we will reap, if we do not give up." (Galatians 6:9)

"Situations can change; people can change. Be the first to seek to bring good. Do not grow accustomed to evil, but defeat it with good." Pope Francis

"Give your hands to serve and your hearts to love." Mother Teresa

"A tree is known by its fruit; a man by his deeds. A good deed is never lost; he who sows courtesy reaps friendship, and he who plants kindness gathers love." Saint Basil

"Do all the good you can, by all the means you can, in all the ways you can, in all the places you can, at all the times you can, to all the people you can, as long as ever you can." John Wesley

"There is no higher religion than human service." Albert Schweitzer

Islam

"Do unto all men as you would wish to have done unto you, and reject for others what you would reject for yourselves." Muhammad (Abu Dawud)

"To whoever, male or female, does good deeds and is a believer, We shall give a good life and reward them according to the best of their actions." (Qur'an 16:97)

"None of you have faith until you love for your neighbour what you love for yourself." Muhammad (Sahih Muslim)

"Those who believe and do good deeds - the Gracious God will create love in their hearts." (Qur'an 19:97)

"Do good to the people for the sake of God or for the peace of your own soul that you may always see what is pure and save your heart from the darkness of hate." Rumi

Judaism

"Do not neglect to do good and to share what you have, for such sacrifices are pleasing to God." (Hebrews 13:16)

"What is hateful to you, do not do to your neighbour. This is the whole Torah; all the rest is commentary. Go and learn it." (Talmud, Shabbath 31a)

"Do not be wise in words - be wise in deeds." (Jewish proverb)

"The whole worth of a kind deed is in the love that inspires it." (The Talmud)

"The end result of wisdom is... good deeds." (The Talmud)

Hinduism

"This is the sum of duty: do not do to others what would cause pain if done to you." (Mahabharata 5:1517)

"Strive constantly to serve the welfare of the world; by devotion to selfless work one attains the supreme goal of life. Do your work with the welfare of others always in mind." (The Bhagavad Gita)

"The best way to find yourself is to lose yourself in the service of others." Gandhi

"They alone live, who live for others." Swami Vivekananda

"Doing good to others is the one great universal religion." Swami Vivekananda

"Service broadens your vision, widens your awareness, deepens your compassion." Sathya Sai Baba

"To the degree we cultivate the spirit of selfless service; to that degree we'll actually find bliss in life." Radhanath Swami

"Life is short. Time is fleeting. Realise the Self. Purity of the heart is the gateway to God. Aspire. Renounce. Meditate. Be good; do good. Be kind; be compassionate. Inquire, know Thyself." Swami Sivananda

Buddhism

"Ceasing to do evil, cultivating the good, purifying the heart: This is the teaching of the Buddhas." The Buddha (Dhammapada, verse 183)

"Should a person do good, let him do it again and again. Let him find pleasure therein, for blissful is the accumulation of good." The Buddha (Dhammapada, verse 118)

"Be kind whenever possible. It is always possible." Dalai Lama

"It is not enough to be compassionate - you must act." Dalai Lama

Sikhism

"Through selfless service, eternal peace is obtained." (Guru Granth Sahib)

"Cruelty, material attachment, greed and anger are the four rivers of fire. Nanak says, one is burned by falling into them. One is saved only by holding tight to good deeds." (Guru Granth Sahib 147).

"Without the karma of good deeds, they are only destroying themselves." (Guru Granth Sahib)

"The God-conscious being delights in doing good to others." (Guru Granth Sahib p273)

Bahá'í Faith

"Lay not on any soul a load which ye would not wish to be laid upon you, and desire not for any one the things ye would not desire for yourselves." Bahá'u'lláh (Gleanings from the Writings of Bahá'u'lláh, p. 128)
"Service to humanity is service to God." 'Abdu'l-Bahá (The Promulgation of Universal Peace, p. 8)
"This is worship: to serve mankind and to minister to the needs of the people. Service is prayer." 'Abdu'l-Bahá (Paris Talks, p. 177)

Taoism

"If you would take, you must first give, this is the beginning of intelligence." Lao Tzu

Paganism

"Since profligate lifestyles in the developed world are the primary force behind the destruction of natural eco systems there are plenty of opportunities for action and few excuses for unthinking business-as-usual." John Michael Greer

FINDING DEEPER HAPPINESS

If we take this spiritual guidance on how to find lasting happiness then our behaviour will not contribute to climate change.

Christianity

"I know that there is nothing better for people than to be happy and to do good while they live." (Ecclesiastes 3:12-13)
"Happy is the man who finds wisdom, and the man who gains understanding." (Proverbs 3:13-24)
"The secret of happiness is to live moment by moment and to thank God for all that He, in His goodness, sends to us day after day." St. Gianna Molla
"There is within every soul a thirst for happiness and meaning." Thomas Aquinas

"The great secret of true success, of true happiness, is this: the man or woman who asks for no return, the perfectly unselfish person, is the most successful." Pope Francis

Islam

"Acquire knowledge. It enables its possessor to distinguish right from wrong; it lights the way to Heaven; it is our friend in the desert, our society in solitude, our companion when friendless; it guides us to happiness; it sustains us in misery; it is an ornament among our friends and an armour against enemies." Muhammad
"He who knows himself is truly happy." al-Ghazali
"O, happy the soul that saw its own faults." Rumi

Judaism

"Who is the wealthy person? The one who is happy with his portion!" (Pirkei Avot 4:1).
"The Holy Spirit rests on one who has a joyous heart." (Jerusalem Talmud, Sukkah)
"We cannot make our happiness dependent on things we don't have." Rabbi Yitzchak Berkowitz
"The happiest people I know are people who don't even think about being happy. They just think about being good neighbours, good people. And then happiness sort of sneaks in the back window while you are busy doing good." Rabbi Harold Kushner
"Clear knowledge of God's existence generates happiness." (Chazon Ish, Emunah U'Bitachon)

Bahá'í Faith

"Happy the soul that shall forget his own good, and like the chosen ones of God, vie with his fellows in service to the good of all." 'Abdu'l-Bahá (The Secret of Divine Civilisation, p. 113)
"Your utmost desire must be to confer happiness upon each other. Each one must be the servant of the others, thoughtful of their comfort and welfare." 'Abdu'l-Bahá (The Promulgation of Universal Peace, p. 214)

257

"Man is, in reality, a spiritual being, and only when he lives in the spirit is he truly happy." 'Abdu'l-Bahá (Paris Talks, p. 72.)

"Human happiness is founded upon spiritual behaviour." 'Abdu'l-Bahá, (Selections from the Writings of 'Abdu'l-Bahá, p. 127)

"…man's supreme honour and real happiness lie in self-respect, in high resolves and noble purposes, in integrity and moral quality, in immaculacy of mind." 'Abdu'l-Bahá (The Secret of Divine Civilisation, p. 18)

"We desire but the good of the world and the happiness of the nations". Bahá'u'lláh, (The Proclamation of Bahá'u'lláh p.8)

Hinduism

"The happiness obtained by him who is contented and who seeks joy within himself is many times more than the happiness of that person who, under the influence of desires and greed, runs in all the four directions and obtains a lot of wealth." (Purāṇa 7.15.16)

"Happiness is when what you think, what you say, and what you do are in harmony." Mahatma Gandhi

"Judge nothing, you will be happy. Forgive everything, you will be happier. Love everything, you will be happiest." Sri Chinmoy

"I am very happy because I have conquered myself and not the world. I am very happy because I have loved the world and not myself." Swami Vivekananda

"When your happiness is dependent upon what is happening outside of you, constantly you live as a slave to the external situation." Sadhguru

"No matter what you are doing, keep the undercurrent of happiness. Learn to be secretly happy within your heart in spite of all circumstances." Paramahansa Yogananda

"Happiness depends on what you can give, not on what you can get." Swami Chinmayananda

Buddhism

"It is felt that a disciplined mind leads to happiness and an undisciplined mind leads to suffering, and in fact it is said that bringing about discipline within one's mind is the essence of the Buddha's teaching." Dalai Lama (The Art of Happiness)

"The secret of happiness lies in the mind's release from worldly ties." Buddha

"One who acts on truth is happy in this world and beyond." Buddha

"Happiness is not having a lot. Happiness is giving a lot." Buddha

"If you want others to be happy, practise compassion. If you want to be happy, practise compassion." Dalai Lama

"There is no way to happiness - happiness is the way." Thich Nhat Hanh

Taoism

"If you look to others for fulfilment, you will never be fulfilled. If your happiness depends on money, you will never be happy with yourself. Be content with what you have; rejoice in the way things are. When you realise there is nothing lacking, the world belongs to you." Lao Tzu (Tao Te Ching)

"Happiness is the absence of the striving for happiness." Chuang Tzu

PRACTISING LOVE AND COMPASSION

If we take this spiritual advice on love and compassion we will not want to harm others by behaviour which leads to climate change.

Christianity

"As a father has compassion on his children, so the Lord has compassion on his faithful followers." (Psalm 103:13)

"A new commandment I give to you, that you love one another: just as I have loved you, you also are to love one another." (John 13:34)

"God is love. Whoever lives in love lives in God, and God in them." (1 John 4:16)

"Love bears all things, believes all things, hopes all things, endures all things." (1 Corinthians 13:7)

"Do everything in love. He who is filled with love is filled with God himself." Saint Augustine

"You may call God love, you may call God goodness. But the best name for God is compassion." Meister Eckhart

"Until he extends the circle of his compassion to all living things, man will not himself find peace." Albert Schweitzer

"Compassion is the keen awareness of the interdependence of all things." Thomas Merton

"God still loves the world and He sends you and me to be His love and His compassion to the poor." Mother Teresa

Judaism

"Love thy neighbour as thyself!" (Leviticus 18:19)

"Who acts from love is greater than who acts from fear." (Talmud, Sota)

"The purpose of the laws of the Torah are to promote loving kindness, compassion and peace in the world." Maimonides (Yad Sabbath 1180 2.3)

Islam

"Kindness is a mark of faith, and whoever has not kindness has not faith." Muhammad

"The compassionate are near to God, near to men, near to paradise and far from hell." Muhammad

"Love for the people what you love for yourself and you will be a believer. Behave well with your neighbours and you will be a Muslim." (Sunan Ibn Majah 4217)

"Be drunk with love, for love is all that exists." Rumi

"Love is the bridge between you and everything." Rumi

"Treat people in such a way and live amongst them in such a manner that if you die they will weep over you; alive they crave for your company." Nahjul Balagha

Buddhism

"So definitely, it's important that we be able to improve and change our minds and especially, it's important that from now on we develop a real loving connection with each other, whether this be a loving connection between people to people or be loving connection between people and the environment. This is the essence of the Dharma and is very beneficial right now, especially now because we are in an urgent situation." Gyalwang Karmapa, Ogyen Trinley Dorje

"We have the propensity for showing kindness and love from birth. It is part of our nature. However, this has been turned off by our upbringing or different circumstances and we have become habituated to not using it." Gyalwang Karmapa Ogyen Trinley Dorje

"Radiate boundless love towards the entire world - above, below, and across - unhindered, without ill will, without enmity." The Buddha (Metta Sutra)

"All beings wish for happiness, so extend your compassion to all." Buddha

"Ultimately humanity is one, and this small planet is our only home. If we're to protect this home of ours, each of us needs to experience a vivid sense of universal altruism and compassion." Dalai Lama (The Compassionate Life)

"The purpose of all the major religious traditions is not to construct big temples on the outside, but to create temples of goodness and compassion inside, in our hearts." Dalai Lama

"Let us fill our hearts with our own compassion – towards ourselves and towards all living beings." Thich Nhat Hanh

Hinduism

"The essence of Hinduism is the same essence of all true religions: Bhakti or pure love for God and genuine compassion for all beings." Radhanath Swami

"Only through love and compassion is the protection and preservation of Nature possible!" Sri Sri Amritanandamayi Devi

"The person who offers compassion is the first to receive its blessing. Wherever a heart beats with compassion: God is there." Sri Sri Amritanandamayi Devi

"All love is expansion, all selfishness is contraction. Love is therefore the only law of life. He who loves lives, he who is selfish is dying. Therefore love for love's sake, because it is the law of life, just as you breathe to live." Swami Vivekananda

"Love is to human hearts what the sun is to flowers." Swami Chinmayananda

"Affirm divine calmness and peace, and send out only thoughts of love and goodwill if you want to live in peace and harmony." Paramahansa Yogananda

261

Bahá'í Faith

"The Kingdom of God is founded upon equity and justice, and also upon mercy, compassion, and kindness to every living soul. Strive ye then with all your heart to treat compassionately all humankind." 'Abdu'l-Bahá, (Selections from the Writings of 'Abdu'l-Bahá, p. 158)

"It is your duty to be exceedingly kind to every human being, and to wish him well; to work for the upliftment of society...until ye change the world of man into the world of God." 'Abdu'l-Bahá (Selections from the Writings of 'Abdu'l-Baha, Page 90)

"Love is the spirit of life unto the adorned body of mankind, the establisher of true civilisation in this mortal world, and the shedder of imperishable glory upon every high-aiming race and nation." 'Abdu'l-Bahá (Selections from the Writings of 'Abdu'l-Bahá, p. 27).

"Do not be content with showing friendship in words alone, let your heart burn with loving kindness for all who may cross your path." 'Abdu'l-Bahá (Paris Talks, p. 15)

"To be a Bahá'í simply means to love all the world, to love humanity and try to serve it." 'Abdu'l-Bahá (Star of the West - 2 III 3)

"The more we love each other, the nearer we shall be to God." 'Abdu'l-Bahá (quoted in Bahá'í World Vol 5, p547)

"The best way to thank God is to love one another." 'Abdu'l-Bahá (The Promulgation of Universal Peace 140.3)

Sikhism

"Those who have loved are those that have found God." Guru Nanak (Guru Granth Sahib)

"Love is the ultimate state of human behaviour where compassion prevails and kindness rules." Yogi Bhajan

"A life devoid of love is a flower blooming in the wilderness, with nobody to enjoy its fragrance." Kabirji, Gauri Rag

Jainism

"Live and let live. Love all – Serve all." Mahavira

"Have benevolence towards all living beings, joy at the sight of the virtuous, compassion and sympathy for the afflicted, and tolerance towards the indolent and ill-behaved." (Tattvarthasutra *7.11)*

Shamanism

"The world must begin sharing again. We need more kindness." Takua Kawirembeyju, Guarani Shaman of Paraguay
"There is no such thing as tough love. Love is kind, love is compassionate, love is tender." Heather Wolf (Kipnuk the Talking Dog)
"All began in love, all seeks to return in love. Love is the law, the teacher of wisdom, and the great revealer of mysteries." Starhawk (Spiral Dance: Slipcase)

Taoism

"With compassion one becomes courageous. Compassion brings triumph when attacked; it brings security when maintained. Lao Tzu (Tao Te Ching)
"I have just three things to teach: simplicity, patience, compassion. These three are your greatest treasures." Lao Tzu ((Tao Te Ching)

OUR FUTURE IS IN OUR HANDS

Climate change will affect everyone's future as well as our own.... now it is up to each of us to see if we can make the necessary changes in order to produce the best possible result for all of us.
Please list the changes you are going to make (if you haven't already done so) and see what we can achieve together!

References

Ch. 1: The Deeper Causes of Climate Change

1. Robert Henson The Thinking Person's Guide to Climate Change. American Meteorological Society 2019
2. https://climate.nasa.gov/vital-signs/carbon-dioxide/
3. https://en.wikipedia.org/wiki/List_of_countries_by_carbon_dioxide_emissions https://www.statista.com/statistics/271748/the-largest-emitters-of-co2-in-the-world/ https://www.ucsusa.org/resources/each-countrys-share-co2-emissions
4. https://www.c2es.org/content/international-emissions/
5. Global Climate in 2015-2019 : Climate Change accelerates. WMO 2019.
6. The Production Gap Report. The discrepancy between countries' planned fossil fuel production and global production levels consistent with limiting warming to 1.5°C or 2°C. UNEP 2019. http://productiongap.org/wp-content/uploads/2019/11/Production-Gap-Report-2019.pdf
7. Rodney J.Keenan et al. Dynamics of global forest area: Results from the FAO Global Forest Resources Assessment 2015. Forestry Ecology and Management Volume 352, 7 September 2015, Pages 9-20.
8. https://blog.globalforestwatch.org/data-and-research/global-tree-cover-loss-data-2019/
9. https://www.ipcc.ch/sr15/
10. Joseph From .Climate Change What Everyone Needs to Know.. Oxford University Press 2016.
11. Monica de Bolle Lets Look at the Evidence on Tipping Points in the Amazon Rainforest . Peterson Institute for International Economics .Oct 31 ,2019.
12. Monica de Bolle Amazon Deforestation Is Fast Nearing Tipping Point When Rainforest Cannot Sustain Itself. Peterson Institute for International Economics Oct 23 ,2019.
13. Jean Francois Basin et al. The Global Tree Restoration Potential. Science 5th July 2019.
14. https://populationmatters.org/
15. https://www.iufro.org/de/science/divisions/division-6/60000/publications/
16. https://www.un.org/esa/forests/index.html
17. Geoffrey Maslen. Too Late. How we lost the battle with climate change. Hardie Grant books 2019
18. IPCC. Climate Change 2013: The Physical Science Basis. *Contribution of Working Group I to the Fifth Assessment Report of the Intergovernmental Panel on Climate Change.*
19. https://news.cornell.edu/stories/2019/08/study-fracking-prompts-global-spike-atmospheric-methane

20. Louise M. Farquharson et al. Climate Change Drives Widespread and Rapid Thermokarst Development in Very Cold Permafrost in the Canadian High Arctic. Geophysical Research Letters Volume 46, Issue 12, 10th June 2019.
21. https://en.wikipedia.org/wiki/Fluorinated_gases
22. Christopher Wright and Daniel Nyberg Climate Change Capitalism and Corporations processes of creative Self Destruction . Cambridge University Press 2015.
23. David W.Orr. Dangerous Years .Climate Change, the Long Emergency and the Way Forward . Yale University Press 2016.
24. Jonathon Porritt   Hope in Hell- A decade to confront the climate emergency Simon and Schuster 2020.
25. https://www.footprintnetwork.org
26. https://www.breitbart.com/environment/2019/08/10/pope-franciss-greatest-fear-for-the-planet-loss-of-biodiversity/
27. Dieter Helm Net Zero: How we stop Causing Climate Change William Collins 2020

Ch. 2: Extreme Weather Events

1. https://www.ncdc.noaa.gov/sotc/global/201908
   https://climate.nasa.gov/news/2945/nasa-noaa-analyses-reveal-2019-second-warmest-year-on-record/
2. Cheng, L., Abraham, J., Zhu, J. *et al.* Record-Setting Ocean Warmth Continued in 2019. *Adv. Atmos. Sci.* 37, 137–142   2020
   https://link.springer.com/article/10.1007/s00376-020-9283-7
3. https://public.wmo.int/en/media/press-release/greenhouse-gas-concentrations-atmosphere-reach-yet-another-high
4. https://www.youtube.com/watch?v=RawFpMDgJeM
   https://www.youtube.com/watch?v=TObWJt68HGw
   https://www.youtube.com/watch?v=kij4kKSGzCE
   https://www.youtube.com/watch?v=Os4L1ocbbcE
   https://www.youtube.com/watch?v=BSBI4K_WT-c
5. https://www.youtube.com/watch?v=PDxKxnVZtgo
   https://www.youtube.com/watch?v=yRgGmNQVrQg
   https://www.youtube.com/watch?v=8si8hNI8sXs
   https://www.youtube.com/watch?v=BSipoCcB4sU
   https://www.youtube.com/watch?v=88CPLktYzhU
   https://www.youtube.com/watch?v=wwIOpk_f8S0
   https://www.youtube.com/watch?v=d9b315-WyLI
   https://www.youtube.com/watch?v=6H6ZVyUvZXs
   https://www.youtube.com/watch?v=NTdKJdGEQAU
   https://www.youtube.com/watch?v=UKNPJlBolN4
   https://www.youtube.com/watch?v=AKDK08hIgKA
6. https://www.youtube.com/watch?v=ETVDHPpKWWA
   https://www.youtube.com/watch?v=C6a0yVzM1Is
   https://www.youtube.com/watch?v=czN0fzK1LVI
   https://www.youtube.com/watch?v=tji6TomwFlI
   https://www.youtube.com/watch?v=heKGC-uvDT8

https://www.youtube.com/watch?v=Cuc04Og5UAo
https://www.youtube.com/watch?v=Bvy0cRljsds
https://www.youtube.com/watch?v=2bvnigwjY5E
https://www.youtube.com/watch?v=VrbsdTlG2JE
https://www.youtube.com/watch?v=fnyljp3X4jU

7. https://www.youtube.com/watch?v=YbfMRf8yI8E
    https://www.youtube.com/watch?v=zFNeftlC_oQ
    https://www.youtube.com/watch?v=UeZ45FoKcN8
    https://www.youtube.com/watch?v=oQpWAfJa99E
    https://www.youtube.com/watch?v=vRwlygihP7I
    https://www.youtube.com/watch?v=Bk4_BiXb7Wk
    https://www.youtube.com/watch?v=qxxGUBU2ZCc

8. https://www.youtube.com/watch?v=zLSaDVG4yBE
    https://www.youtube.com/watch?v=WKaHN3egFP4
    https://www.youtube.com/watch?v=Q8_tMiLTG1Y
    https://www.youtube.com/watch?v=ut-HykJkqW0
    https://www.youtube.com/watch?v=xFNd6tHyCwI&list=PLseY_NPAZAWf
    A8C4R0FabXp_d6Z1Mqsd_
    https://www.youtube.com/watch?v=1PO3wJXmIR8
    https://www.youtube.com/watch?v=vqg-qcadglU
    https://www.youtube.com/watch?v=0h9hLL3JFnI
    https://www.youtube.com/watch?v=PpRu7s56YkI

9. https://www.youtube.com/watch?v=-AAG4HEsgMQ

10. https://www.nasa.gov/mission_pages/hurricanes/archives/2012/h2012_Boph
    a.html http://disasterphilanthropy.org/disaster/typhoon-bopha-philippines/
    https://www.youtube.com/watch?v=YrTIMxNfsIQ
    https://reliefweb.int/disaster/tc-2014-000092-phl

11. https://www.bbc.co.uk/bitesize/guides/z9whg82/revision/4
    https://www.worldvision.org/disaster-relief-news-stories/2013-typhoon-
    haiyan-facts
    https://www.youtube.com/watch?v=-BnahLG_DmQ

12. https://reliefweb.int/disaster/tc-2014-000092-phl

13. Aslak Grinsted,et. al Normalized US hurricane damage estimates using area of
    total destruction, 1900–2018 PNAS November 26, 2019 116 (48) 23942-23946
    https://www.pnas.org/content/116/48/23942

14. https://www.britannica.com/event/Hurricane-Katrina
    https://www.nationalgeographic.com/environment/natural-
    disasters/reference/hurricane-katrina/
    https://www.youtube.com/watch?v=Wu1en7O4OTE
    https://www.youtube.com/watch?v=s76Qn7bpCsQ
    https://www.youtube.com/watch?v=HbJaMWw4-2Q

15. Dawson Ashley Extreme Cities and the Perils and Promise of Urban Life in
    the age of Climate Change   Verso   2017
    https://www.livescience.com/24380-hurricane-sandy-status-data.html
    https://www.nationalgeographic.com/environment/natural-
    disasters/reference/hurricane-sandy

16. https://www.nhc.noaa.gov/data/tcr/EP202015_Patricia.pdf
    https://weather.com/storms/hurricane/news/things-to-know-hurricane-

patricia https://en.wikipedia.org/wiki/Hurricane_Patricia
https://www.youtube.com/watch?v=IyFJvZ7IWoU
17. https://www.thebalance.com/hurricane-harvey-facts-damage-costs-4150087
https://www.weather.gov/crp/hurricane_harvey
https://www.nhc.noaa.gov/data/tcr/AL092017_Harvey.pdf
https://www.youtube.com/watch?v=PKIv9Cz9WQY
https://www.youtube.com/watch?v=l6V8Kxyvivw
18. https://www.thebalance.com/hurricane-irma-facts-timeline-damage-costs-
4150395 https://www.nhc.noaa.gov/data/tcr/AL112017_Irma.pdf
https://www.weather.gov/tae/Irma2017
https://www.youtube.com/watch?v=k2GqdIISjko
19. https://www.worldvision.org/disaster-relief-news-stories/2017-hurricane-
maria-facts https://www.nhc.noaa.gov/data/tcr/AL152017_Maria.pdf
https://www.washingtonpost.com/national/harvard-study-estimates-
thousands-died-in-puerto-rico-due-to-hurricane-maria/2018/05/29/1a82503a-
6070-11e8-a4a4-c070ef53f315_story.html?noredirect=on
https://www.youtube.com/watch?v=zNFnVIlE6cA
20. https://www.teamcomplete.com/hurricane-michael/
https://weather.com/storms/hurricane/news/2018-10-25-united-states-
hurricane-typhoon-landfalls-category-4-or-5
https://www.youtube.com/watch?v=wSXvcveNSTQ
21. https://www.nhc.noaa.gov/data/tcr/EP242018_Willa.pdf
https://www.youtube.com/watch?v=AnIo6roO1Jc
22. https://en.wikipedia.org/wiki/Hurricane_Dorian
https://www.weather.gov/mhx/Dorian2019
https://blog.ucsusa.org/brenda-ekwurzel/intense-5-remarkable-facts-about-
hurricane-dorian https://www.youtube.com/watch?v=P6ShYNAAyAQ
https://www.youtube.com/watch?v=jxupGXOYTWg
23. https://blog.ucsusa.org/kristy-dahl/hurricane-dorian-what-the-presidential-
candidates-and-all-of-us-need-to-know
24. Scott B. Power and François P. D. Delage   Setting and smashing extreme
temperature records over the coming century Nature Climate Change VOL 9 (
529–534) 2019   https://doi.org/10.1038/s41558-019-0498-
25. Mora, C., Dousset, B., Caldwell, I. *et al.* Global risk of deadly heat. *Nature Clim
Change* **7,** 501–506 2017 https://www.nature.com/articles/nclimate3322
https://www.climatecommunication.org/new/features/heat-waves-and-
climate-change/heat-waves-the-details/#refmark-13
https://www.climate.gov/news-features/understanding-climate/climate-
change-global...
https://www.climatecentral.org/news/half-world-deadly-heat-waves-2100-
21554
26. https://en.wikipedia.org/wiki/Heat_stroke https://www.hsph.harvard.edu/c-
change/subtopics/climate-change-heatwaves-and-health/
https://en.wikipedia.org/wiki/Talk:Wet-bulb_temperature
27. Frank Landis   Hot Earth Dreams   Create Space 2016
28. Steven C. Sherwood and Matthew Huber An adaptability limit to climate
change due to heat stress PNAS May 25, 2010 107 (21) 9552-9555
https://www.pnas.org/content/107/21/9552

29. https://www.metoffice.gov.uk/weather/learn-about/weather/case-studies/heatwave   https://en.wikipedia.org/wiki/2003_European_heat_wave https://www.sciencedirect.com/science/article/pii/S1631069107003770
30. https://en.wikipedia.org/wiki/2010_Northern_Hemisphere_heat_waves https://en.wikipedia.org/wiki/2010_Russian_wildfires
31. David Barriopedro et.al The Hot Summer of 2010: Redrawing the Temperature Record Map of Europe *Science* 08 Apr 2011: Vol. 332, Issue 6026, pp. 220-224 https://science.sciencemag.org/content/332/6026/220.abstract
32. https://en.m.wikipedia.org/wiki/2018_European_heat_wave https://public.wmo.int/en/media/press-release/state-of-climate-2018-shows-accelerating... https://insideclimatenews.org/news/27072018/summer-2018-heat-wave-wildfires-climate-change-evidence-crops-flooding-deaths-records-broken
33. https://en.wikipedia.org/wiki/July_2019_European_heat_wave https://www.theguardian.com/uk-news/2019/jun/28/what-is-causing-the-european-heatwave https://public.wmo.int/en/media/news/july-matched-and-maybe-broke-record-hottest-month-analysis-began https://www.wired.co.uk/article/europe-uk-france-2019-heatwave-news
34. https://en.wikipedia.org/wiki/1995_Chicago_heat_wave https://www.climatesignals.org/events/great-chicago-heat-wave-1995
35. https://en.wikipedia.org/wiki/2006_North_American_heat_wave https://www.liquisearch.com/2006_north_american_heat_wave https://scijinks.gov/heat/
36. https://en.wikipedia.org/wiki/2012_North_American_heat_wave https://www.climatecentral.org/blogs/was-the-heat-wave-an-unprecedented-event
37. https://en.wikipedia.org/wiki/2018_North_American_heat_wave https://www.express.co.uk/news/weather/985270/heatwave-canada-north-america-death-toll-latest-forecast https://www.livescience.com/63195-heat-wave-global-visualization.html
38. https://www.livescience.com/65877-anchorage-alaska-record-breaking-heat.html
39. https://reliefweb.int/report/india/heat-waves-killed-over-6000-2010
40. https://www.ecosia.org/search?p=1&q=2010+Heat+wave+in+India+ https://www.theguardian.com/world/2010/jun/01/pakistan-record-temperatures-heatwave http://archive.indianexpress.com/news/weather-researchers-fear--may-2010-heat-wave--may-return-to-city/944740/
41. https://www.youtube.com/watch?v=0hCMwxpPyJo https://en.m.wikipedia.org/wiki/2015_Indian_heat_wave https://www.britannica.com/event/India-Pakistan-heat-wave-of-2015
42. https://www.indiaspend.com/65-indians-exposed-to-heatwaves-in-may-june-2019-july-2019-was-indias-hottest-ever/ https://en.wikipedia.org/wiki/2019_heat_wave_in_India_and_Pakistan https://earthobservatory.nasa.gov/images/145167/heatwave-in-india
43. https://www.news.com.au/technology/environment/climate-change/heatwaves-in-australia-this-natural-killer-just-got-deadlier/news-story/7876bd4840e7cbc126c7a04dfa5c8973

44. https://en.wikipedia.org/wiki/2009_southeastern_Australia_heat_wave
45. https://www.climatecouncil.org.au/uploads/6d06af6b4198fd83aed7c3019d71e5a2.pdf
46. http://www.bom.gov.au/state-of-the-climate/2016/
47. https://www.npr.org/2019/01/25/688755024/australias-heatwave-is-taking-a-toll-on-people-animals-infrastructure-and-land?t=1580499883602
    https://www.bbc.co.uk/news/world-australia-46886798
48. https://en.wikipedia.org/wiki/Black_Saturday_bushfires
49. https://bushfiresaustralia.blogspot.com/2013/
    https://theconversation.com/uk/topics/nsw-bushfires-2013-7580
50. https://en.wikipedia.org/wiki/2014%E2%80%9315_Australian_bushfire_season https://www.youtube.com/watch?v=5Cq6_5R0qkI
51. https://en.wikipedia.org/wiki/2015%E2%80%9316_Australian_bushfire_season
52. https://www.climatesignals.org/events/australia-bushfire-season-2019-2020
    https://disasterphilanthropy.org/disaster/2019-australian-wildfires/
53. Richard C. J. Somerville, Wildfires and climate change Bulletin of Atomic Scientists October 29, 2019
    https://www.scientificamerican.com/article/heres-what-we-know-about-wildfires-and-climate-change/
54. https://www.ncdc.noaa.gov/sotc/fire/201107
55. https://earthobservatory.nasa.gov/images/79921/us-fires-2012
    https://www.ncdc.noaa.gov/sotc/fire/201213
56. https://earthsky.org/earth/2015-worst-us-wildfire-year-on-record
    https://www.youtube.com/watch?v=QiY4x_MXALY
    https://www.theguardian.com/us-news/2015/sep/13/california-lake-county-wildfire-size
57. https://en.wikipedia.org/wiki/2017_California_wildfires
    https://www.youtube.com/watch?v=_aK_p_jw_OY
58. https://www.huffingtonpost.co.uk/entry/fire-fire-everywhere-the-2018-global-wildfire-season-is-already-disastrous-
    https://www.youtube.com/watch?v=F28CRnpcQzQ
    https://en.wikipedia.org/wiki/2018_California_wildfires
59. https://en.wikipedia.org/wiki/June_2017_Portugal_wildfires
60. https://www.bbc.co.uk/news/world-europe-44932366
    https://en.wikipedia.org/wiki/2018_Greek_forest_fires
    https://www.youtube.com/watch?v=xtupDvz1WVI
    https://www.youtube.com/watch?v=T-Qcj6M73gk
61. https://www.climatehotmap.org/global-warming-effects/drought.html
    https://en.wikipedia.org/wiki/Drought
    https://wg1.ipcc.ch/presentations/Sbsta_drought.pdf
62. https://en.wikipedia.org/wiki/Drought_in_Australia
    https://en.wikipedia.org/wiki/2000s_Australian_drought
    https://www.csiro.au/en/Research/Environment/Extreme-Events
63. https://en.wikipedia.org/wiki/2010_Sahel_drought
    https://www.researchgate.net/publication/236867522_The_causes_effects_and_challenges_of_Sahelian_droughts_A_critical_review
    https://www.youtube.com/watch?v=c-MYQYKQXhI

64. https://en.wikipedia.org/wiki/2011_East_Africa_drought
    https://www.youtube.com/watch?v=B2YVRNbQy6c
    https://www.youtube.com/watch?v=_Hr7wSDNgxI
65. https://en.wikipedia.org/wiki/2012_Sahel_drought
    https://www.huffpost.com/entry/sahel-drought-2012_n_1403884
66. https://www.livescience.com/30085-amazon-drought-2010-climate-change-
    110203.html https://www.youtube.com/watch?v=M_7yxVv39uI
67. https://en.wikipedia.org/wiki/2010%E2%80%9311_China_drought
    https://www.youtube.com/watch?v=i2M_GqTGSr0
68. Thomas C. Peterson, Peter A. Stott and Stephanie Herring, Editors Explaining
    Extreme Events of 2011 from a Climate Perspective American Meteorological
    Society May 2012 https://earthobservatory.nasa.gov/images/51684/drought-
    across-the-united-states https://www.youtube.com/watch?v=tK-YATetLPI
    https://www.weather.gov/tsa/weather-event_2011drought
    https://www.youtube.com/watch?v=mrzj74VE764
69. https://en.wikipedia.org/wiki/2012_North_American_drought
    https://www.youtube.com/watch?v=7AKb-piXctw
    https://www.ncdc.noaa.gov/sotc/drought/201213
70. https://en.wikipedia.org/wiki/Droughts_in_California
    https://en.wikipedia.org/wiki/2011%E2%80%932017_California_drought
    https://www.youtube.com/watch?v=WCxpxOr0gt8
    https://www.youtube.com/watch?v=1BPCg1WtviM
71. Geoffrey Maslen Too Late ; How we lost the battle with climate change
    Hardie Grant books 2017
    https://www.climatecentral.org/gallery/graphics/warmer-air-means-more-
    evaporation-and-precipitation https://www.c2es.org/content/extreme-
    precipitation-and-climate-change/
72. https://www.theguardian.com/world/2017/sep/02/flood-waters-rising-urban-
    development-climate-change
73. https://www.unwater.org/water-facts/disasters/
74. https://www.pik-potsdam.de/news/press-releases/record-breaking-heavy-
    rainfall-events-increased-under-global-warming
75. https://en.wikipedia.org/wiki/2010_Pakistan_floods
    https://www.youtube.com/watch?v=3pl6p_tPqC8
76. https://en.wikipedia.org/wiki/2011_Southeast_Asian_floods
    https://www.unocha.org/media-centre/humanitarian-reports
    https://www.youtube.com/watch?v=-ZhkPFqWsSs
77. https://en.wikipedia.org/wiki/2013_North_India_floods
    https://www.youtube.com/watch?v=ZlBV7UczlV0
78. https://en.wikipedia.org/wiki/2017_South_Asian_floods
    https://www.youtube.com/watch?v=rgu1OANdbCw
79. https://en.wikipedia.org/wiki/2018_Kerala_floods
    https://www.youtube.com/watch?v=-kHEI_76Bnc&t=2s
80. https://en.wikipedia.org/wiki/2019_Indian_floods
    https://en.wikipedia.org/wiki/2019_Kerala_floods
    https://www.youtube.com/watch?v=Oc9FwUrm-IY&t=29s
81. https://en.wikipedia.org/wiki/2010_China_floods
    https://www.youtube.com/watch?v=G-x6i3g1U_Q

82. https://en.wikipedia.org/wiki/2011_China_floods
    https://www.youtube.com/results?search_query=China+Floods+2011
83. https://en.wikipedia.org/wiki/2016_China_floods
    https://www.youtube.com/watch?v=n1dO8A-8SZI
    https://www.youtube.com/watch?v=_mY2Eo__xlk
84. https://en.wikipedia.org/wiki/2017_China_floods
    https://www.youtube.com/watch?v=SgFrl-KwyPs
    https://www.youtube.com/watch?v=Deo1wc3OEA8
85. https://en.wikipedia.org/wiki/2010_Central_European_floods
    http://floodlist.com/europe/report-floods-europe-increase-fivefold-2050
    https://www.youtube.com/watch?v=plOJFXH5Afs
    https://www.youtube.com/watch?v=c5rtWcoWk-s
86. https://en.wikipedia.org/wiki/2012_Great_Britain_and_Ireland_floods
    https://www.youtube.com/watch?v=fH9obMbLu0w
87. https://en.wikipedia.org/wiki/2013–2014_United_Kingdom_winter_floods
    https://www.youtube.com/watch?v=mRWq8p8qUKY
    https://www.youtube.com/watch?v=TkGmeOiZ0cc
88. https://www.ceh.ac.uk/news-and-media/news/uk-winter-20152016-floods-
    one-century%E2%80%99s-most-extreme-and-severe-flood-episodes
    https://www.youtube.com/watch?v=M7MgnGinAOY
89. https://en.wikipedia.org/wiki/2019_UK_floods
    https://www.youtube.com/watch?v=XXYFXKtE6ps
90. https://nca2014.globalchange.gov/report https://www.epa.gov/climate-
    indicators/climate-change-indicators-heavy-precipitation
    https://rockymountainclimate.org/reports_3.htm Stephen Saunders Dan
    Findlay Tom Easley Theo Spencer Double Trouble more Midwestern
    Extreme Storms The Rocky Mountain Climate Organization Natural
    Resources Defense Council 2012
    https://www.youtube.com/watch?v=M_b2YpkJsUs
    https://www.youtube.com/watch?v=mMnUhJ3RUHk
91. https://en.wikipedia.org/wiki/2015_Texas%E2%80%93Oklahoma_flood_and
    _tornado_outbreak   https://www.youtube.com/watch?v=6NybRG6pa3c
92. https://en.wikipedia.org/wiki/2016_Louisiana_floods
    https://www.youtube.com/watch?v=_1UpniAy51E
93. https://en.wikipedia.org/wiki/2017_California_floods
    https://www.youtube.com/watch?v=mXEza6kPyFk
94. https://en.wikipedia.org/wiki/2019_Midwestern_U.S._floods
    https://www.youtube.com/watch?v=fbYxXrJQeag

Ch. 3: Water Shortages

1. https://www.surrey.ac.uk/people/jonathan-chenoweth
2. Aarhus University. "Worldwide water shortage by 2040." Science Daily, 29 July
   2014. www.sciencedialy.com/releases/2104/07/140729093112.htm
   Mesfin M. Mekonnen and Arjen Y. Hoekstra Four billion people facing severe
   water scarcity. *Science Advances* 12 Feb 2016: Vol 2, no 2.

3. http://www.fao.org/aquastat/en/geospatial-information/global-maps-irrigated-areas/latest-version
    https://en.wikipedia.org/wiki/List_of_countries_by_irrigated_land_area

4. https://watrefootprint.org/en/water-footprint/product-water-footprint/water-footprint-crop-and-animal-products
    FAO. Water use of livestock production systems and supply chains – Guidelines for assessment FAO 2018. www.fao.org/3/I9692en.pdf

5. https://www.un.org/en/sections/issues-depth/population
    https://en.wikipedia.org/wiki/Projections_of_population_growth
    https://pai.org/wp-content/uploads/2012/04/PAI-1293-WATER-4PG.pdf

6. Hugo Valin et.al The future of food demand: understanding differences in global economic models   Agricultural Economics December 2013
    http://www.futuredirections.org.au/publication/global-food-and-water-security-in-2050-demographic-change-and-increased-demand/

7. https://www.forbes.com/sites/marshallshepherd/2016/06/20/water-vapor-vs-carbon-dioxide-which-wins-in-climate-warming/#5da5fb943238

8. https://www.unwater.org/publications/world-water-development-report-2017/ https://www.theguardian.com/environment/2018/mar/19/water-shortages-could-affect-5bn...
    https://waterfootprint.org/en/about-us/news/news/water-stress-affect-52-worlds-population-2050/

9. Neil Berg Alex Hall Anthropogenic warming impacts on California snowpack during drought Geophysical Research Letters Vol.44 Issue 5 March   2017
    https://agupubs.onlinelibrary.wiley.com/action/doSearch?AllField=Hall+and+Berg+&SeriesKey=19448007

10. Bradley Udall and Jonathon Overpeck The twenty-first century Colorado River hot drought and implications for the future   Water Resources Research Volume 53, Issue 3 March 2017
    https://agupubs.onlinelibrary.wiley.com/doi/full/10.1002/2016WR019638

11. https://www.ipcc.ch/report/ar5/wg1/
    https://www.iucn.org/regions/mediterranean/our-work/climate-change-mediterranean

12. L. Samaniego et al, Anthropogenic warming exacerbates European soil moisture droughts, *Nature Climate Change* 2018

13. Joel Guiot, Wolfgang Cramer Climate change: The 2015 Paris Agreement thresholds and Mediterranean basin ecosystems   *Science* 28 Oct 2016: Vol. 354, Issue 6311, pp. 465-468
    https://science.sciencemag.org/content/354/6311/465

14. https://ec.europa.eu/environment/water/quantity/about.htm
    https://ec.europa.eu/environment/water/quantity/scarcity_en.htm

15. https://ec.europa.eu/jrc/en/news/europe-hit-one-worst-droughts-2003

16. https://www.climate.gov/news-features/event-tracker/hot-dry-summer-has-led-drought-europe-2018 https://public.wmo.int/en/media/news/july-sees-extreme-weather-high-impacts
    https://www.theguardian.com/environment/2018/jul/20/crop-failure-and-bankruptcy-threaten-farmers-as-drought-grips-europe

17. https://ourworldindata.org/co2-and-other-greenhouse-gas-emissions

18. https://cdkn.org/wp-content/uploads/2014/04/AR5_IPCC_Whats_in_it_for_Africa.pdf
19. https://borgenproject.org/the-water-crisis-in-sub-saharan-africa/ https://en.wikipedia.org/wiki/Water_scarcity_in_Africa
20. https://cdkn.org/wp-content/uploads/2014/04/AR5_IPCC_Whats_in_it_for_Africa.pdf
21. https://www.climate.gov/news-features/event-tracker/not-so-rainy-season-drought-southern-africa-january-2016 https://www.theguardian.com/environment/2016/mar/16/drought-high-temperatures-el-nino-36m-people-africa-hunger https://www.theguardian.com/global-development/2016/may/22/africa-worst-famine-since-1985-looms-for-50-million https://www.youtube.com/watch?v=8B7JToTyeNM
22. https://www.actionaid.org.uk/about-us/what-we-do/emergencies-disasters-humanitarian-response/east-africa-crisis-facts-and-figures https://www.youtube.com/watch?v=Ft6WwlXYbVM https://www.worldvision.org/hunger-news-stories/africa-hunger-famine-facts
23. https://earthobservatory.nasa.gov/images/146015/drought-threatens-millions-in-southern-africa https://en.wikipedia.org/wiki/2018%E2%80%9320_Southern_Africa_drought https://www.thenewhumanitarian.org/analysis/2019/06/10/drought-africa-2019-45-million-in-need https://www.youtube.com/watch?v=F6ChpsmTSnI https://www.youtube.com/watch?v=Z6UxTTrdsZo
24. https://www.scidev.net/south-asia/environment/news/south-asia-running-out-of-groundwater
25. https://en.wikipedia.org/wiki/Water_resources_in_India https://www.wri.org/blog/2015/02/3-maps-explain-india-s-growing-water-risks https://www.hindustantimes.com/mumbai-news/groundwater-depletion-owing-to-exceptionally-high-demand-in-india/story-
26. Wenju Cai, Xiao-Tong Zheng, Evan Weller, Mat Collins, Tim Cowan et al. Projected response of the Indian Ocean Dipole to greenhouse warming Nature Geoscience Nov 28, 2013
27. https://countercurrents.org/2016/08/indian-drought-2015-16-lessons-to-be-learnt https://www.youtube.com/watch?v=V7EOD3OkW3c
28. https://www.indiaspend.com/worldenvironmentday-600-million-indians-face-acute-water-crisis/ https://www.aljazeera.com/news/2019/06/india-reels-worst-drought-decades-heat-kills-dozens-190617084139066.html https://www.youtube.com/watch?v=gqINv1cA2_w https://www.youtube.com/watch?v=a5pcEniBwf0 https://www.youtube.com/watch?v=v9LcJBG2Zh0

Ch. 4: Food Supply

1. https://ourworldindata.org/land-use
2. www.fao.org/resources/infographics/infographics-details/en/c/218650
3. http://www.fao.org/soils-portal/soil-management/soil-carbon-sequestration/en/

4. http://www.fao.org/news/story/en/item/216137/icode/
http://www.fao.org/gleam/results/en/ http://www.fao.org/soils-portal/soil-management/soil-carbon-sequestration/en/
https://en.wikipedia.org/wiki/Soil_carbon

5. http://www.fao.org/organicag/oa-mandate/en/
https://en.wikipedia.org/wiki/Organic_farming
UNCTAD Trade and Environment Review 2013 Wake up before it's too late
UN Publications
https://unctad.org/en/pages/PublicationWebflyer.aspx?publicationid=666

6. https://en.wikipedia.org/wiki/Methane_emissions
https://insideclimatenews.org/news/14122016/agriculture-methane-emissions-climate-change
Lynch, J. Agricultural methane and its role as a greenhouse gas. Food Climate Research Network, University of Oxford 2019
https://foodsource.org.uk/sites/default/files/building-blocks/pdfs/2019_fcrn_explainer...

7. https://www.theguardian.com/commentisfree/2017/nov/07/big-meat-big-dairy-carbon-emmissions-exxon-mobil

8. Philip Lymbery and Isabel Oakeshott Farmageddon Bloomsbury 2014

9. http://www.fao.org/save-food/resources/keyfindings/en/
https://feedbackglobal.org/knowledge-hub/food-waste-scandal/
www.fao.org/fileadmin/templates/nr/sustainability_pathways/docs/Factsheet_FOOD-WASTAGE.pdf https://www.wri.org/our-work/project/food-loss-waste-protocol https://www.wri.org/blog/2019/11/theres-no-time-or-food-waste

10. F. Alice Cang ,Ashley A. Wilson and John J. Wiens Climate change is projected to outpace rates of niche change in grasses Royal Society journal Biology Letters September 2016
https://royalsocietypublishing.org/doi/10.1098/rsbl.2016.0368

11. https://www.ipcc.ch/assessment-report/ar5

12. Challinor, A., Watson, J., Lobell, D. et al. A meta-analysis of crop yield under climate change and adaptation Nature Clim Change 4, 287–291 2014
https://www.nature.com/articles/nclimate2153#citeas

13. https://en.wikipedia.org/wiki/Sea_level_rise
https://www.ipcc.ch/report/ar1/wg1/sea-level-rise/

14. https://en.wikipedia.org/wiki/Fisheries_and_climate_change
https://www.ipcc.ch/srocc/
FAO The State of the Worlds Fisheries and Aquaculture 2018 FAO
www.fao.org/documents/card/en/c/I9540EN

15. FAO The State of Food Security and Nutrition in the world FAO 2019

16. Dr Marco Springmann, PhD et.al Global and regional health effects of future food production under climate change: a modelling study The Lancet March 02, 2016 https://www.thelancet.com/journals/lancet/article/PIIS0140-6736(15)01156-3/fulltext

17. https://www.ipcc.ch/report/ar5/wg2/africa/
https://en.wikipedia.org/wiki/Climate_change_in_Africa
https://theconversation.com/climate-change-is-hitting-african-farmers-the-hardest-of-all-40845

https://oxfordre.com/environmentalscience/view/10.1093/acrefore/9780199389414.001.0001/acrefore-9780199389414-e-292
https://www.hoover.org/research/climate-change-and-africas-future
18. https://www.ipcc.ch/report/ar5/wg2/africa/
https://www.worldhunger.org/africa-hunger-poverty-facts-2018/
https://www.bbc.co.uk/news/world-africa-35054300
19. https://www.worldbank.org/en/news/feature/2013/06/19/india-climate-change-impacts
20. Akter, N., Rafiqul Islam, M. Heat stress effects and management in wheat. A review. *Agron. Sustain. Dev.* 37, 37 2017
https://link.springer.com/article/10.1007%2Fs13593-017-0443-9#citeas .
21. Chuang Zhao et.al Temperature increase reduces global yields of major crops in four independent estimates PNAS August 29, 2017 114 (35) 9326-9331
https://www.pnas.org/content/114/35/9326
22. https://news.globallandscapesforum.org/27357/indo-gangetic-plain-rice-wheat-landscapes-get-climate-smart-makeover/
https://www.downtoearth.org.in/news/climate-change/derailment-of-climate-action-will-be-catastrophic-for-india-s-agriculture-sector-58018
23. https://en.wikipedia.org/wiki/Agriculture_in_China
24. https://www.theguardian.com/environment/2018/jul/31/chinas-most-populous-area-could-be-uninhabitable-by-end-of-century
http://news.mit.edu/2018/china-could-face-deadly-heat-waves-due-climate-change-0731
25. https://globalriskinsights.com/2017/08/shocks-china-growing-water-crisis/
Charlie Parton China's looming water crisis China Dialogue April 2018
https://chinadialogue-production.s3.amazonaws.com/uploads/content/file_en/10608/China..
https://us-issues.com/2018/10/02/china-in-water-crisis/comment-page-1/
26. Shilu Tong et al. Climate, food, water and health in China Bulletin of the World Health Organisation. 2016;94:759–765
Yi Zhang et al Prediction of Maize Yield Response to Climate Change with Climate and Crop Model Uncertainties American Meteorological Society Journal April 2015 https://journals.ametsoc.org/doi/10.1175/JAMC-D-14-0147.1
27. Strauss, B. H., Kulp, S. and Levermann,. Mapping Choices: Carbon, Climate, and Rising Seas, Our Global Legacy. Climate Central Research Report 2015
https://sealevel.climatecentral.org/research/reports/mapping-choices-carbon-climate-and-rising-seas-our-global-legacy https://gbtimes.com/china-reports-overall-rise-in-sea-level

Ch. 5: Loss of Biodiversity

1. https://ipbes.net/sites/default/files/2020-02/ipbes_global_assessment_report_summary_for_policymakers_en.pdf
https://www.iucn.org/
https://portals.iucn.org/library/sites/library/files/documents/2019-007-En.pdf https://www.iucnredlist.org/about/background-history

https://www.iucn.org/resources/conservation-tools/iucn-red-list-threatened-species

2. https://www.un.org/sustainabledevelopment/blog/2019/05/nature-decline-unprecedented-report/

3. FranciscoSánchez-Bayo. Worldwide decline of the entomofauna: A review of its drivers. Biological Conservation Volume 232, April 2019, Pages 8-27

4. Warren[1] et al, The projected effect on insects, vertebrates, and plants of limiting global warming to 1.5°C rather than 2°C. *Science* 18 May 2018: Vol. 360, Issue 6390, pp. 791-795 .

5. Caleb P. Roberts et al Shifting avian spatial regimes in a changing climate. Nature Climate Change volume 9, pages562–566.2019.

6. https://www.ipcc.ch/report/ar4/syr/

7. Michael Allen. Earlier migration shows how some species are responding to climate change. EU Horizon EU Research and Innovation Magazine. 12 March 2015

8. Forchhammer MC. Climate change reduces reproductive success of an Arctic herbivore through trophic mismatch. Philos Trans R Soc Lond B Biol Sci. 2008 Jul 12;363(1501):2369-75.

9. Steffen, W., Broadgate, W., Deutsch, L., Gaffney, O. & Ludwig, C. The trajectory of the Anthropocene: The Great Acceleration. The Anthropocene Review 2: 81-98, 2015.

10. https://www.footprintnetwork.org

11. https://en.wikipedia.org/wiki/List_of_mammals_of_South_America
https://en.wikipedia.org/wiki/Category:Reptiles_of_South_America
https://en.wikipedia.org/wiki/List_of_birds_of_South_America
https://en.wikipedia.org/wiki/Category:Amphibians_of_South_America

12. https://www.wwf.org.uk/where-we-work/places/amazon
https://www.worldatlas.com/articles/what-animals-live-in-the-amazon-rainforest.html
https://wwf.panda.org/knowledge_hub/where_we_work/amazon/about_the_amazon/wildlife_amazon/

13. https://phys.org/news/2016-07-drought-stalls-tree-growth-amazon.html

14. R. Warren et al . The implications of the United Nations Paris Agreement on climate change for globally significant biodiversity areas. Climatic Change March 2018 147:395–409

15. Elizabeth Kolbert. The Sixth Extinction: An Unnatural History Bloomsbury Publishing 2014.

16. https://teara.govt.nz/en/native-plants-and-animals-overview/page-1

17. https://www.activewild.com/australian-animals-list/
https://animalsake.com/a-z-list-of-native-australian-animals-with-pictures

18. https://www.nccarf.edu.au/search/node/Climate%20Change%20and%20species?page=1

19. https://www.ipcc.ch/site/assets/uploads/2018/02/WGIIAR5-Chap25_FINAL.pdf

20. https://climatechange.environment.nsw.gov.au/

21. Sun newspaper. "Hundreds of koalas burned alive after breeding ground is wiped out by bushfires ravaging parts of south east Australia ." 30 Oct 2019

22. https://www.tai.org.au/

23. The Climate Council . Lethal Consequences: Climate Change Impacts on the Great Barrier Reef. 2019.
24. https://science2017.globalchange.gov/
25. https://www.natureserve.org/biodiversity-science/publications/natureserve-annual-report-fy17
26. https://environment.princeton.edu/news/study-helps-pinpoint-what-makes-species-vulnerable-to-environmental-change/
27. https://www.nwf.org/Educational-Resources/Reports/Archive
28. National Audubon Society. Birds and Climate Change. Conservation Science September 2015. http://climate.audubon.org/sites/default/files/NAS_EXTBIRD_V1.3_9.2.15%20lb.pdf
29. Kenneth V. Rosenberg et al. Birds Decline of the North American avifauna. *Science* 04 Oct 2019: Vol. 366, Issue 6461, pp. 120-124.
30. https://www.carbonbrief.org/polar-bears-and-climate-change-what-does-the-science-say
31. S. G. Hamilton A. E. Derocher. Assessment of global polar bear abundance and vulnerability. Animal Conservation Pages 83-95 August 2018. https://zslpublications.onlinelibrary.wiley.com/doi/full/10.1111/acv.12439
32. Regehr EV et al. Conservation status of polar bears(Ursus maritimus) in relation to projected sea-ice declines. Biology. Letters.12: 2 October 2016. https://royalsocietypublishing.org/doi/pdf/10.1098/rsbl.2016.0556
33. https://www.ipcc.ch/site/assets/uploads/2018/02/WGIIAR5-Chap22_FINAL.pdf
34. https://www.ioes.ucla.edu/ctr/
35. https://www.iucnredlist.org/
36. https://www.worldwildlife.org/pages/living-planet-report-2014
37. https://www.wwf.org.uk/learn/wildlife/african-lions
38. https://www.wwf.org.uk/learn/wildlife/african-elephants
39. https://www.telegraph.co.uk/news/2019/11/11/drought-hit-zimbabwe-readies-mass-wildlife-migration-thousands/
40. https://www.valuewalk.com/2016/12/hunting-giraffes-silent-extinction/
41. https://www.eea.europa.eu/soer-2015/europe/climate-change-impacts-and-adaptation#tab-based-on-indicators
42. https://www.iucn.org/regions/europe/our-work/european-red-list-threatened-species
43. http://datazone.birdlife.org/userfiles/file/Species/erlob/EuropeanRedListOf Birds_June2015.pdf
44. https://www.currentresults.com/Endangered-Animals/europe.php
45. https://www.eea.europa.eu/publications/climate-change-impacts-and-vulnerability-2016

Ch. 6: The Effects on Health

1. https://www.who.int/news-room/fact-sheets/detail/climate-change-and-health IPCC, 2014: Summary for Policymakers. In: Climate Change 2014: Mitigation of Climate Change

2. Jay Lemery and Paul Auerbach The Impact of Climate Change on Human Health Rowen and Littlefield 2017
3. Ruth Lorenz et al Detection of a Climate Change Signal in Extreme Heat, Heat Stress, and Cold in Europe From Observations Geophysical Research Letters 17th July 2019 https://doi.org/10.1029/2019GL082062
4. https://en.wikipedia.org/wiki/2003_European_heat_wave
5. https://en.wikipedia.org/wiki/June_2019_European_heat_wave
6. https://www.eea.europa.eu/data-and-maps/indicators/heat-and-health-2/assessment
7. Juan-Carlos Ciscar et al Physical and economic consequences of climate change in Europe PNAS February 15, 2011 https://doi.org/10.1073/pnas.1011612108
8. https://www.parliament.uk/business/committees/committees-a-z/commons-select/environmental-audit-committee/inquiries/parliament-2017/heatwaves-17-19/
9. https://health2016.globalchange.gov/temperature-related-death-and-illness/content/projected-deaths-and-illness-temperature-exposure
10. https://www.ipcc.ch/report/ar5/wg2
11. http://www.bom.gov.au/state-of-the-climate/2016/
12. https://en.wikipedia.org/wiki/Skin_cancer_in_Australia https://www.aihw.gov.au/reports/cancer/skin-cancer-in-australia/summary
13. https://www.skincancer.org/skin-cancer-information/skin-cancer-facts/
14. https://www.who.int/publications-detail/world-malaria-report-2019
15. https://www.who.int/globalchange/climate/summary/en/index5.html
16. A. S. Siraj et al Altitudinal Changes in Malaria Incidence in Highlands of Ethiopia and Colombia *Science* 07 Mar 2014: Vol. 343, Issue 6175, pp. 1154-1158 https://science.sciencemag.org/content/343/6175/1154 E. T. Ngarakana-Gwasira et al Assessing the Role of Climate Change in Malaria Transmission in Africa   Malaria Research and Treatment March 2016 https://www.hindawi.com/journals/mrt/2016/7104291/
17. Messina, J.P., Brady, O.J., Golding, N. *et al.* The current and future global distribution and population at risk of dengue. *Nat Microbiol* 4, 1508–1515 (2019). https://doi.org/10.1038/nrmicro3430
18. Melinda K. Butterworth et al An Analysis of the Potential Impact of Climate Change on Dengue Transmission in the Southeastern United States Environmental health Perspectives Vol. 125, No. 4 April 2017 https://ehp.niehs.nih.gov/doi/10.1289/EHP218
19. James Hadfield et al Twenty years of West Nile virus spread and evolution in the Americas visualized by Nextstrain PLOS PATHOGENS journal   October 31, 2019 https://doi.org/10.1371/journal.ppat.1008042 https://en.wikipedia.org/wiki/WestNile_virus_in_the_United_States
20. David C.E. Philpott et al Acute and Delayed Deaths after West Nile Virus Infection, Texas, USA, 2002–2012 Emerging Infectious Diseases Volume 25, Number 2—February 2019   https://wwwnc.cdc.gov/eid/article/25/2/18-1250_article

21. James Hadfield et al Twenty years of West Nile virus spread and evolution in the Americas visualized by Nextstrain PLOS PATHOGENS journal October 31, 2019 https://doi.org/10.1371/journal.ppat.1008042

22. Sadie J. Ryan et al   Global expansion and redistribution of *Aedes*-borne virus transmission risk with climate change PLOS Neglected Tropical Diseases March 28, 2019 https://journals.plos.org/plosntds/article?id=10.1371%2Fjournal.pntd.0007213

23. Moritz U.G. Kraemer et al Past and future spread of the arbovirus vectors *Aedes aegypti* and *Aedes albopictus Nature Microbiology* volume 4, pages854–863(2019)

24. Micah B Hahn Reported Distribution of *Aedes* (*Stegomyia*) *aegypti* and *Aedes* (*Stegomyia*) *albopictus* in the United States, 1995-2016 (Diptera: Culicidae) *Journal of Medical Entomology*, Volume 53, Issue 5, September 2016, Pages 1169–1175, https://doi.org/10.1093/jme/tjw072

25. Sadie J. Ryan et al   Global expansion and redistribution of *Aedes*-borne virus transmission risk with climate change PLOS Neglected Tropical Diseases March 28, 2019 https://journals.plos.org/plosntds/article?id=10.1371%2Fjournal.pntd.0007213

26. https://www.thelancet.com/journals/lancet/article/PIIS0140-6736%2819%2932790-4/fulltext

27. https://lymediseaseassociation.org

28. https://www.cdc.gov/lyme/

29. Igor Dumic and Edson Severnini "Ticking Bomb": The Impact of Climate Change on the Incidence of Lyme Disease Canadian Journal of Infectious Diseases and Medical Microbiology Volume 2018 Article ID 5719081 2018 https://doi.org/10.1155/2018/5719081

30. https://www.unwater.org/new-publication-whounicef-joint-monitoring-programme-2017-report/

31. . https://www.who.int/news-room/fact-sheets/detail/drinking-water

32. https://www.who.int/news-room/fact-sheets/detail/cholera

33. https://www.path.org/articles/typhoid-fever-past-present-and-future-threat/

34. https://en.wikipedia.org/wiki/1993_Milwaukee_Cryptosporidiosis_outbreak https://waterandhealth.org/safe-drinking-water/drinking-water/milwaukee-1993-largest..

35. https://en.wikipedia.org/wiki/Walkerton_E._coli_outbreak

36. Vikram Kapoor et al Real-Time Quantitative PCR Measurements of Fecal Indicator Bacteria and Human-Associated Source Tracking Markers in a Texas River following Hurricane Harvey. *Environmental Science & Technology Letters*, 2018 10.1021/acs.estlett.8b00237 https://www.chron.com/news/houston-texas/houston/article/harvey-flood-surface-water-map-contamination-12214453.php?utm_campaign=moengage&cmpid=email-desktop

37. https://www.vox.com/energy-and-environment/2017/10/26/16523868/toxic-waste-hurricane-maria-epa-superfund-puerto-rico https://www.nrdc.org/experts/mekela-panditharatne/over-2-million-puerto-ricans-risk-bacteria-water

279

Ch. 7: Choices in Daily Life

1. McLoughlin, N, Corner, A., Clarke, J., Whitmarsh, L., Capstick, S. and Nash N. *Mainstreaming low-carbon lifestyles.* Oxford: Climate Outreach 2019

2. Meat Eaters Guide: Report - Reducing Your Footprint. *EWG* 2011
https://www.theguardian.com/environment/2018/oct/08/climate-change-what-you-can-do-campaigning-installing-insulation-solar-panels
https://static.ewg.org/reports/2011/
https://www.un.org/sustainabledevelopment/biodiversity

3. https://veganadvisors.com/veganism-and-climate-change/
https://www.ecotricity.co.uk/news/news-archive/2018/climate-change-is-veganism-the-answer https://www.bbc.co.uk/news/science-environment-49238749

4. https://www.oxfordmartin.ox.ac.uk/food/

5. https://www.ifpri.org/ https://borgenproject.org/eating-less-meat-can-reduce-poverty/

6. http://www.fao.org/state-of-food-security-nutrition/en/ FAO The State of Food Security and Nutrition in the World FAO 2019

7. https://academic.oup.com/af/article/1/1/19/4638592
https://en.wikipedia.org/wiki/Environmental_impact_of_meat_production

8. Lymbery P and Oakeshott I Farmageddon Blooms bury 2014

9. Springmann, M. *et al.* Options for keeping the food system within environmental limits *Nature* 562, 519–525 2018.

10. https://en.wikipedia.org/wiki/Food_miles
http://www.pollutionissues.co.uk/food-miles-environmental-impact-food.html
https://www.ethical.org.au/3.4.2/get-informed/issues/food-miles-buying-local/
Wholefood cookery books
Rose Elliot's New Complete Vegetarian - Rose Elliot
Cheap and Easy: Vegetarian Cooking on a Budget - Rose Elliot
The Bean Book - Rose Elliot
River Cottage Veg Every Day! - Hugh Fearnley-Whittingstall
River Cottage Much More Veg - Hugh Fearnley-Whittingstall
Deliciously Ella The Plant-Based Cookbook - Ella Mills (Woodward)
EatingWell Whole Foods Now - The Editors of EatingWell
The Simply Vegetarian Cookbook - Susan Pridmore
How to Cook Everything Vegetarian - Mark Bittman

11. http://www.fao.org/food-loss-and-food-waste/en/
https://lovefoodhatewaste.com

12. Kustermann et al (2008) 'Modelling carbon cycles and estimation of greenhouse gas emissions from organic and conventional systems', Renewable Agriculture and Food Systems,23(1) 38-52
http://www.researchgate.net/publication/231904442_Modeling_carbon_cycles_and_estimation_of_greenhouse_gas_emissions_from_organic_and_conventional_farming_systems

13. Skinner, C, A. Gattinger, A. Mueller, P. Mäder, A. Fliessbach, R. Ruser, and U. Niggli 2014 Greenhouse gas fluxes from agricultural soils under organic and

non-organic management – a global meta-analysis. Science of the Total Environment, 468-469, 553-563

14. https://en.wikipedia.org/wiki/Community-supported_agriculture https://www.localharvest.org/csa https://www.ams.usda.gov/local-food-directories/csas https://communitysupportedagriculture.org.uk https://communitysupportedagriculture.org.uk/find-csa https://www.canalsidecommunityfood.org.uk
15. https://rodaleinstitute.org https://www.gardenorganic.org.uk/growing-advice https://www.facebook.com/AustralianOrganicGardening https://www.rhs.org.uk/advice/pdfs/Organic-gardening
16. https://www.iea.org/reports/tracking-transport-2019
17. https://ec.europa.eu/clima/policies/transport_en
18. https://www.epa.gov/ghgemissions/sources-greenhouse-gas-emissions
19. http://walkit.com/ https://tfl.gov.uk/modes/walking
20. https://www.cyclinguk.org/advice https://www.cyclinguk.org/article/cycling-guide/top-ten-tips-for-cycling-in-traffic https://www.cyclescheme.co.uk https://www.britishcycling.org.uk/knowledge https://www.cyclingweekly.com/news/product-news/buying-new-bike-12-point-plan-138372 https://usacycling.org https://www.theactivetimes.com/bike/bikes-gear/top-25-bike-brands http://www.bicyclinglife.com/ https://www.cyclingforums.com/
21. https://www.carsguide.com.au/car-advice/how-many-cars-are-there-in-the-world-70629
22. https://www.defensivedriving.org/.../18-tips-for-reducing-your-cars-carbon-footprint thediscoveryblog.com/how-to-reduce-carbon-footprint-caused-by-your-car https://chooseyourcurrent.org/2018/04/how-to-reduce-your-carbon-footprint-in-the-car/
23. https://www2.deloitte.com/uk/en/insights/industry/automotive/battery-electric-vehicles...
24. European Joint Research Centre Well -to -Wheels Analysis of Future Automotive Fuels and Power Trains in the European context European Commission 2014. https://www.theguardian.com/football/ng-interactive/2017/dec/25/how-green-are-electric-cars https://www.thisismoney.co.uk/money/cars/article-6963195/Electric-cars-SMALLER-carbon-footprints-lifetime-says-VW.html https://cleantechnica.com/2018/02/19/electric-car-well-to-wheel-emissions-myth/
25. IPCC Aviation and the Global Atmosphere IPCC 1999 https://www.ipcc.ch/report/aviation-and-the-global-atmosphere-2/
26. https://friendsoftheearth.uk/climate-change/saving-energy-home-heating-and-insulation https://energysavingtrust.org.uk/blog/climate-change-what-can-you-do-help http://www.preventclimatechange.co.uk/double-glazing-effect-on-climate-change.html https://www.thegreenage.co.uk/replace-double-glazing/
27. https://www.eia.gov/ https://energysavingtrust.org.uk/home-energy-efficiency https://www.thebalance.com/boost-home-energy-efficiency-2395215 https://www.energy.gov/energysaver/design/energy-efficient-home-design https://www.theguardian.com/environment/2014/nov/18/how-to-make-old-homes-energy-efficient

281

28. https://www.c2es.org/content/home-energy-use/
https://www.eia.gov/energyexplained/use-of-energy/homes.php
https://smarterhouse.org/appliances-energy/home-electronics
https://www.visualcapitalist.com/what-uses-the-most-energy-home/
29. https://theecoguide.org/benefits-using-motion-sensor-light-switches
https://www.energy.gov/energysaver/save-electricity-and-fuel/lighting-choices-save-you-money/lighting-controls
https://energysavingtrust.org.uk/home-energy-efficiency/lighting
https://www.carbontrust.com/resources/guides/energy-efficiency/lighting
30. https://energysavingtrust.org.uk/blog/take-control-your-heating-home
https://energysavingtrust.org.uk/home-energy-efficiency/heating-and-hot-water https://energysavingtrust.org.uk/home-energy-efficiency/thermostats-and-controls https://www.hivehome.com
https://www.thegreenage.co.uk/tech/heating-controls/
31. https://energysavingtrust.org.uk/home-energy-efficiency/boiler-replacement
https://www.cse.org.uk/advice/advice-and-support/upgrading-your-boiler
https://www.energy.gov/energysaver/home-heating-systems/furnaces-and-boilers
32. https://energysavingtrust.org.uk/renewable-energy/heat/air-source-heat-pumps https://www.greenmatch.co.uk/blog/2016/02/pros-and-cons-of-air-source-heat-pumps
33. https://energysavingtrust.org.uk/renewable-energy/heat/ground-source-heat-pumps https://www.which.co.uk/reviews/ground-and-air-source-heat-pumps/article/ground-source...
https://www.youtube.com/watch?v=f8GcqW_4KVg
https://www.greenmatch.co.uk/.../ground-source-heat-pump/ground-source-heat-pump-prices https://www.greenmatch.co.uk/.../ground-source-heat-pump/ground-source-heat-pump-prices
https://www.cse.org.uk/advice/renewable-energy/ground-source-heat-pumps
https://www.energy.gov/energysaver/heat-and-cool/heat-pump-systems/geothermal-heat-pumps
34. https://energysavingtrust.org.uk/renewable-energy/electricity/solar-panels
https://energysavingtrust.org.uk/renewable-energy/heat/solar-water-heating
https://www.greenmatch.co.uk/blog/2014/08/how-to-save-money-with-solar-energy https://www.youtube.com/watch?v=Hyg8CNxW4wo
https://www.youtube.com/watch?v=xKxrkht7CpY
https://www.youtube.com/watch?v=HiOLan8J0cE
https://www.youtube.com/watch?v=ZsARidBjgHs
https://www.youtube.com/watch?v=wHOulpxI4Us
https://www.dezeen.com/2015/05/01/elon-musk-launches-tesla-powerwall-battery-replace... www.spiritenergy.co.uk https://www.solarguide.co.uk/solar-batteries
35. https://energysavingtrust.org.uk/renewable-energy/heat/solar-water-heating
https://www.youtube.com/watch?v=WZygrBbj9qA
https://www.youtube.com/watch?v=NsCZD1MZPPo
https://www.energy.gov/energysaver/water-heating/solar-water-heaters
36. https://www.energystar.gov https://www.energystar.gov/about

37. https://en.wikipedia.org/wiki/European_Union_energy_label
https://energysavingtrust.org.uk/home-energy-efficiency/home-appliances
38. https://www.uswitch.com/energy-saving/guides/energy-efficient-cooking/
https://www.greenlivingtips.com/articles/saving-energy-when-cooking.html
http://www.ecolife.com/reno-energy/saving-energy-tips/save-energy-cooking.html
39. Homi Kharas   The Unprecedented Expansion of the Global Middle Class
Brookings Institution. 2017
https://www.brookings.edu/.../uploads/2017/02/global_20170228_global-middle-class.pdf
40. Kai Whiting , Luis Gabriel Carmona   Here's the hidden carbon cost behind
everyday products The Independent Newspaper 23rd May 2018.
https://www.independent.co.uk/news/science/plastic-waste-carbon-emissions-pollution-manufacturing-everyday-products-a8366071.html
41. https://www.carbonbrief.org/mapped-worlds-largest-co2-importers-exporters
42. https://factspy.net/an-average-us-citizens-carbon-footprint/
43. Hugues Ferreboeuf et al Lean ICT towards digital sobriety Shift Project 2019
https://drive.google.com/file/d/1CFFQh0fmtOvGoIl1bw6URoW9rSLyZiB9/view
44. Bawden Tom - Global warming: Data centres to consume three times as much
energy in next decade, experts warn - Independent newspaper 23rd January
2016 https://www.independent.co.uk/environment/global-warming-data-centres-to-consume-three-times-as-much-energy-in-next-decade-experts-warn-a6830086.html
45. https://www.greenpeace.org.uk/news/fast-fashion-this-industry-needs-an-urgent-makeover/
46. https://www.ellenmacarthurfoundation.org/our-work/activities/new-plastics-economy
47. www.action21.co.uk
48. https://en.wikipedia.org/wiki/Local_exchange_trading_system
www.letslinkuk.net https://www.investopedia.com/terms/l/local-exchange-trading-systems-lets.asp
49. https://uk.freecycle.org
https://www.moneysavingexpert.com/shopping/freecycle
50. https://repaircafe.org/en   wiseuptowaste.org.uk/reuse/repair-cafés
https://news.warwickshire.gov.uk/blog/2018/07/17/warwickshires-first-repair-cafe... https://www.facebook.com/RepairCafeLSpa

Ch. 8: The Path of Protest

1. https://en.wikipedia.org/wiki/Campaign_against_Climate_Change
https://www.campaigncc.org
2. https://en.wikipedia.org/wiki/Campaign_against_Climate_Change
www.climatecrisiscoalition.org/video.html
http://www.nbcnews.com/id/10283388/ns/us_news-environment/t/protests-focus-attention-global-warming/#.XfEibfynyUk

https://unfccc.int/.../montreal-climate-change-conference-december-2005/cop-11

3. https://campaigncc.org/node/298 https://www.campaigncc.org/node/299
4. https://www.theguardian.com/commentisfree/2006/aug/31/drax
   https://en.wikipedia.org/wiki/Camp_for_Climate_Action
   www.indymedia.org.uk/en/actions/2006/climatecamp
   https://www.youtube.com/watch?v=oH1bHnAPa7Q
   https://www.youtube.com/watch?v=Uf1yzjjE7go
   https://infogalactic.com/info/Campaign_against_Climate_Change
5. https://www.indymedia.org.uk/en/actions/2007/climatecamp/
   https://en.m.wikipedia.org/wiki/Climate_Camp
   https://en.wikipedia.org/wiki/Plane_Stupid
   https://archive.org/details/climatecampfilm2007
   https://www.theguardian.com/business/gallery/2007/aug/13/theairlineindustry.activists https://www.youtube.com/watch?v=nMQr1AetRBs
6. https://www.campaigncc.org/international/GDA/GDA_history
   www.indymedia.org.uk/en/2007/12/387497.html
7. https://en.wikipedia.org/wiki/350.org https://350.org/about
8. https://en.wikipedia.org/wiki/Camp_for_Climate_Action
   https://www.indymedia.org.uk/en/actions/2008/climatecamp
   https://www.theguardian.com/environment/gallery/2008/aug/05/kingsnorth
   https://www.theguardian.com/environment/2008/aug/08/kingsnorthclimatecamp.climatechange1climatecamp
   https://www.theguardian.com/environment/2008/aug/11/kingsnorthclimatecamp.activists socialistresistance.org/kingsnorth-climate-camp-2008/215
   https://www.youtube.com/watch?v=t8DUC5WiFeg
   https://www.youtube.com/watch?v=ocZxq0WkbNQ
9. https://campaigncc.org/content/national-climate-march-2008
   https://en.wikipedia.org/wiki/Campaign_against_Climate_Change
   https://www.youtube.com/watch?v=yyyHrZXjgP0
   https://www.youtube.com/watch?v=yyyHrZXjgP0
10. https://en.wikipedia.org/wiki/350.org https://350.org/bill
11. https://socialistworker.co.uk/art/18539/Climate+Camp+established+at+Blackheath+in+London https://www.youtube.com/watch?v=y7CRGkqxcr0
    https://www.youtube.com/watch?v=FWk6_iN3o2Y
    news.bbc.co.uk/2/hi/uk_news/8232522.stm
12. https://www.theguardian.com/world/gallery/2009/dec/06/protest-climate-change https://en.m.wikipedia.org/wiki/Stop_Climate_Chaos
13. https://www.campaigncc.org/climatemarch2009
14. https://www.campaigncc.org/copenhagen.shtml
    https://en.wikipedia.org/wiki/Copenhagen_2009
    https://www.indymedia.org.uk/en/actions/2009/cop15/
    https://www.theguardian.com/environment/2009/dec/16/copenhagen-protest
15. https://www.theguardian.com/environment/2010/aug/19/climate-camp-royal-bank-of-scotland
    https://www.theguardian.com/environment/blog/2010/aug/23/climate-

camp-day-action-edinburgh https://www.bbc.com/news/uk-scotland-edinburgh-east-fife-11020007

16. https://campaigncc.org/climatemarch2010 https://campaigncc.org/node/381 https://www.youtube.com/watch?v=QmecPpNu6F8
17. https://en.wikipedia.org/wiki/Occupy_movement https://www.occupy.com/about https://www.youtube.com/watch?v=235qHnTI8tI
18. http://occupywallst.org/ occupywallst.org/about https://www.theatlantic.com/politics/archive/2015/06/the-triumph-of-occupy-wall-street/...
19. https://en.wikipedia.org/wiki/Occupy_Canada
20. https://www.youtube.com/watch?v=iGfYcTee_1U
21. https://en.wikipedia.org/wiki/Occupy_London https://www.theguardian.com/uk/occupy - https://www.telegraph.co.uk/news/uknews/law-and-order/9110341/Occupy-London-timeline.html London   https://www.mirror.co.uk/news/uk-news/occupy-london-st-pauls-cathedral-173310 https://www.youtube.com/watch?v=61qd1PfIEMI https://www.youtube.com/watch?v=ickrqpGWAmE https://www.youtube.com/watch?v=0T3GkxGcD1s https://www.youtube.com/watch?v=DKRpbU_BES0
22. https://link.springer.com/chapter/10.1007/978-3-662-44766-6_10 https://en.wikipedia.org/wiki/Landless_Workers'_Movement https://www.britannica.com/event/Landless-Workers-Movement https://pulitzercenter.org/reporting/occupy-buenos-aires-workers-movement-transformed https://www.theguardian.com/cities/2016/mar/10/occupy-buenos-aires-argentina-workers.. https://www.youtube.com/watch?v=QtAoAlYMxBM www.globalissues.org/news/2011/11/03/11761
23. https://en.wikipedia.org/wiki/Occupy_protests_in_New_Zealand https://www.youtube.com/watch?v=cd2_kfnbIqE https://en.wikipedia.org/wiki/Occupy_Sydney https://www.youtube.com/watch?v=In7BjJOyCFg
24. https://www.youtube.com/watch?v=AwJsj6RHKiQ https://thediplomat.com/2011/10/occupy-singapore-flop https://anilnetto.com/democracy-2/asean/occupy-movement-reaches-south-east-asia https://asiancorrespondent.com/topic/occupy-movement
25. https://www.youtube.com/watch?v=qR5TqEyQLJ4&feature=youtu.be news.cornell.edu/stories/2019/07/howarth-advised-methane-portions-nys-new-climate-law
26. fracking.com/ https://www.youtube.com/watch?v=DVBGLd00MtI https://www.theguardian.com/environment/2012/apr/17/whats-the-truth-about-fracking https://www.theguardian.com/environment/2018/oct/15/fracking-in-uk-what-is-it-and-why.. https://www.gov.uk/government/news/government-ends-support-for-fracking https://inews.co.uk/news/environment/fracking-uk-ban-climate-change-government-policy.. https://en.wikipedia.org/wiki/Hydraulic_fracturing_in_the_United_Kingdom

https://www.independent.co.uk/news/uk/politics/fracking-suspension-earthquake...

27. https://350.org/about https://en.wikipedia.org/wiki/350.org
    https://m.youtube.com/user/350org

28. https://en.wikipedia.org/wiki/Fossil_fuel_divestment
    https://350.org/category/topic/divestment

29. https://en.wikipedia.org/wiki/Keystone_Pipeline

30. https://www.youtube.com/watch?v=CQOSiKUcko0
    https://www.youtube.com/watch?v=09_nCKcbgg0
    https://vimeo.com/80006743 https://www.cbc.ca/news/canada/british-columbia/climate-change-rallies-staged-across...
    https://montreal.ctvnews.ca/protesters-speak-out-against-climate-change-pipeline.

31. https://thinkprogress.org/thousands-in-canada-and-australia-protest-anti-climate.. https://en.m.wikipedia.org/wiki/Climate_change_in_Australia

32. https://en.wikipedia.org/wiki/2014_People's_Climate_March
    https://www.theguardian.com/environment/live/2014/sep/21/peoples-climate-march-live https://www.youtube.com/watch?v=5HEae9MCJxA
    https://www.youtube.com/watch?v=JmRnOi9jtNA
    https://www.theguardian.com/.../2014/sep/21/optimist-peoples-climate-march-melbourne https://www.youtube.com/watch?v=iaySl5Xkh4c

33. https://campaigncc.org/climatemarchlondon
    https://www.theguardian.com/.../2015/mar/07/time-to-act-climate-change-protest-london https://campaigncc.org/climatemarchlondon
    https://www.theguardian.com/environment/live/2015/nov/29/global-peoples-climate-change... https://www.theguardian.com/australia-news/video/2015/nov/30/climate-change-protest..
    https://www.smh.com.au/environment/climate-change/paris-2015-climate-change-rally-in...

34. https://en.wikipedia.org/wiki/People's_Climate_March_(2017)
    https://www.youtube.com/watch?v=8e3xDBxpMm0
    https://www.theguardian.com/us-news/2017/apr/30/peoples-climate-march-thousands-rally... https://350.org/press-release/peoples-climate-march-a-huge-success-200000-march-in-d-c...

35. https://riseforclimate.org https://350.org/press-release/rise-for-climate-september-8th https://350.org/10-years/rise-for-climate-jobs-and-justice-2
    https://350.org/press-release/rise-for-climate-massive-global-mobilisation-concludes... https://www.youtube.com/watch?v=8MQttpGOs78
    https://actionnetwork.org/event_campaigns/rise-for-climate

36. https://www.youtube.com/watch?v=QUCqyqNI5U0
    https://www.youtube.com/watch?v=W6hVZVJwM50
    https://www.youtube.com/watch?v=Emr_r9xrTkY
    https://en.wikipedia.org/wiki/Extinction_Rebellion

37. https://www.youtube.com/watch?v=WTILQFaREZ4

38. https://www.youtube.com/watch?v=WTILQFaREZ4https://www.youtube.com/watch?v=jAH3IQwHKag
    https://www.youtube.com/watch?v=vS1pnNTJiXc

https://www.youtube.com/watch?v=HQurFEJO1SI
https://www.bbc.co.uk/news/uk-england-london-46252619
39. https://www.youtube.com/watch?v=pNJieCMiKbE
https://www.youtube.com/watch?v=HDhNORiTtOU
https://www.dailymotion.com/video/x76hc5r
https://www.youtube.com/watch?v=0Fj6iobDVu
https://www.youtube.com/watch?v=owe11NAF0-0
https://www.youtube.com/watch?v=IIuImZvBPr0
40. https://rebellion.earth
41. https://www.facebook.com/pg/ExtinctionRebellionWarwickDistrict/posts/
42. https://www.youtube.com/watch?v=Tc9MfDfOZfk
https://www.youtube.com/watch?v=9UBx11bx_Kc
https://www.youtube.com/watch?v=WcCAvV5kGYE
https://www.youtube.com/watch?v=OY_DrjDF4_0
43. https://www.youtube.com/watch?v=uRI5c5Jl-ew
https://www.youtube.com/watch?v=ECIcmh3DVjk
44. https://www.youtube.com/results?search_query=Extinction+Rebellion+Lam
bth+bridge+Inter-faith+protest
https://www.youtube.com/watch?v=69NwikuQERI
45. https://www.youtube.com/watch?time_continue=49&v=Ski8LcjvwVo
https://www.youtube.com/watch?v=Ski8LcjvwVo&t=49s
https://www.youtube.com/watch?v=bSbxAMK9ma4&t=47s
46. https://www.youtube.com/watch?v=ew-MxXnx83A
47. https://www.youtube.com/watch?v=dSFgdUgL0FM
48. https://www.youtube.com/watch?v=m7y3xp6sOmk
49. https://www.youtube.com/watch?v=Hk6Q8wshPTI
https://www.bbc.co.uk/news/world-49959227
https://www.youtube.com/watch?v=SjRRUk2SCZ4
https://www.youtube.com/watch?v=eaUr4t3BmV0
https://www.youtube.com/watch?v=2YNsu2IgeXE
https://www.youtube.com/watch?v=L_DFFna5IvE
https://www.youtube.com/watch?v=7ky0iBHnDEM
https://www.youtube.com/watch?v=EpoVFe7Ey1g
https://www.youtube.com/watch?v=deJwMhee6hU
https://www.youtube.com/watch?v=eFiGScCEQVw
https://www.youtube.com/watch?v=3aU1KMJx1iA
https://www.youtube.com/watch?v=Oq0gP1Yr8to
https://www.youtube.com/watch?v=xoKws5Q7aZ0
https://www.youtube.com/watch?v=6bEnlvtulM0
https://www.youtube.com/watch?v=eFX7AC0DBk0
https://www.youtube.com/watch?v=3OK7fLmGptM
https://www.youtube.com/watch?v=emEAE27ehic
https://www.youtube.com/watch?v=Mt6sqhmd_5M
https://www.youtube.com/watch?v=RN8xn-p6pWg
https://www.youtube.com/watch?v=uGUymi9emlI
https://www.youtube.com/watch?v=eC3c0ELnsSk
https://www.youtube.com/watch?v=83P6eEovL7s

Ch. 9: Supporting Non-Governmental Organisations

1. https://services.parliament.uk/bills/2007-08/climatechangehl.html
   https://en.wikipedia.org/wiki/Climate_Change_Act_2008
   https://foe.org/resources/friends-of-the-earth-annual-report-2005/
   https://foe.org/resources/friends-of-the-earth-annual-report-2006/
   https://foe.org/resources/friends-of-the-earth-annual-report-2007/
   https://foe.org/resources/friends-of-the-earth-annual-report-2008/

2. https://www.24hoursofreality.org/ https://www.climaterealityproject.org
   https://www.youtube.com/watch?v=rUO8bdrXghs
   https://www.climaterealityproject.org/video/video-case-optimism-climate-change

3. Marshall George Don't Even Think About it Bloomsbury 2014
   https://en.wikipedia.org/wiki/George_Marshall_(environmentalist)
   https://www.theguardian.com/profile/george-marshall
   https://climatedenial.org   https://climateoutreach.org/
   https://climateoutreach.org/resources/how-to-have-a-climate-change-conversation-talking-climate/ https://climateoutreach.org/the-guardian-rethinking-climate-imagery/
   https://climateoutreach.org/resources/recommendations-for-engaging-young-people-with-climate-change-campaigns-climates/
   https://climateoutreach.org/resources/ipcc-communications-handbook/
   https://climatevisuals.org/sites/default/files/2018-03/Climate-Visuals-Report-Seven-principles-for-visual-climate-change-communication.pdf
   https://www.youtube.com/watch?v=5cw710DgM1s
   https://www.youtube.com/watch?v=D1EDmFglU8U
   https://www.youtube.com/watch?v=wBlTu9Tpvvo

4. https://www.theguardian.com/environment/2008/sep/11/activists.kingsnorth
   climatecamp https://www.greenpeace.org/archive-international/en/news/features/armada-kingsnorth...
   news.bbc.co.uk/2/hi/uk_news/england/kent/7608054.stm
   https://vimeo.com/14062778 https://www.greenpeace.org/archive-international/Global/international/briefings/other/Using%20the%20Law%20action%20version%20-%20July%202010.pdf

5. http://www.greenpeace.org/archive-international/en/campaigns/climate-change/arctic-impacts/ https://www.greenpeace.org/usa/issues/protect-the-arctic/ https://en.wikipedia.org/wiki/Greenpeace_Arctic_Sunrise_ship_case
   https://www.youtube.com/watch?v=EMyd4rwEkp4
   https://www.theguardian.com/.../12/trump-arctic-national-wildlife-refuge-oil-gas-drilling

6. https://en.wikipedia.org/wiki/Fossil_fuel_divestment
   https://en.wikipedia.org/wiki/350.org https://350.org/about
   https://350.org/category/topic/divestment/v
   https://gofossilfree.org/usa/divest-usa https://gofossilfree.org/usa/what-is-fossil-fuel-divestment https://www.youtube.com/watch?v=mzdlpMfoHFs

7. https://www.theguardian.com/environment/fossil-fuel-divestment
   https://www.greenhousepr.co.uk/keep-it-in-the-ground-guardian-campaign-

288

on-fossil-fuel... https://gofossilfree.org/uk
https://campaigncc.org/divestment
https://www.desmog.co.uk/2019/07/16/only-seven-uk-universities-are-committed-investing... https://peopleandplanet.org/fossil-free

8. https://www.theguardian.com/environment/2014/apr/16/pope-francis-back-fossil-fuel-divestment-campaign-religions-groups
https://www.youtube.com/watch?v=XxWpPEigPLE
www.vatican.va/.../francesco/en/speeches/2018/june/...20180609_imprendito
ri-energia.html

9. https://www.theguardian.com/environment/2018/jul/12/ireland-becomes-worlds-first... https://www.nytimes.com/2018/07/12/climate/ireland-fossil-fuels-divestment.html

10. https://www.theguardian.com/commentisfree/2018/sep/10/london-new-york-cities-divest... https://www.newyorker.com/news/dispatch/the-divestment-movement-to-combat-climate...

11. https://gofossilfree.org/europe https://europeangreens.eu/content/fossil-fuel-divestment

12. https://en.wikipedia.org/wiki/Australian_Local_Government_Fossil_Fuel_Di
vestment https://www.theguardian.com/.../2013/may/21/fossil-fuel-divestment-campaign-australia
https://www.thesaturdaypaper.com.au/opinion/topic/2016/12/17/australia-leads-way... https://globalclimatefinance.org/news/divestment-campaign-spreads-to-new-zealand

13. https://en.wikipedia.org/wiki/Fossil_fuel_divestment https://350.org/11-trillion-divested/ https://350.org/investing-in-fossil-fuels-means-burying-your-money-because-last-centurys-fuel-is-staying-in-the-ground/

14. https://www.mirror.co.uk/news/politics/bank-england-governor-mark-carneys-21185300 https://www.dailymail.co.uk/news/article-7835641/amp/Climate-change-tragedy-horizon...
https://www.energyvoice.com/otherenergy/214729/carney-warns-firms-assets-could-become-worthless-if-climate-crisis-not-realised/

15. https://en.wikipedia.org/wiki/AvaazOrg https://secure.avaaz.org
https://www.youtube.com/watch?v=zWrstBidAXg&feature=youtu.be
https://www.theguardian.com/environment/live/2015/nov/29/global-peoples-climate-change... https://www.youtube.com/watch?v=xOejFe-7Nss

16. https://www.worldwildlife.org
https://en.wikipedia.org/wiki/World_Wide_Fund_for_Nature
https://www.worldwildlife.org/about
https://wwf.panda.org/knowledge_hub/history/50_years_of_achievements/
https://wwf.panda.org/our_work/climate_and_energy/

17. https://wwf.panda.org/our_work/forests/deforestation_fronts2/deforestation
_in_the_amazon/
https://wwf.panda.org/our_work/forests/deforestation_fronts2/deforestation
_in_the_amazon/?270070/Region%2Dwide%2Dcooperation%2Dcritical%2Dt
o%2Dfuture%2Dof%2Dthe%2DAmazon

18. https://www.wwf.gr/en/wwf-history-en

19. https://en.wikipedia.org/wiki/Corcovado_National_Park
https://corcovado.com/places-to-visit/corcovado-national-park-costa-rica

20. www.arcworld.org/downloads/THE ASSISI DECLARATIONS.pdf
    https://www.wwf.org.uk/updates/keeping-faith
    arcworld.org/news.asp?pageID=484
21. https://en.wikipedia.org/wiki/Debt-for-Nature_Swap
22. https://www.fsc.org
    https://en.wikipedia.org/wiki/Forest_Stewardship_Council
    https://fsc.org/en/page/about-us
23. http://www.wwf-congobasin.org/
24. https://wwf.panda.org/knowledge_hub/where_we_work/amazon/vision_amazon/models/amazon_protected_areas/financing/arpa/
    https://www.newscientist.com/article/dn2712-worlds-largest-tropical-forest-park-created
    wwf.panda.org/.../where_we_work/amazon/species/tumucumaque_brazilian_national_park
25. wwf.panda.org/wwf_news/?270437/Living-Amazon-Report-2016
26. https://en.wikipedia.org/wiki/Chiribiquete_Natural_National_Park
    https://www.wwf.org.uk/updates/colombian-reserve-becomes-worlds-largest-protected... https://www.independent.co.uk/environment/colombia-rainforest-national-park-world-heritage-site-serrania-del-chiribiquete-a8428371.html

Ch. 10: The Path of Politics

1. https://www.globalgreens.org/
2. https://www.greenparty.org.uk/?q
3. https://greens.scot/
4. https://en.wikipedia.org/wiki/Alliance_'90/The_Greens
   https://www.theguardian.com/commentisfree/2019/jun/24/german-greens-rise-nation-divided
   https://en.wikipedia.org/wiki/2019_European_Parliament_election_in_Germany https://www.dw.com/en/german-eu-election-results-ramp-up-pressure-on-merkels-coalition/a-48884360
5. https://www.gp.org
6. https://brandongaille.com/32-stunning-green-party-demographics /
7. https://www.greens.fi/artikkeli/2017/03/greens-finland
   https://en.wikipedia.org/wiki/Green_League
   http://environmentalprogress.org/big-news/2018/6/26/the-greens-are-no-longer-anti-nuclearin-finland-1
   https://en.wikipedia.org/wiki/2019_Finnish_parliamentary_election
8. https://energia.fi/en/advocacy/energy_policy/renewable_energy
   https://en.wikipedia.org/wiki/Renewable_energy_in_Finland
9. https://greens.org.au
10. https://en.wikipedia.org/wiki/Renewable_energy_in_Australia
11. https://www.greens.org.nz/about
    https://en.wikipedia.org/wiki/Renewable_energy_in_New_Zealand

Ch. 11: The Path of a Spiritual Life

1) Walpola Rahula What the Buddha Taught Grove 1969

2) Shunryu Suzuki Zen Mind, Beginner's Mind Weatherhill Inc; 1973
Alan Watts The Way of Zen Vintage Books; Vintage Books 1999   Roshi
Kennet Zen Is Eternal Life Dharma Publishing 1976 Daishan Morgan Sitting
Buddha: Zen Meditation for Everyone Throssel Hole Press 2005

3) Life in Zen Monastery
https://www.youtube.com/watch?v=6pllQ_-ZxEA
https://www.youtube.com/watch?v=3FwGd8dSBp4
https://www.youtube.com/watch?v=akcGlShaklA
https://www.youtube.com/watch?v=St-Qn3TvLxQ
https://www.youtube.com/watch?v=jwLBrwDTq50
https://www.youtube.com/watch?v=nIiydvJ2eC8
Zazen Meditation
https://www.youtube.com/watch?v=dBtFnQrC7kw
https://www.youtube.com/watch?v=8T-Z1WoFXkk
https://www.youtube.com/watch?v=W6R1SfJ0Cgc
https://throssel.org.uk/

4) Ann E. Kessler   Benedictine Men and Women of Courage: Roots and History
Lean   Scholar Press 2014
Laura Swan The Benedictine Tradition   Liturgical Press U.S. . . . 2007
John McQuiston II   Always We Begin Again: The Benedictine Way of Living
Morehouse Publishing   2011

5) https://asirvanambenedictines.org/about-us/

6) www.benedictinenuns.org.uk

7) Martin Lings Muhammad: His Life Based on the Earliest Sources
Inner Traditions 2006

8) M. A. S. Abdel Haleem The Qur'an Oxford University Press 2008
https://www.youtube.com/channel/UCmOzgWOz_OfwBShm-q3eekg

9) https://www.learnreligions.com/islamic-prayer-timings-2003811
https://www.islamreligion.com/articles/2642/prayer-in-islam/
https://en.wikipedia.org/wiki/Salah
https://www.youtube.com/watch?v=tqFfge1K0fs

10) https://www.youtube.com/watch?v=czN0fzK1LVI&t=608s
Jeananne Fowler   Hinduism: Beliefs & Practices   Sussex Academic Press
1996 Thomas J. Hopkins The Hindu Religious Tradition Wadsworth 1971
Dwarika Nath Raina   A Synoptic Panorama of the Hindu Thought and
Practice Notion Press 2020

11) https://en.wikipedia.org/wiki/Mata_Amritanandamayi
https://www.youtube.com/watch?v=YsxZI0PBl_A
https://www.youtube.com/watch?v=AEEGpLWjjsw
https://www.youtube.com/watch?v=N85ymWS9mRE

Ch. 12: Global Warming Below 2 degrees

1. https://www.ipcc.ch
2. https://www.ipcc.ch/2018/10/08/summary-for-policymakers
   https://www.climaterealityproject.org/blog/why-15-degrees-danger-line-global-warming
   https://e360.yale.edu/features/what_would_a_global_warming_increase_15_degree_be_like
   https://www.theguardian.com/environment/2018/oct/08/global-warming-must-not-exceed-15c-warns-landmark-un-report
   https://www.youtube.com/watch?v=_8hXv5p_OUQ
3. https://public.wmo.int/en/media/press-release/wmo-confirms-past-4-years-were-warmest-record
4. https://www.ipcc.ch/sr15/download
5. Brajesh K. Singh   *Soil Carbon Storage: Modulators, Mechanisms and Modeling*
   Elsevier Inc. 2018.   María Ángeles
   Muñoz and Raúl Zornoza   Soil Management and Climate Change Elsevier Inc .
   2018.   Jacqueline E. Mohan Eco
   System Consequences of Soil Warming   Elsevier Inc . 2019.
   Carlos Garcia, Paolo Nannipieri and Teresa Hernandez   The Future of Soil
   Carbon   Elsevier Inc . 2018
   http://www.fao.org/soils-portal/soil-management/soil-carbon-sequestration/en/ http://www.soilquality.org.au/factsheets/how-much-carbon-can-soil-store https://climatenexus.org/climate-issues/food/soil-carbon-storage/
6. UNCCD   Global Land Outlook   UNNCD Publications 2017.
   https://www.unccd.int/publications/global-land-outlook
   Global Environment Facility Secretariat Land Degradation Global
   Environment Facility 2019
   IPBES Secretariat   Global Assessment Report on Biodiversity and Ecosystem
   Services   IPBES 2019
   https://www.theguardian.com/environment/2017/sep/12/third-of-earths-soil-acutely-degraded-due-to-agriculture-study
7. UNCCD   Global Land Outlook   UNNCD Publications 2017.
   https://www.unccd.int/publications/global-land-
   https://en.wikipedia.org/wiki/Organic_farming
   UNCTAD Secretariat Wake Up Before Its Too Late UN publications 2013
   https://unctad.org/en/PublicationsLibrary/ditcted2012d3_en.pdf
   https://www.scientificamerican.com/article/only-60-years-of-farming-left-if-soil-degradation-continues/
   http://www.fao.org/organicag/oa-specialfeatures/oa-climatechange/en/
   https://rodaleinstitute.org/why-organic/issues-and-priorities/carbon-sequestration/
8. WMO   Provisional Statement on the State of the Global Climate in 2019
   WMO Publications 2019
   WMO Global Climate in 2015-2019: Climate change accelerates WMO
   Publications 2019 https://public.wmo.int/en/media/press-release/global-climate-2015-2019-climate-change-accelerates

IPCC Global Warming of 1.5 degrees IPCC Publications 2018
https://www.ipcc.ch/sr15/

9.   IPCC Global Warming of 1.5 degrees IPCC Publications 2018
      https://www.ipcc.ch/sr15/ https://scied.ucar.edu/longcontent/predictions-
      future-global-climate

10.   https://www.washingtonexaminer.com/news/noaa-scientists-claim-that-
      flooding-in-the-us-will-increase-in-coming-years
      https://science2017.globalchange.gov/chapter/7/
      https://nca2014.globalchange.gov/report/our-changing-climate/precipitation-
      change

11.   IPCC Global Warming of 1.5 degrees IPCC Publications 2018
      https://www.ipcc.ch/sr15/

12.   Bevacqua Emanuele et al   Higher probability of compound flooding from
      precipitation and storm surge in Europe under anthropogenic climate change
      JRC Publication https://ec.europa.eu/jrc/en/publication/higher-probability-
      compound-flooding-precipitation-and-storm-surge-europe-under-
      anthropogenic
      EU Science Hub Global warming poses substantial flood risk increase for
      Central and Western Europe   EU Science Hub newsletter 2018
      https://ec.europa.eu/jrc/en/news/global-warming-poses-substantial-flood-
      risk-increase-central-and-western-europe

13.   https://www.ipcc.ch/sr15/https://www.spri.cam.ac.uk/research/projects/gre
      enlandicesheet/
      https://www.esa.int/ESA_Multimedia/Images/2019/05/Antarctic_ice_loss_1
      992_2019
      Eric Rignot et al. Four decades of Antarctic Ice Sheet mass balance from
      1979–2017 PNAS January 22, 2019 116 (4)
      https://www.pnas.org/content/116/4/1095

14.   https://www.ipcc.ch/report/ar1/wg1/sea-level-rise/

15.   Kristina Dahl et. al Underwater: Rising Seas, Chronic Floods and the
      Implications for U.S. Coastal Real Estate Union of Concerned Scientists 2018
      https://www.ucsusa.org/sites/default/files/attach/2018/06/underwater-
      analysis-full-report.pdf

16.   Barbara Neumann et.al   Future Coastal Population Growth and Exposure to
      Sea-Level Rise and Coastal Flooding - A Global Assessment   PLOS ON
      JOURNAL 2015.
      https://journals.plos.org/plosone/article?id=10.1371/journal.pone.0118571
      Climate Central   Global Vulnerability to Sea Level Rise Far Worse Than
      Previously Understood Climate Central 2019
      https://climatecentral.org/pdfs/2019CoastalDEMReport.pdf

17.   http://displacementsolutions.org/ds-initiatives/climate-change-and-
      displacement-initiative/bangladesh-climate-displacement/
      https://displacementsolutions.org/ds-initiatives/climate-change-and-
      displacement-initiative/maldives-climate-displacement/
      https://www.youtube.com/watch?v=-eFnyb7_kaA

18.   IPCC Global Warming of 1.5 degrees IPCC Publications 2018
      https://www.ipcc.ch/sr15/ https://scied.ucar.edu/longcontent/predictions-
      future-global-climate

19. Nick Watts et. al The 2019 report of The *Lancet* Countdown on health and climate change: ensuring that the health of a child born today is not defined by a changing climate The Lancet https://www.thelancet.com/journals/lancet/article/PIIS0140-6736(19)32596-6/fulltext

20. Anna Maria Vicedo-Cabrera et. al Temperature-related mortality impacts under and beyond Paris Agreement climate change scenarios Climatic Change volume 150, pages 391–402(2018) https://www.lshtm.ac.uk/newsevents/news/2018/implementation-paris-agreement-critical-avoid-large-increase-temperature

21. Steffen Will , Hughes Lesley, Perkins Sarah Heatwaves: Hotter, Longer, more often Climate Council of Australia Limited 2014 http://www.bom.gov.au/state-of-the-climate/State-of-the-Climate-2018.pdf https://www.abc.net.au/news/2018-01-18/heatwaves-australias-deadliest-hazard-why-you-need-plan/9338918

22. Constible Juanita Killer Summer Heat: Paris Agreement compliance could avert hundreds of thousands of needless heat deaths in America's cities. Natural Resources Defence Council 2017 https://www.nrdc.org/sites/default/files/killer-summer-heat-paris-agreement-compliance-ib.pdf

23. Hosmay Lopez et. al Early emergence of anthropogenically forced heat waves in the western United States and Great Lakes Nature Climate Change volume 8, pages414–420 2018 https://www.nature.com/articles/s41558-018-0116-y

24. https://www.who.int/en/news-room/fact-sheets/detail/vector-borne-diseases

25. https://www.ecdc.europa.eu/en/climate-change/climate-change-europe/vector-borne-diseases

26. IPCC Global Warming of 1.5 degrees IPCC Publications 2018 https://www.ipcc.ch/sr15/ https://scied.ucar.edu/longcontent/predictions-future-global-climate https://www.climatesignals.org/climate-signals/wildfire-risk-increase

27. https://www.abc.net.au/news/2019-11-12/cause-of-bushfires-is-complex-but-climate-change-is-part-of-it/11692176 https://www.abc.net.au/news/2019-10-04/the-bushfires-of-the-future-are-here-black-swan/11559930

28. https://en.wikipedia.org/wiki/Wildfires_in_the_United_States

29. https://www.upi.com/Science_News/2017/07/12/Climate-change-could-mean-more-wildfires-in-Alaska-northwest-Canada/2641499893084/

30. IPCC Global Warming of 1.5 degrees IPCC Publications 2018 https://www.ipcc.ch/sr15/

31. Xu L et al Global drought trends under 1.5 C and 2 C warming. International Journal of Climatology 39, 2375-85 2019

32. IPCC Global Warming of 1.5 degrees IPCC Publications 2018 https://www.ipcc.ch/sr15/

33. Richard A. Bettset al Changes in climate extremes, fresh water availability and vulnerability to food insecurity projected at 1.5°C and 2°C global warming with a higher-resolution global climate model Philosophical Transactions of the Royal Society A: Mathematical, Physical and Engineering Sciences Volume 376,

Issue 2119 Published:02 April 2018
https://www.exeter.ac.uk/news/research/title_649617_en.html
34. https://www.ifpri.org/
35. https://www.ipcc.ch/report/ar5/wg2 https://www.ipcc.ch/report/ar4
https://www.ipcc.ch/site/assets/uploads/2018/02/WGIIAR5-
Chap7_FINAL.pdf
36. Wheeler Tim et. al Climate Change Impacts on Global Food Security *Science*
02 Aug 2013: Vol. 341, Issue 6145, pp. 508-513
https://science.sciencemag.org/content/341/6145/508.full
37. Éva Plagányi Climate change impacts on fisheries *Science* 01 Mar 2019:
Vol. 363, Issue 6430, pp. 930-931 http://www.fao.org/fisheries/en/
http://www.fao.org/in-action/globefish/news-events/details-
news/en/c/1032635/ https://science.sciencemag.org/content/363/6430/930
38. IPCC Global Warming of 1.5 degrees IPCC Publications 2018
https://www.ipcc.ch/sr15/
39. Geoffrey Maslen Too Late How we lost the battle with climate change
Hardie Grant books 2017
40. https://en.wikipedia.org/wiki/Ocean_acidification
https://www.pmel.noaa.gov/co2/story/What+is+Ocean+Acidification?
https://www.eartheclipse.com/environment/causes-effects-solutions-of-ocean-
acidification.html 41.
41. IPCC AR5 Synthesis Report: Climate Change 2014 IPPC 2014
42. https://www.ipcc.ch/assessment-report/ar5/
https://www.un.org/ruleoflaw/un-and-the-rule-of-law/united-nations-high-
commissioner-for-refugees/
43. Rigaud Kumari et al Groundswell: Preparing for Internal Climate Migration.
Washington, DC: The World Bank.2018
https://www.worldbank.org/en/news/infographic/2018/03/19/groundswell--
-preparing-for-internal-climate-migration
44. IPCC Global Warming of 1.5 degrees IPCC Publications 2018
https://www.ipcc.ch/sr15/
45. https://www.uea.ac.uk/about/-/climate-change-risk-for-half-of-plant-and-
animal-species-in-biodiversity-hot-spots
Warren, R., Price, J., VanDerWal, J. *et al.* The implications of the United
Nations Paris Agreement on climate change for globally significant biodiversity
areas. *Climatic Change* 147, 395–409 2018

Ch. 13: Global Warming Beyond 2 Degrees

1. Bill McKibben Falter: Has the Human Game Begun to Play Itself Out
Headline Publishing Group 2019.
2. Mark Lynas Our Final Warning- Six Degrees of Climate Emergency 4th Estate
2020
3. Jonathon Porritt Hope in Hell- a decade to confront the climate emergency
Simon and Schuster 2020
4. Climate Action Tracker, December 2019.
https://climateactiontracker.org/global/temperatures/
https://en.wikipedia.org/wiki/4_Degrees_and_Beyond_International_Climate

_Conference www.climatecodered.org/2010/09/what-would-3-degrees-mean.html https://interactive.carbonbrief.org/impacts-climate-change-one-point-five-degrees-two-degrees/ https://www.greenfacts.org/en/impacts-global-warming/l-2/1.htm
https://www.sciencedaily.com/releases/2009/09/090930174655.htm

5. Karhu, K., Auffret, M., Dungait, J. *et al.* Temperature sensitivity of soil respiration rates enhanced by microbial community response. *Nature* 513, 81–84 (2014) https://www.nature.com/articles/nature13604

6. https://www.gfdl.noaa.gov/global-warming-and-hurricanes/#summary-statement

7. Mei, W., Xie, S. Intensification of landfalling typhoons over the northwest Pacific since the late 1970s. *Nature Geoscience* 9, 753–757 2016.
https://www.nature.com/articles/ngeo2792
https://www.ipcc.ch/srccl/ https://www.carbonbrief.org/explainer-desertification-and-the-role-of-climate-change

8. Kazuhisa Tsuboki et al Future increase of supertyphoon intensity associated with climate change *Geophysical Research Letters* 19 December 2014 https://doi.org/10.1002/2014GL061793

9. Guilang Wang et.al The peak structure and future changes of the relationships between extreme precipitation and temperature Nature Climate Change 7 , 268–274 2017 https://www.nature.com/search?q=Guiling+Wang

10. Hirabayashi Y. et al Global Risk under climate change. *Nature Climate Change, 3,* 816-21 2013

11. https://www.eea.europa.eu/data-and-maps/indicators/precipitation-extremes-in-europe-3/assessment-1

12. Thober S. Et al multi-model ensemble projections of European river floods and high flows at 1.5, 2 and 3 degrees of global warming *Environmental research letters* 13,014003 2018

13. Andreas Prein et.al Increased rainfall volume from future convective storms in the US Nature Climate Change 7 , 880–884 2017
https://www.nature.com/search?q=Andreas+Prein%2C+

14. https://nca2014.globalchange.gov/report/our-changing-climate/heavy-downpours-increasing https://www.climate.gov/news-features/featured-images/heavy-downpours-more-intense-frequent-warmer-world
Alexandra Witze Why extreme rains are gaining strength as the climate warms Nature 563 , 458–460 2018
https://www.nature.com/search?q=Nature+563%2C+458-460+%282018%29

15. https://www.worldbank.org/en/news/press-release/2012/11/18/new-report-examines-risks-of-degree-hotter-world-by-end-of-century

16. Svetlana Jevrejeva et al Coastal sea level rise with warming above 2 °C PNAS November 22 2016 https://www.pnas.org/content/113/47/13342

17. https://www.ipcc.ch/report/ar5/wg2/

18. https://www.scientificamerican.com/article/seas-may-rise-23-meters-per-degree/

19. Kirezci, E., Young, I.R., Ranasinghe, R. *et al.* Projections of global-scale extreme sea levels and resulting episodic coastal flooding over the 21st Century. *Sci Rep* 10, 11629 (2020). https://doi.org/10.1038/s41598-020-67736-6

20. Clark, P., Shakun, J., Marcott, S. *et al.* Consequences of twenty-first-century policy for multi-millennial climate and sea-level change. *Nature Climate Change* 6, 360–369 (2016). https://doi.org/10.1038/nclimate2923

21. DeConto, R., Pollard, D. Contribution of Antarctica to past and future sea-level rise. *Nature* 531, 591–597 (2016). https://doi.org/10.1038/nature17145

22. Garbe, J., Albrecht, T., Levermann, A. *et al.* The hysteresis of the Antarctic Ice Sheet. *Nature* 585, 538–544 (2020). https://doi.org/10.1038/s41586-020-2727-5

23. Brown S. et al. Quantifying land and people exposed to sea-level rise with no mitigation and 1.5 and 2 degree C rise in global temperatures to year 2300. Earth's Future 6 583-600 2018

24. Ashley Dawson Extreme Cities - the perils and promise of urban life in the age of Climate Change Verso 2017

25. Kulp, S.A., Strauss, B.H. New elevation data triple estimates of global vulnerability to sea-level rise and coastal flooding. *Nat Commun* 10, 4844 2019

    https://www.nature.com/articles/s41467-019-12808-z#citeas
    https://sealevel.climatecentral.org/uploads/research/Global-Mapping-Choices-Report.pd

26. https://news.cornell.edu/stories/2017/06/rising-seas-could-result-2-billion-refugees-2100

27. Jeff Goodell The Water Will Come Black Inc. 2017

28. https://www.gov.uk/government/publications/future-flooding

29. Mora, C., Dousset, B., Caldwell, I. *et al.* Global risk of deadly heat. *Nature Clim Change* 7, 501–506 2017. https://doi.org/10.1038/nclimate3322

30. WHO Quantitative risk assessment of the effects of climate change on selected causes of death, 2030s and 2050s WHO 2014 https://www.who.int/globalchange/publications/quantitative-risk-assessment/en 1

31. https://www.ipcc.ch/report/ar5/wg2/

32. https://www.maplecroft.com/insights/analysis/heat-stress-to-cut-labour-productivity-in-30-years/ https://www.theguardian.com/world/2015/oct/28/too-hot-to-work-climate-change-south-east-asia-economies-at-risk

33. Eun-Soon Im, Jeremy S. Pal, Elfatih A. B. Eltahir.   Deadly heat waves projected in the densely populated agricultural regions of South Asia Science Advances August 2nd 2017 https://advances.sciencemag.org/content/3/8/e1603322

34. https://www.ipcc.ch/report/ar5/wg2/

35. Kang, S., Eltahir, E.A.B.   North China Plain threatened by deadly heatwaves due to climate change and irrigation. *Nat Commun* 9, 2894 (2018). https://doi.org/10.1038/s41467-018-05252-y

36. Dahl, Kristina et al. 2019. *Killer Heat in the United States: Climate Choices and the Future of Dangerously Hot Days.* Cambridge, MA: Union of Concerned Scientists. https://www.ucsusa.org/resources/killer-heat-united-states-0

37. Wobus C. et al Reframing future risks of extreme heat in the United States Earths Future, 6 1313-35   2018

38. The Interagency Working Group on Climate Change and Health *A Human Health Perspective on Climate Change* Centre for Disease Control 2009

39. Sheridan, S.C., Allen, M.J., Lee, C.C. *et al.* Future heat vulnerability in California, Part II: projecting future heat-related mortality. *Climatic Change* 115, 311–326 (2012). https://doi.org/10.1007/s10584-012-0437-1

40. Elisaveta P. Petkova et al Heat-Related Mortality in a Warming Climate: Projections for 12 U.S. Cities *Int. J. Environ. Res. Public Health 11*(11), 11371-11383; 2014 https://doi.org/10.3390/ijerph111111371

41. Y. T. Eunice Lo et al Increasing mitigation ambition to meet the Paris Agreement's temperature goal avoids substantial heat-related mortality in U.S. cities *Science Advances* 05 Jun 2019:
    Vol. 5, no. 6 https://advances.sciencemag.org/content/5/6/eaau4373

42. https://www.eea.europa.eu/data-and-maps/indicators/heat-and-health-2/assessment

43. Antonio Gasparinni et al Projections of temperature-related excess mortality under climate change scenarios Lancet Planetary Health Volume 1, ISSUE 9, Pe360-e367, December 01, 2017
    https://www.thelancet.com/journals/lanplh/article/PIIS2542-5196%2817%2930156-0/fulltext

44. Committee on Climate Change 2017 Report to Parliament – Progress in preparing for climate change Committee on Climate Change 2017

45. https://www.carbonbrief.org/daily-brief/heat-related-deaths-projected-to-triple-in-the-uk-by-2050

46. Sadie J. Ryan et al Global expansion and redistribution of *Aedes*-borne virus transmission risk with climate change PLOS journal March 28, 2019 https://journals.plos.org/plosntds/article?id=10.1371/journal.pntd.0007213

47. Messina, J.P., Brady, O.J., Golding, N. *et al.* The current and future global distribution and population at risk of dengue. *Nat Microbiol* 4, 1508–1515 (2019). https://doi.org/10.1038/s41564-019-0476-8

48. Paaijmans, K.P., Blanford, J.I., Crane, R.G. *et al.* Downscaling reveals diverse effects of anthropogenic climate warming on the potential for local environments to support malaria transmission. *Climatic Change* 125, 479–488 (2014). https://doi.org/10.1007/s10584-014-1172-6

49. https://www.ipcc.ch/report/managing-the-risks-of-extreme-events-and-disasters-to-advance-climate-change-adaptation/
    https://www.ipcc.ch/report/ar5/wg1/

50. John T. Abatzoglou and A. Park Williams Impact of anthropogenic climate change on wildfire across western US forests PNAS October 18, 2016 https://doi.org/10.1073/pnas.1607171113

51. Adam M. Young et al   Climatic thresholds shape northern high-latitude fire regimes and imply vulnerability to future climate change Ecography Volume40, Issue5 09 April 2016
    https://onlinelibrary.wiley.com/doi/full/10.1111/ecog.02205

52. https://www.ipcc.ch/report/managing-the-risks-of-extreme-events-and-disasters-to-advance-climate-change-adaptation/
    https://www.ipcc.ch/report/ar5/wg1/

53. https://www.worldweatherattribution.org/bushfires-in-australia-2019-2020/

54. Park C. et al Keeping Warming within 1.5 degrees constrains the emergence of aridification Nature Climate Change ,8 70-4   2018

55. Koutroulis A. Global availability under high-end climate change: A vulnerability based assessment. Global and Planetary Change 175, 52-63 2019

56. Tianbao Zhao Aiguo Dai The Magnitude and Causes of Global Drought Changes in the Twenty-First Century under a Low–Moderate Emissions Scenario American Meteorological Society May 2015 https://doi.org/10.1175/JCLI-D-14-00363.1

57. https://www.unwater.org/publications/world-water-development-report-2019/

58. The World Bank   High and Dry *Climate Change, Water, and the Economy* World Bank 2016 https://www.worldbank.org/en/topic/water/publication/high-and-dry-climate-change-water-and-the-economy

59. https://www.ipcc.ch/report/managing-the-risks-of-extreme-events-and-disasters-to-advance-climate-change-adaptation/

60. https://www.wri.org/blog/2019/08/17-countries-home-one-quarter-world-population-face-extremely-high-water-stress

61. World Bank   Beyond Scarcity Water Security in the Middle East and North Africa World Bank 2018 https://www.worldbank.org/en/topic/water/publication/beyond-scarcity-water-security-in...

62. https://www.unwater.org/publications/world-water-development-report-2019/

63. Future warming increases probability of globally synchronized maize production shocks. PNAS, 2018. https://www.pnas.org/content/115/26/6644https://www.nature.com/articles/ncomms13931
    Kotir, J.H. Climate change and variability in Sub-Saharan Africa: a review of current and future trends and impacts on agriculture and food security. *Environ Dev Sustain* 13, 587–605 (2011). https://doi.org/10.1007/s10668-010-9278-0http://news.mit.edu/2017/climate-change-drought-corn-yields-africa-0316

64. https://www.ifpri.org/blog/climate-change-adversely-impact-grain-production-china-2030

65. https://www.wri.org/blog/2015/02/3-maps-explain-india-s-growing-water-risks

66. https://www.weforum.org/agenda/2019/06/this-city-in-india-is-running-out-of-water/

67. UNCCD Desertification: The Invisible Frontline (second edition) United Nations Convention to Combat Desertification 2014 https://www.unccd.int/publications/desertification-invisible-frontline-second-edition

68. World Bank   Groundswell: Preparing for Internal Climate Migration World Bank 2018 https://openknowledge.worldbank.org/handle/10986/29461

69. Richard Pearson Driven to Extinction The Impact of Climate Change on Biodiversity Natural History Museum 2011

70. Elizabeth Kolbert The Sixth Extinction An Unnatural History Blooms bury 2014

71. Ashraf M.T. Elewa Ahmed A. Abdelhady Past, present, and future mass extinctions Journal of African Earth Sciences Volume 162, February 2020

72. Mark C. Urban Accelerating extinction risk from climate change *Science* 01 May 2015: Vol. 348, Issue 6234, pp. 571-573
https://science.sciencemag.org/content/348/6234/571.full

73. Cristian Román-Palacios and John J. Wiens   Recent responses to climate change reveal the drivers of species extinction and survival PNAS February 25, 2020 117 (8) 4211-4217 https://doi.org/10.1073/pnas.1913007117

74. R. Warren et al The implications of the United Nations Paris Agreement on climate change for globally significant biodiversity areas *Climatic Change* volume 147, pages395–409(2018)
https://link.springer.com/article/10.1007/s10584-018-2158-6

75. Francisco Sanchez-Bayo Worldwide decline of the entomofauna: a review of its drivers .Biological Conservation Volume 232 , April 2019

76. https://www.climate.gov/news-features/featured-images/ocean-acidification-today-and-future

77. Geoffrey Maslen Too Late How we lost the battle with climate change Hardie Grant books 2017

Definitions and Frequently Used Abbreviations

PERSONAL PLEDGE PAGE

To help avoid climate catastrophe, I will:

_____

_____

_____

_____

_____

_____

_____

_____

_____

_____

Printed in Great Britain
by Amazon